Essential Grammar

Daphne West

For UK order enquiries: please contact
Bookpoint Ltd, 130 Milton Park,
Abingdon, Oxon OX14 4SB.
Telephone: +44 (0) 1235 827720. *Fax:* +44 (0) 1235 400454.
Lines are open 09.00–17.00, Monday to Saturday, with a 24-hour message
answering service. Details about our titles and how to order are available at
www.teachyourself.com

For USA order enquiries: please contact
McGraw-Hill Customer Services, PO Box 545,
Blacklick, OH 43004-0545, USA.
Telephone: 1-800-722-4726. *Fax:* 1-614-755-5645.

For Canada order enquiries: please contact
McGraw-Hill Ryerson Ltd, 300 Water St, Whitby,
Ontario L1N 9B6, Canada.
Telephone: 905 430 5000. *Fax:* 905 430 5020.

Long renowned as the authoritative source for self-guided learning – with more
than 50 million copies sold worldwide – the *Teach Yourself* series includes over
500 titles in the fields of languages, crafts, hobbies, business, computing and
education.

British Library Cataloguing in Publication Data: a catalogue record for
this title is available from the British Library.

Library of Congress Catalog Card Number: on file.

First published in UK 2000 as Teach Yourself Russian Grammar by
Hodder Education, part of Hachette UK,
338 Euston Road, London NW1 3BH.

First published in US 2000 by The McGraw-Hill Companies, Inc.

This edition published 2010.

The *Teach Yourself* name is a registered trade mark of Hachette UK.

Copyright © 2000, 2003, 2010 Daphne West

Typeset by MPS Limited, A Macmillan Company.

Printed in Great Britain for Hodder Education, an Hachette UK Company,
338 Euston Road, London NW1 3BH, by CPI Cox & Wyman, Reading,
Berkshire, RG1 8EX.

The publisher has used its best endeavours to ensure that the URLs for external
websites referred to in this book are correct and active at the time of going to
press. However, the publisher and the author have no responsibility for the websites and can make no guarantee that a site will remain live or that the content will
remain relevant, decent or appropriate.

Hachette UK's policy is to use papers that are natural, renewable and
recyclable products and made from wood grown in sustainable forests.
The logging and manufacturing processes are expected to conform to the
environmental regulations of the country of origin.

Impression number 10 9 8 7 6 5 4 3 2

Year 2014 2013 2012 2011

Contents

....

Credits

Meet the author

The author's passion for Russian began when it was offered at her school as an alternative to O-level Physics. At the University of Durham she gained a first-class honours degree in Russian with distinction in spoken Russian, followed by a PhD on the poet Mandelstam. She has taught in schools and further education colleges; she was Head of Modern Languages at Sherborne School for Girls and Sevenoaks School, and Headmistress of the Maynard School in Exeter. She has been Chief Examiner for GCSE and A-level Russian and her publications include three Teach Yourself titles, as well as A-level textbooks (*Poshli dalshe, Tranzit, Kompas*). In1993 she was awarded the Pushkin Medal by the Pushkin Insitute, Moscow, for contributions to the teaching of Russian. In the early 1990s she established an exchange which has flourished for nearly twenty years with School No.7 in Perm (a city in the Urals closed to foreigners in Soviet times). Now a freelance teacher and writer, her former Russian students include teachers of Russian in schools and universities, as well those who have made their careers in Russia working for businesses and charitable organisations. In January 2010 she became the editor of Rusistika, the Russian journal of the Association of Language Learning.

Acknowledgements

The author would like to thank Elena Kelly for her help in the preparation of the manuscript and Tatyana Izmailova for her constant support.

Only got a minute?

Russian is one of the most commonly spoken languages in the world: approximately 270 million speak it worldwide, with just over 140 million living in the Russian Federation.

Russian is a Slavonic language which belongs to the same Indo-European family as English. Its grammar and vocabulary have been influenced by a range of languages, including Old Church Slavonic, English, French, German, Latin and Greek.

Can you speak/understand/read/write Russian without a knowledge of its grammar? Only at a most basic level, and even then not completely, since the meaning of Russian words depends on their endings. The better you understand and know the grammar, the more effective your use and understanding of the language will be. Russian is a highly structured language, and, although there are a lot of grammatical rules, they can be divided into convenient categories, and there are relatively few irregularities.

After a summary of the Russian (Cyrillic) alphabet, this course divides the study of Russian grammar into specific sections, giving clear explanations of what grammatical terms mean in English, with lots of examples, exercises, tips and points to remember. The vocabulary used in the examples and exercises aims to teach useful, contemporary language as well as covering the grammatical points.

Like Latin and Classical Greek, Russian has case endings – in other words, the endings of the nouns/adjectives/pronouns change according to the way they are used in a sentence; there are six case endings in Russian and there are three genders of noun (masculine, feminine and neuter), but there are no articles ('the', 'a').

Russian verbs have the interesting feature of aspects (e.g. in the past and future tenses it distinguishes between process and result); this might sound a bit complicated, but to compensate Russian has a straightforward tense system.

Only got five minutes?

One of the official languages of the United Nations and UNESCO, Russian is spoken by approximately 270 million people worldwide, with about 140 million living in the Russian Federation; it is the most widespread of the Slavic languages and continues to be the main language in much of eastern Europe and northern Asia. Russian is still widely spoken in countries which used to be part of the Soviet Union and which still have large Russian communities (Estonia, Kazakhstan and Ukraine, for example); more than 25% of the world's scientific literature is in Russian.

The Russian Federation straddles Europe and Asia, but Russian, like English, belongs to the Indo-European family of languages and it developed from Eastern Slavic, a language spoken by Slavs who migrated eastwards after the seventh century BC. Although the roots of the Russian language lie in Old East Slavonic and Old Church Slavonic, it has also been influenced by Greek and Latin, Dutch, English, French and German. Russian's closest relatives, in the spoken language at least, are Belorussian and Ukrainian.

So how difficult a language is Russian? For the English speaker, it is less straightforward initially (particularly from the point of view of vocabulary) than Western European languages such as French, German, Italian and Spanish. However, Russian shares a significant amount of vocabulary and grammatical structures with modern Western European languages, as well as with Classical Greek and Latin, so that students encounter lots of reassuringly familiar items as their study progresses.

The first striking difference between English and Russian is that Russian uses the Cyrillic alphabet (named after the ninth-century monk, St Cyril, its reputed author). Cyrillic is not completely different from English: some letters look and sound like their English equivalents: the letters т, a, м, for example, spell the word

там, which means '*there*'. Some letters look familiar to the English speaker, but they sound different: e.g.: **e** is pronounced like the '*ye*' in the word '*yet*', **p** like '*r*' in '*rat*', but rolled, so **театр**, which means '*theatre*' is pronounced '*tyeatr*'. A third group of letters do not look like English letters; some are connected with Greek, like **ф** (sounds like '*f*' in '*far*') and others cannot be rendered by one English sound – **ш** is pronounced 'sh' – and the word **шарф** (*sharf*) means '*scarf*'. The first section of this course summarizes and gives some practice in using Cyrillic.

Pronunciation in Russian is straightforward: if you pronounce each letter individually, you will produce the whole word, i.e. the spelling represents the sound, which is not always the case in English (think of '*draft*' and '*draught*', for example.) 'Stress' is an important feature in Russian pronunciation – however many syllables there are in a word, only one of them can be emphasized.

Without knowledge and understanding of the alphabet and pronunciation, reading, writing, speaking and understanding Russian is not possible. But what about grammar? Because Russian is such a highly structured language, without an understanding of how it functions, it is only possible to access Russian at the most basic of levels, and even then not completely. To use and understand Russian, whether spoken or written, it is the understanding of how the language fits together through its grammatical patterns which enables effective written and spoken communication.

So how difficult is Russian grammar? It is true that there is a lot of detail in it, but once understood, the grammatical rules do not let you down, as there are relatively few irregularities. This course works carefully through each grammatical 'category' – nouns, adjectives, adverbs, numerals, pronouns, verbs, conjunctions, prepositions – explaining each grammatical item in English, giving you lots of information, examples and practice, and using language which is of practical, contemporary use.

As in many languages, in Russian there are genders of nouns (masculine, feminine and neuter), but there are no articles ('*the*', '*a*'). Like Classical Greek, Latin and German, Russian has a case system, according to which the endings of words change, depending on their meaning: by looking at the endings of the words, we can be clear about the meaning of the whole phrase/sentence. For example, notice how the Russian word for *actress* (актри́са) changes in the following sentences:

Актри́са о́чень изве́стная.	*The actress is very famous.*
Вы не зна́ете э́ту изве́стную актри́су?	*Don't you know this famous actress?*
Расскажи́те мне об актри́се!	*Tell me about the actress!*

Thanks to the case system, Russian word order is very flexible, as the meaning is made clear by the endings of words. There are six cases: nominative, accusative, genitive, dative, instrumental and prepositional, and the cases apply to nouns, adjectives and pronouns. This course aims to help you feel confident about recognizing and using the patterns involved in the case system for nouns, adjectives and pronouns.

Verbs in Russian have a straightforward tense system. There is just one form of the present tense verb in Russian, which gives the equivalent of I read, I am reading, I do read, I have been reading. Perhaps the most interesting feature about Russian verbs is the concept of imperfective and perfective aspects: the essential difference between imperfective and perfective is that the former is interested in process and the latter in result, e.g.:

Process: I am reading her letter; I was reading her letter when the phone rang; I always used to read/will always read every single one of her letters.

Result: I will read her letter as soon as it arrives; I read her letter as soon as it arrived; I had already read her letter when you rang.

In recent years Russian vocabulary may have undergone significant changes, and been more subject to Western European influences since the collapse of the Soviet Union, but its grammatical system has not changed, and a knowledge of Russian grammar will help you use and understand the language of today, as well as the language of Russia's great cultural heritage – the language described by the great Russian writer Turgenev as the 'great, powerful, true and free Russian language!'

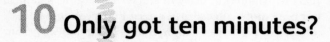

10 Only got ten minutes?

According to the great eighteenth-century Russian scientist and writer, Mikhail Lomonosov, the Russian language has 'the greatness of Spanish, the liveliness of French, the force of German, the tenderness of Italian, and, in addition, the richness and strong terse descriptiveness of Greek and Latin'. Quite a recommendation! This course aims to help you acquire a strong grammatical foundation so that you can appreciate the variety of the Russian language, and use it confidently.

One of the official languages of the United Nations and UNESCO, Russian is spoken by approximately 270 million people worldwide, with about 140 million living in the Russian Federation; it is the most widespread of the Slavic languages and continues to be the main language in much of eastern Europe and northern Asia. Russian is still widely spoken in countries which used to be part of the Soviet Union and which still have large Russian communities (Estonia, Kazakhstan and Ukraine, for example); more than 25% of the world's scientific literature is in Russian.

The Russian Federation straddles Europe and Asia, but Russian, like English, belongs to the Indo-European family of languages and it developed from Eastern Slavic, a language spoken by Slavs who migrated eastwards after the seventh century BC.

Although the roots of the Russian language lie in Old East Slavonic and Old Church Slavonic, it has also been influenced by Greek and Latin, Dutch, English, French and German. Russian's closest relatives, in the spoken language at least, are Belorussian and Ukrainian.

So how difficult a language is Russian? For the English speaker, it is less straightforward initially (particularly from the point of view of vocabulary) than Western European languages such as French, German, Italian and Spanish. However, Russian shares a significant amount of vocabulary and grammatical structures with modern

Western European languages, as well as with Classical Greek and Latin, so that students encounter lots of reassuringly familiar items as their study progresses.

The Cyrillic alphabet, named after the ninth-century monk, St Cyril, its reputed author, was influenced primarily by Greek, with extra letters created to represent Slavic sounds. The first examples of written Russian date from the tenth century, after which the alphabet developed various cursive forms, until the reign of Peter the Great in the eighteenth century, when the alphabet was regularized; after the Revolution in 1917, the alphabet was further 'tidied up' and unnecessary characters deleted, leaving the alphabet as we have it today. Cyrillic has much in common with the Latin alphabet (as used in English), whilst some letters may be familiar already (via Greek and mathematics) and those letters created to represent Slavic sounds are so intriguing that it is difficult <u>not</u> to remember them!

Pronunciation in Russian is achieved simply by pronouncing each letter individually – i.e. words sound as they are spelt; this makes Russian pronunciation a good deal easier than English, where very often a word is not pronounced as it is written (e.g. '*cough*') or may mean different things when pronounced differently ('*Have you read this book? It's a good read.*')

A characteristic feature of the 'sound' of Russian is due to its system of 'hard' and 'soft' vowels. So, for example, Russian has both the 'hard' sounding vowel **a** (which sounds like the English '*a*' in '*far*') and **я** which is pronounced like the letters '*ya*' in '*yak*'. 'Soft' vowels 'soften' (or 'palatalize') the consonants which precede them. This may sound complicated, but it is not unlike English: try saying these two words and listen to the difference caused by the hard 'oo' sound and the soft 'u':

Hard: moon   *Soft*:   music

Now try saying these two Russian words. which both start with the letter **н** (which sounds like the English letter *n*)

Hard: **на** (which means "on/onto")   *Soft*:   **няня** (which means "nanny").

Another very important feature of Russian pronunciation is stress: however many syllables there are in a Russian word, only one of them can be emphasized. To achieve authentic pronunciation it is very important to get the stress right – just think how strange it would sound in English if you emphasized the second syllable of the word *'purchase'* instead of the first.

Without a knowledge of the alphabet and pronunciation, using and understanding Russian is impossible; without a knowledge of grammar, using and understanding Russian effectively is impossible, since it is a highly structured language, where precise meaning is conveyed by case endings, aspects and tenses, prepositions and prefixes.

After a summary of the alphabet and the rules of stress and spelling, this course works through each major component of the Russian language: nouns, adjectives, adverbs, numerals, pronouns, verbs, conjunctions and prepositions. In the explanations, examples, exercises and author insight boxes, the vocabulary used is of a practical and contemporary nature, and there is deliberate repetition of vocabulary items, to aid learning of the grammatical points.

As in many languages, Russian has genders of nouns (masculine, feminine and neuter), but there are no articles (*'the'*, *'a'*). It is usually possible to identify the gender of a noun by looking at its last letter – so, for example, the majority of nouns ending in a consonant or **-й** are masculine, whilst the majority of those ending in **-а** or **-я** are feminine and those ending in **-о** or **-е** are neuter. Russian has a case system, according to which the endings of nouns, adjectives and pronouns change, depending on their meaning. Thanks to the case system, Russian word order is very flexible, as the meaning is made clear by the endings of words. There are six cases: nominative, accusative, genitive, dative, instrumental and prepositional. Notice how the Russian word for *situation* ситуа́ция changes in the following examples, according to the sense of each phrase:

Ситуа́ция сло́жная.	*The situation is complicated.*
Вы не понима́ете ситуа́цию!	*You don't understand the situation!*
Из-за э́той ситуа́ции она́ не смо́жет прийти́.	*Because of this situation, she won't be able to come.*

This course aims to help you feel confident about recognizing the patterns involved in the case system, through careful explanations in English, with lots of examples and opportunities for practice.

The good news is that, compared with some other languages, there are reassuringly few irregularities in Russian. This applies to verbs as well as to nouns. There is just one form of the present tense verb in Russian, which gives the equivalent of *I read, I am reading, I do read, I have been reading*. Perhaps the most interesting feature about Russian verbs is the concept of *imperfective* and *perfective aspects*: so, for example, in the past tense, the first decision to make is whether the action being described was habitual/general/unspecific or specific/completed. In the former case, the past tense is made from the *imperfective infinitive* and in the latter, from the *perfective infinitive*. This is very different from English, which has lots of different ways of expressing the past tense (*I was reading, I used to read, I read, I have read, I had read, I had been reading*). Once the decision about aspect has been made, the formation of the past tense is easy and involves only four possible endings for non-reflexive verbs, and four for reflexives, depending on whether the subject of the verb is masculine singular, feminine singular, neuter singular or plural.

Verbs of Motion offer more possibilities than other verbs, in that they have an *indefinite imperfective infinitive* and *a definite imperfective infinitive*, as well as a *perfective infinitive*; this allows for even more layers of meaning to be conveyed in the verb:

Indefinite imperfective = generalization about movement, movement in more than one direction, habitual movement, return journeys.

Definite imperfective = one occasion, one direction.
Perfective = single action, completion, beginning of a journey.

Russian makes considerable use of prefixes; understanding the meaning of prefixes can be very helpful in identifying the meaning of nouns and verbs:

The prefix **до-** implies *as far as*, up to and this meaning is reflected in the following words, for example:

догово́р	*agreement (i.e. something 'talked through' until agreement reached)*
догоня́ть	*to catch up with (i.e. to drive until you reach something/someone)*
доеда́ть	*to eat up (i.e. to eat until you have finished)*
долета́ть	*to reach (i.e. to fly as far as)*
дохо́д	*income (i.e. your earnings 'walk until they reach you'!)*

Russian has a rich selection of prepositions, some of which have more than one meaning; for example the preposition **к** when used the dative can be connected with movement (*towards, to the house of*) or it can indicate feelings and attitudes:

Он подбежа́л к вы́ходу.	*He ran towards the exit.*
Мы е́дем к ба́бушке.	*We're going to granny's.*
Как они́ отно́сятся к студе́нтам?	*How do they treat (behave towards) the students?*

Two important spelling rules apply to all aspects of Russian grammar, and you will find them mentioned in many sections of this course:

after the letters **г, к, х, ж, ч, ш, щ** never write **ы, ю, я**, but instead always write **и, у, а**

never write an unstressed **о** after the letters **ж, ч, ш, щ, ц**, but instead write **е** (very occasionally, you may see **о** after these letters in words of foreign origen e.g. **шоссé**, *highway*; **шотлндие**, Scotland.)

In other words, Russian grammar rules are really worth learning, because they are applied with reassuring consistency!

Although there have been many changes in Russia since the collapse of the Soviet Union in 1991, and many new items of vocabulary have entered the language, its grammatical system has changed very little, so that the secure knowledge of Russian grammar this course can give you will enable you to make confident use of Russian today, as well as give you access to the vast world of Russia, its culture and heritage. The Russian Federation covers an area of over 10 million square kilometres, with eleven time zones and the longest continuous railway on earth (the Trans-Siberian), and yet it is the same language, with the same grammatical system, which is spoken in St Petersburg in the far west and Vladivostok on the eastern Pacific coast. Russia has an astonishingly rich history and culture, studded with dramatic, tumultuous characters and events ever since the founding of Kievan Rus' in the tenth century, with some well-known characters to read about (Ivan the Terrible, Peter the Great, Catherine the Great, Rasputin, Lenin, Trotsky, Stalin) and some of the world's greatest authors to read (e.g. Chekhov, Dostoevsky, Gogol, Mandelshtam, Pushkin, Tolstoy, Turgenev).

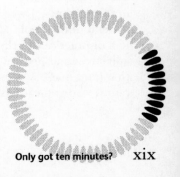

Introduction

Essential Russian Grammar is a reference and a practice book in one. It is intended for learners with very little Russian, but will also be useful for anyone who feels they need more explanation and practice of basic Russian grammar. The explanations are clear and simple, and answers to the exercises are provided in the key at the end, making it an ideal book for self-study. Throughout the course you will find cross-references to other units on the same or related points. In the course of each unit you will find 'author insight boxes' with tips to help you understand and remember essential or tricky points and the final part of each unit will give you ten key points to remember.

How to use this book

You can either work through the book progressively, or dip into specific grammar points which you need to clarify and practise. You can select the grammar items you have found difficult while using the language, or units which supplement the material in the coursebook you are working with. The opening unit gives some practice in recognizing the letters of the Cyrillic printed and handwritten alphabets; if you feel you need more practice in mastering the alphabet, there are lots of exercises which would help in *Learn to Read & Write Russian Script*, also part of the *Teach Yourself* series. You will find all the grammar points listed in the contents. There is also a glossary of grammatical terms at the end of the book. Most students of Russian find that they need lots of practice to help them master the case endings of nouns, adjectives and pronouns, so this book gives lots of opportunity for that (and that's why each case is treated separately, singular and plural – so you can just practise the points you feel you need to reassure yourself about). English translations are given for most of the examples in the grammar explanations and for most of the material used in the exercises.

Abbreviations

sing.	singular
pl.	plural
masc.	masculine
fem.	feminine
adj.	adjective
nom.	nominative
acc.	accusative
gen.	genitive
dat.	dative
instr.	instrumental
prep.	prepositional
infin.	infinitive

1

....

Getting started

1.1 The Cyrillic alphabet

The Cyrillic alphabet is made up of 33 letters. Here they are in their printed and handwritten forms.

ру́сский алфави́т – printed		ру́сский алфави́т – cursive	
А а	*a* in f*a*ther	*A*	*a*
Б б	*b* in *b*ank	*Б*	*б*
В в	*v* in *v*isit	*В*	*в*
Г г	*g* in *g*oat	*Г*	*г*
Д д	*d* in *d*aughter	*Д*	*g ∂*
Е е	*ye* in *ye*t	*Е*	*е*
Ё ё	*yo* in *yo*nder	*Ё*	*ё*
Ж ж	*s* in plea*s*ure	*Ж*	*ж*
З з	*z* in *z*oo	*З*	*з*
И и	*ee* in f*ee*t	*И*	*и*
Й й	*y* in bo*y*	*Й*	*й*
К к	*k* in *k*ite	*К*	*к*
Л л	*l* in bott*l*e	*Л*	*л*
М м	*m* in *m*otor	*М*	*м*
Н н	*n* in *n*ovel	*Н*	*н*
О о	*aw* in l*aw* (when stressed; otherwise like *a* in sof*a*)	*О*	*о*
П п	*p* in *p*each	*П*	*п*
Р р	*r* in *r*at	*Р*	*р*
С с	*s* in *s*ip	*С*	*с*
Т т	*t* in *t*ired	*Т*	*m, т*
У у	*oo* in sh*oo*t	*У*	*у*
Ф ф	*f* in *f*unny	*Ф*	*ф*

Х х	*ch* in lo*ch*		$\mathcal{X}$	*x*
Ц ц	*ts* in ra*ts*		$\mathcal{U}$	*u*
Ч ч	*ch* in *ch*eese		$\mathcal{U}$	*ч*
Ш ш	*sh* in *sh*eep		$\mathcal{W}$	*ш*
Щ щ	*shsh* in English *sh*ampoo		$\mathcal{W}$	*щ*
ъ*	hard sign – makes a tiny pause between syllables			*ъ*
ы*	approximately like *i* in *i*ll			*ы*
ь*	soft sign – adds a soft, gentle 'y' sound after a consonant			*ь*
Э э	*e* in l*e*t		$\mathcal{Э}$	*э*
Ю ю	*u* in *u*niversity		$\mathcal{10}$	*ю*
Я я	*ya* in *ya*rd		$\mathcal{Я}$	*я*

* Do not occur at the beginning of words.

1 Match the Russian words on the left with their English meaning on the right.

1	компью́тер		**a**	*website*
2	веб-са́йт		**b**	*laser printer*
3	ла́зерный при́нтер		**c**	*Internet*
4	онла́йн		**d**	*on-line*
5	Интерне́т		**e**	*computer*

Insight

The Russian words in Exercise 1 are all 'cognates' – in other words, they sound roughly the same as their English equivalent. If you find a word difficult to recognize, you may find it helpful to say it out loud.

Now try the following exercises to practise your familiarity with alphabet.

2 The words in the following list all sound like their English equivalents. Fill in the missing letter from each word. (Cover up the list on the right unless you are stuck!)

1	т_ри́ст	*tourist*
2	с_уде́нт	*student*

3	_урнали́ст	*journalist*
4	ба_ки́р	*banker*
5	бале_и́на	*ballerina*
6	пи_ни́ст	*pianist*
7	про_е́ссор	*professor*
8	а_три́са	*actress*
9	ме́недж_р	*manager*
10	д_ктор	*doctor*

Insight

Being familiar with the Cyrillic alphabet is a key factor in making progress in the language, so it can be unhelpful to rely on representing the sound of a Russian word with English letters ('transliterating') – e.g. 'stood*уе*nt' for студе́нт. Try to avoid doing this unless you are really stuck!

3 Look at the following details of what's on television and answer the questions:

1 At what time is the dog show?
2 On which channel is there a film about Hollywood?

I	OPT	2	HTB
10.15	Макси-шоу	10.00	Сегодня
10.40	Каламбур. Юмористический журнал	10.25	Сериал «Комиссар Рекс»
11.25	Сериал «Дженни едет в Голливуд»	11.30	Дог-шоу «Я и моя собака»
12.00	Новости	12.00	Сегодня

4 Which of the following countries is not in Europe?

1 Герма́ния **4** Кана́да
2 Ирла́ндия **5** Ита́лия
3 Фра́нция

1.2 The stressed syllable

If a Russian word has more than one syllable, it is important in terms of both pronunciation and grammar to know which syllable is 'stressed'. For example, in the Russian word for *engineer* there are three syllables: инженéр and an acute accent over the relevant letter (*e*) shows you that the third syllable is the one to emphasize. The good news is that you never need to write the 'stress mark' in – it's just there to help you, while you're learning. In this book stress marks are always indicated, unless an exercise is based on a real advertisement or ticket, as you would not normally see them in printed materials.

Of course, Russian isn't the only language where emphasis is important. In English, emphasizing the wrong part of the word can sometimes change the meaning (think of *record* and *record*), and there are many words where it would sound odd if we emphasized each syllable equally (think how we emphasize the first syllable of *ever*, *everything* and *father* and how we 'throw away' the second or the second and third). This is what happens in Russian: pronounce the stressed syllable clearly and deliberately, but skim over the others – don't give them any emphasis (much as we deal with the last syllable, the *-er* of *ever*). The stress mark is perhaps most important of all in words which feature the letter o. If the o occurs in a word of only one syllable, or if it is the stressed syllable in a word composed of several syllables, then it will be pronounced, like *aw* in 'law':

нос   *nose*   нóвый   *new*

If the letter o is not stressed it is pronounced like the 'a' in 'sof*a*', for example, водá *water*.

1 Here is a list of 15 of the words you have seen in stressed form so far in Unit 1. Mark in their stresses and, when you have checked your answers in the Key, practise saying each word.

1	актриса	*actress*
2	балерина	*ballerina*
3	банкир	*banker*
4	вода	*water*
5	доктор	*doctor*
6	журналист	*journalist*
7	Италия	*Italy*
8	компьютер	*computer*
9	менеджер	*manager*
10	новый	*new*
11	пианист	*pianist*
12	профессор	*professor*
13	собака	*dog*
14	студент	*student*
15	турист	*tourist*

Insight

Getting the stress right will make your spoken Russian sound much more authentic. For example, it is very important for Russian students to know how to pronounce the words for *Moscow* (**Москва́**) and *Russia* (**Росси́я**) – remember to 'throw away' the unstressed o, like the 'a' in *sofa*.)

2 More practice with the alphabet – match the Russian words on the left with their English meaning on the right; read each Russian word aloud, making sure you stress the correct syllable.

1	университе́т	**a**	*theatre*
2	суперма́ркет	**b**	*university*
3	теа́тр	**c**	*museum*
4	рестора́н	**d**	*supermarket*
5	музе́й	**e**	*restaurant*

• For change of stress, see Sections 2.5, 2.7, 2.10.

1.3 Spelling rules

There are two important spelling rules in Russian:

1 Never write ы, ю, я after г, к, х, ж, ч ш, щ; instead write и, у, а

2 Never write an unstressed o after ж, ч, ш, щ, ц

In order to apply Rule 2 accurately, it is important to know which syllable of a word is stressed. Unfortunately, there is no foolproof way of knowing where a word is stressed ... other than to make a point of learning where the stress is when you first come across the word!

1 Vladimir has been writing a story for homework, but has made five serious spelling mistakes. Underline and explain them. (A translation of Vladimir's masterpiece can be found in the Key.)

Ваня наконец спрашивает Машю
«Где собакы? Почему они молчят?»
Маша не отвечает, Ваня берёт
свои книгы и уходит к лучшому другу, Саше.

> **Insight**
> The first spelling rule came about because it is quite difficult to pronounce the 'prohibited' vowels (ы, ю, я) after г, к, х, ж, ч, ш, щ and easier to say the alternatives (и, у, а). Try repeating г, к, х, ж, ч, ш, щ out loud to memorize them.

1.4 Ten things to remember

1 To make the sound of a Russian word, all you need to do is make the sound of each letter and join them together.

2 For Russian words which have more than one syllable, it is important to know which syllable is stressed. (In this course, the stressed vowel is marked with an acute accent.)

3 Look carefully at each new word and pronounce it out loud, making sure you emphasize the stressed syllable.

4 The sound of the letter *o* is very different when it is stressed and when it is unstressed: like the *aw* in l*aw* when it is stressed, but like the *a* in so*fa* when it is unstressed.

5 Don't be caught out by the letters which look like English letters, but sound different: в, е, н, р, с, у, х.

6 After the letters г, к, х, ж, ч, ш, щ never write ы (always и).

7 After the letters г, к, х, ж, ч, ш, щ never write ю (always у).

8 After the letters г, к, х, ж, ч, ш, щ never write я (always а).

9 Never write an unstressed о after ж, ч, ш, щ, ц.

10 In the handwritten (cursive) Cyrillic alphabet some case letters differ more significantly from the lower case letters than in the printed alphabet.

2

....

Nouns

2.1 Using nouns

Nouns are words which name someone or something –
people, places, animals, objects, concepts: e.g. журналист
journalist, Россия *Russia*, собака *dog*, сумка *bag*, понимание
understanding. Nouns are a vital part of sentences, helping to
make statements and answer questions about who, what, where
and when.

2.2 Gender of nouns

All Russian nouns have a 'gender' and are randomly divided into
three groups: *masculine, feminine* and *neuter*. In some languages,
you need to look at the direct article (*the*) or indirect article (*a*) to
work out the gender of a noun. There are no words for *the* and *a*
in Russian, so just look at the ending of a word to determine its
gender:

Gender	Endings	Example	
Masculine	consonant	журнал	*magazine*
(dictionary symbol м)	й	музей	*museum*
	ь	автомобиль	*car*

Feminine (dictionary symbol ж)	а я ия ь	газе́та неде́ля Росси́я дочь	*newspaper* *week* *Russia* *daughter*
Neuter (dictionary symbol ср)	о е ие	ме́сто по́ле зда́ние	*place* *field* *building*

So, the only ending 'shared' by more than one gender is the soft sign (ь). These are the only nouns where you have to *learn* the gender, but they are a small group (and three-quarters of them are feminine); often they are 'naturally' masculine or feminine – e.g. царь (*tsar*) is masculine and дочь (*daughter*) is feminine.

1 Look at the endings of the words that follow and decide on their gender; write м, ж or ср (or if you prefer to do it in English: m, f, or n) in the brackets which follow each word.

1 ра́дио	*radio*	( )		**6** письмо́	*letter*	( )
2 телеви́зор	*television*	( )		**7** де́рево	*tree*	( )
3 ма́рка	*stamp*	( )		**8** дочь	*daughter*	( )
4 ку́хня	*kitchen*	( )		**9** царь	*tsar*	( )
5 А́нглия	*England*	( )		**10** геро́й	*hero*	( )

Insight

It will be helpful when you are learning case endings to distinguish between feminine nouns which end in я and those which end in ия as they often behave differently (and similarly for neuter nouns ending in е and ие).

2 Match the words from the box to the pictures and indicate the gender (м, ж, ср).

1	**4**
2	**5**
3	**6**

ла́мпа ра́дио соба́ка автомоби́ль компью́тер де́рево

There are a few exceptions to these patterns.

- The following nouns are masculine (because of their meaning):

де́душка	*grandfather*	мужчи́на	*man*
дя́дя	*uncle*	па́па	*daddy*

- The diminutive form of men's first names have feminine endings (e.g. Алекса́ндр → Са́ша).

- Nouns ending in -мя are neuter (вре́мя, *time*); ко́фе is masculine.

Insight

To help you remember the genders of words like вре́мя and ко́фе, learn a phrase which includes an adjective (because the adjective ending points clearly to the gender of the noun – see Unit 3): e.g. свобо́дное вре́мя (*free time*) and чёрный ко́фе (*black coffee*).

3 There is one 'rogue' word in each of the following gender lists. Which words are in the wrong lists and which list should they be in?

М		Ж		СР	
па́спорт	*passport*	медсестра́	*nurse*	окно́	*window*
докуме́нт	*document*	инжене́р	*engineer*	ме́сто	*place*
ме́сяц	*month*	биоло́гия	*biology*	понима́ние	*understanding*
ви́за	*visa*	шко́ла	*school*	эне́ргия	*energy*
гид	*guide*	газе́та	*newspaper*	метро́	*metro*
ю́ноша	*young man*	деклара́ция	*declaration*	письмо́	*letter*

2.3 Cases

Russian is an 'inflected' language: this means that words change their form according to the role they play in a sentence; the word 'case' refers to the changing endings of nouns, adjectives and pronouns. For example, the ending of a noun will change depending on whether it is describing someone/something performing an action or whether someone/something is having an action done to them. There are six cases in Russian and since the relationship between words can be worked out from the case endings, the word order can be much more flexible. In the English phrase *Andrei has eaten the fish*, the word order cannot be changed (without altering the meaning to the rather unlikely *The fish has eaten Andrei*), whereas in Russian we may say either:

| Андрей съел рыбу | *Andrei has eaten the fish* |
| Рыбу съел Андрей | *It's Andrei who has eaten the fish* |

As you can see, the meaning is basically the same, with just a little change of emphasis.

2.4 Nominative case – singular

The nominative case 'names' the person or the thing doing the action of the verb – i.e. it shows us who or what is performing the action of a verb (known as 'the subject of the verb'); singular means there's only one actor/subject. The nominative case of a noun is the form you find in a dictionary, vocabulary or glossary. The endings for each gender are:

masculine: consonant, й, ь
feminine: а, я, ия, ь
neuter: о, е, ие

There are no words for *the* or *a* in Russian. A noun in the nominative case can mean either:

ме́сяц (м) *a month or the month*
медсестра́ (ж) *a nurse or the nurse*
окно́ (ср) *a window or the window*

Subject	Verb	Meaning
Студе́нт	чита́ет	*The/a student is reading*
О́льга	рабо́тает	*Olga is working*
Письмо́	лежи́т (на столе́)	*The/a letter is lying (on the/a table)*

1 Look at the English sentences that follow and underline the subject of each sentence.

e.g. <u>Moscow</u> is the capital of Russia.

   1 My husband works in the centre of town.
   2 Viktor always stays at home on a Friday evening.
   3 Is Olga a journalist?
   4 Where is the dog?
   5 Does the student know the new teacher?

Since there is no present tense of the verb 'to be' in Russian, the nominative case will appear with no apparent verb.

Subject	No verb 'to be'	Meaning
Борис	студе́нт	*Boris (is a) student*
Медсестра́	о́чень до́брая	*(The) nurse (is) very kind*
Письмо́	интере́сное	*(The) letter (is) interesting*

2 Look at the Russian sentences that follow and underline the subject of each sentence (translations of these sentences are given in the Key):

e.g. Обы́чно <u>Влади́мир</u> отдыха́ет в Я́лте.

1 Соба́ка игра́ет в саду́.
2 Теа́тр о́чень краси́вый.
3 Когда́ начина́ется конце́рт?
4 Где моя́ кни́га?
5 Мой сын о́чень хоро́ший футболи́ст.

Insight

The key questions to ask yourself when deciding whether or not you should be using a word in the nominative singular are:

- Does it refer to the 'subject' of the verb (is it the person or the thing doing the action?)
- Is there just one person or thing doing the action?

3 Complete the following sentences with the appropriate nominative singular noun, using the English sentences as a guide.

e.g. _____ начина́ется в семь часо́в. *The concert begins at seven o'clock.* (Конце́рт начина́ется в семь часо́в)

1 _____ не о́чень интере́сная. *The lecture is not very interesting.*

2 К сожале́нию э́то _____ не свобо́дно. *Unfortunately this place is not free.*

3 _____ чита́ет кни́гу по фи́зике. *The student is reading a book on physics.*

4 _____ смо́трит телеви́зор. *Grandfather is watching TV.*

5 _____ до́рого сто́ит. *The car is (costs) expensive.*

6 Где нахо́дится _____? *Where is (situated) the stadium?*

2.5 Nominative case – plural

If you want to talk about more than one subject, you use the plural. In Russian there are different forms of the plural, depending on the gender of the noun.

Regular masculine nouns end in either a consonant, -й or -ь. The plural ending depends on which of these three kinds of noun you are using:

To a consonant, add ы:	студе́нт	→ студе́нты	*students*
Remove й, then add и:	музе́й	→ музе́и	*museums*
Remove ь, then add и:	автомоби́ль	→ автомоби́ли	*cars*

Regular feminine nouns end in either -а, -я, -ия or ь. The plural ending depends on which of these four kinds of noun you are dealing with:

Remove а, add ы:	актри́са	→ актри́сы	*actresses*
Remove я, add и:	неде́ля	→ неде́ли	*weeks*
	ста́нция	→ ста́нции	*stations*
Remove ь, add и:	дверь	→ две́ри	*doors*

NB Remember that you can never write ы after г, к, х, ж, ч, ш, щ, so the plural of both masculine and feminine nouns is affected by this rule: So, for example, парк → па́рки *parks* and кни́га → кни́ги *books*.

1 In the following sentences which nouns are in the plural form? Note that they are all either masculine or feminine. Underline them. (Translations of these sentences are given in the Key.)

1 Бо́льше всего́ Ви́ктор лю́бит чита́ть газе́ты.
2 Ма́рки до́рого сто́ят.
3 Я не зна́ю, где компью́теры.
4 Да, я ча́сто смотрю́ кинофи́льмы.
5 Я не понима́ю, почему́ он смо́трит телесериа́лы.

Regular neuter nouns end in either -о, -е or -ие. The plural ending depends on which of these three kinds of noun you are dealing with:

Remove о, add а:	ме́сто	места́	*places*
Remove е, add я:	по́ле	поля́	*fields*
	зда́ние	зда́ния	*buildings*

Insight

Two key questions to ask yourself when making the nominative plural:

- What is the gender of the noun?
- For masculine and feminine nouns, do you need to apply the spelling rule? (Never write ы after г, к, х, ж, ч, ш, щ).

2 Match up each noun with a suitable plural ending.

e.g. конце́рт + ы → концерты

```
-ы -и -а -я
```

1	балери́на	*ballerina*	**6**	свида́ние	*appointment*
2	журнали́ст	*journalist*	**7**	инжене́р	*engineer*
3	соба́ка	*dog*	**8**	ме́сяц	*month*
4	самолёт	*plane*	**9**	буты́лка	*bottle*
5	исто́рия	*story*	**10**	письмо́	*letter*

3 Write the plural form of the following nouns.

1	же́нщина	*woman*	**6**	ло́шадь (ж)	*horse*
2	ма́льчик	*boy*	**7**	мо́ре	*sea*
3	де́вушка	*girl*	**8**	деклара́ция	*(currency) declaration*
4	мужчи́на	*man*	**9**	зда́ние	*building*
5	ко́шка	*cat*	**10**	геро́й	*hero*

Insight

The change of ending in the nominative plural for masculine singular nouns which end in -й may look tiny, but it affects the pronunciation as well as the writing; so, the singular ending on трамва́й is one sound (like *ai* in Th*ai*land), but for the plural ending, pronounce each letter: трамва́и.

The stress in some regular nouns changes in the nominative plural, as you can see in the word ме́сто. This can happen in all genders.

For example:

Masculine:	стол (*table*) столы́	стари́к (*old man*) старики́	
Feminine:	игра́ (*game*) и́гры	рука́ (*hand, arm*) ру́ки	
		сестра́ (*sister*) сёстры	
Neuter:	окно́ (*window*) о́кна	мо́ре (*sea*) моря́	

Dictionaries usually indicate any movement of stress in the Russian–English section and the best thing is to look out for this when you first come across a word (and try to learn it by saying both singular and plural out loud).

Some regular nouns 'lose' a vowel from their last syllable in all forms except nominative singular. (Vowels which disappear in this way are called 'fleeting vowels'.) Some common ones are: оте́ц → отцы́ (*fathers*); ковёр → ковры́ (*carpets*); це́рковь → це́ркви (*churches*).

> **Insight**
>
> It is worth a special effort to learn some of the most commonly
> used words which have stress changes (e.g. *arm/hand*, *place*,
> *window*, *sister*) or fleeting vowels (e.g. *church*, *father*), because
> these features also apply to case endings other than the
> nominative plural.

4 Match the sentences on the left with the appropriate nominative
plural noun phrase on the right.

1 Óльга и Ви́ктор игра́ют в те́ннис.   **a** Они́ журнали́сты
2 Они́ беру́т интервью́.   **b** Они́ программи́сты
3 Они́ лю́бят компью́теры.   **c** Они́ теннисси́сты

2.6 Nominative case – irregular plurals

Some nouns do not work in the way described in Section 2.5.
Fortunately, irregular plural nouns in Russian fit into convenient
groups.

One group of irregular masculine nouns all behave in the same
way. Instead of ending in ы or и they must end in a stressed á (or,
in the case of учи́тель, a stressed я́). Here are the most common
nouns which behave in this way:

а́дрес	→ адреса́	*addresses*	но́мер	→ номера́	*hotel rooms*
бе́рег	→ берега́	*banks/ shores*	о́стров	→ острова́	*islands*
ве́чер	→ вечера́	*evenings/ parties*	па́спорт	→ паспорта́	*passports*
глаз	→ глаза́	*eyes*	по́езд	→ поезда́	*trains*
го́род	→ города́	*towns*	профе́ссор	→ профессора́	*professors*
дом	→ дома́	*houses*	тра́ктор	→ трактора́	*tractors*
до́ктор	→ доктора́	*doctors*	учи́тель	→ учителя́	*teachers*
лес	→ леса́	*forests*	цвет	→ цвета́	*colours*

Try not to confuse the last word on this list with the plural noun цветы́ (*flowers*, singular: цвето́к).

A second group of masculine nouns takes the nominative plural ending -ья:

брат	→	бра́тья	*brothers*	лист	→	ли́стья	*leaves*
друг	→	друзья́	*friends*	стул	→	сту́лья	*chairs*
сын	→	сыновья́	*sons*			

1 Match the categories on the left with the appropriate plural nouns on the right.

1	университе́т	**a**	поезда́
2	тра́нспорт	**b**	бра́тья
3	гости́ница	**c**	профессора́
4	семья́	**d**	доктора́
5	больни́ца	**e**	номера́

A third group of masculine nouns ends in the singular in -анин or -янин. To make the nominative plural of these nouns, simply remove -ин and add -е:

англича́нин	→	англича́не	*Englishmen*
граждани́н	→	гра́ждане	*citizens*

Feminine and neuter nouns have very few irregulars. The most common are:

дочь (ж)	→	до́чери	*daughters*	коле́но (ср)	→	коле́ни	*knees*
мать (ж)	→	ма́тери	*mothers*	плечо́ (ср)	→	пле́чи	*shoulders*
вре́мя (ср)	→	времена́	*times*	у́хо (ср)	→	у́ши	*ears*
де́рево (ср)	→	дере́вья	*trees*	я́блоко (ср)	→	я́блоки	*apples*
и́мя (ср)	→	имена́	*names*				

2 Translate the following irregular nominative plural words into Russian.

1 brothers   **2** names   **3** children

18

4 mothers	**7** trees	**10** towns
5 addresses	**8** friends	
6 eyes	**9** people	

The good news is that some neuter nouns do not change at all in the plural, so the following are both the singular and the plural forms:

бюро́	*office*	метро́	*metro*	такси́	*taxi*
ви́ски	*whisky*	пиани́но	*piano*		
кафе́	*cafe*	ра́дио	*radio*		

Note that all these 'indeclinable' words (i.e. words that do not change) have been borrowed by Russian from western European languages.

The nouns for 'children' and 'people' are the most strikingly irregular of all:

ребёнок → де́ти *children*   челове́к → лю́ди *people*

Кроссво́рд

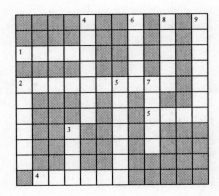

По вертика́ли
2 More than one train
3 Lots of forests
4 Plural of teacher

5 More than one son
6 Underground railway(s)
7 Radio(s)
8 More than one colour
9 Times

По горизонта́ли
1 Scottish drink in singular or plural
2 More than one top university teacher
4 Not sisters, but ...
5 More than one house

> ➤ **For spelling rules see Section 1.3; for change of stress, see Sections 1.2, 2.5, 2.7.**

2.7 Accusative case – singular

The accusative case is used for the direct object of a sentence. The direct object is the person or thing that has an action done to it.

Sentences often include the formula:
Subject (person or thing performing an action) + Verb (action performed) + Direct Object (person or thing that has action done to it)

1 Underline the object noun in each of the following sentences.

e.g. Always buy comfortable <u>shoes</u>.
1 I often watch the television.
2 Pass the water, please.
3 Have you seen the cat anywhere?
4 I've never visited the Kremlin.
5 He bought the least expensive watch available.

For example: Last year I (*subject*) visited (*verb*) the Hermitage Museum (*direct object*) in St Petersburg. In Russian, the ending of some nouns will change when they are the direct object in a sentence. In the table below, notice that only the asterisked nouns have changed:

Subject	Verb	Object	Meaning
А́нна	чита́ет	журна́л	*Anna is reading a magazine*
Врач	понима́ет	пацие́нта*	*The doctor understands the patient*
Бори́с	чита́ет	газе́ту*	*Boris is reading the newspaper*
Мы	чита́ем	письмо́	*We are reading the letter*

In the singular, **masculine singular nouns** only change in the accusative case if they are animate (i.e. a person or an animal). All inanimate nouns (i.e. things) remain the same as in the nominative:

Хорошо́, я возьму́ журна́л. *OK, I'll take the magazine.*

If masculine singular nouns are animate (i.e. a person or an animal), their endings in the accusative are formed as follows:

To a consonant, add а:	студе́нт →	студе́нта
Remove й, then add я:	Андре́й →	Андре́я
Remove ь, then add я:	учи́тель →	учи́теля

Вы зна́ете Бори́са?
Do you know Boris?

Мы ви́дим учи́теля ка́ждый день.
We see the teacher every day.

The overwhelming majority of **neuter singular nouns** are inanimate, and they do not change in the accusative case: Письмо́ интере́сное? Да́йте мне письмо́, пожа́луйста. *Is the letter interesting? Give me the letter, please.* A common animate neuter noun is лицо́ (when it means *person*, not *face*); its animate accusative is лица́.

Feminine singular nouns always change in the accusative case, whether animate or inanimate, except for soft-sign nouns (e.g. дверь *door*). Accusative endings of feminine nouns are formed as follows:

Remove a, add y:	актри́са	→	актри́су
Remove я, add ю:	неде́ля	→	неде́лю
Soft sign stays the same:	дверь	→	дверь

Вы зна́ете Татья́ну?   *Do you know Tatyana?*

2 Match the two halves of each sentence, then find the English translation below.

1 Я предпочита́ю фи́зику	**a**	но его́ бра́та я не зна́ю.
2 Я зна́ю его́ сестру́,	**b**	А́ню и Вади́ма
3 Вы ви́дите апте́ку напра́во	**c**	и врача́.
4 Я хочу́ пригласи́ть	**d**	и не люблю́ хи́мию.
5 Мы уже́ зна́ем медсестру́	**e**	и по́чту нале́во?

1 *I know his sister, but I don't know his brother.*
2 *I want to invite Anya and Vadim.*
3 *We already know the nurse and the doctor.*
4 *I prefer physics and I don't like chemistry.*
5 *Do you (can you) see the chemist's on the right and the post office on the left?*

3 Put the following words into the accusative case.

e.g. инжене́р → инжене́ра

1	дочь (ж)	*daughter*
2	ба́бушка	*grandmother*
3	мать (ж)	*mother*
4	дя́дя	*uncle*
5	тётя	*aunt*
6	стол	*table*
7	по́ле	*field*
8	откры́тка	*postcard*
9	ло́шадь (ж)	*horse*
10	брат	*brother*

Some very common feminine nouns which are stressed on the ending in the nominative singular have a change of stress in the accusative singular, e.g.:

вода́	→ во́ду	*water*
земля́	→ зе́млю	*earth*
нога́	→ но́гу	*foot, leg*
рука́	→ ру́ку	*arm, hand*
спина́	→ спи́ну	*back*
среда́	→ сре́ду	*Wednesday*

➤ **For change of stress, see Sections 1.2, 2.5, 2.7; for use of the accusative with prepositions, see Sections 11.3, 11.4, 11.5, 11.6.**

2.8 Accusative case – plural

If a plural noun is the direct object in a phrase or sentence its endings must change. The endings depend on whether the noun is animate (a person or an animal) or inanimate (a thing).

The good news is that if a noun is inanimate (i.e. a thing), the ending for the accusative plural is exactly the same as the ending for the nominative plural. This applies to all three genders.

Subject	Verb	Object	Meaning
А́нна	чита́ет	журна́лы	*Anna is reading the magazines*
Бори́с	чита́ет	газе́ты	*Boris is reading the newspapers*
Мы	чита́ем	пи́сьма	*We are reading the letters*

1 Write sentences saying what you want to buy, adding the correct accusative plural ending to each singular noun (they're all inanimate).

e.g. биле́т (*ticket*) → Я хочу́ купи́ть биле́ты

1 телефо́н
2 зда́ние
3 буты́лка
4 по́ле
5 ма́рка

If a noun is **animate**, then its ending must change and this applies to all three genders. The animate accusative plural and the genitive plural are the only cases where the endings are different for the three genders. So, the bad news is that there are quite a few endings to learn for the animate accusative, but the good news is that by the time you get to Section 2.11 you will already know the endings of the genitive plural!

Masculine animate accusative plural:

To a consonant, add ов	студе́нт	→	студе́нтов
Remove й, then add ев	геро́й *(hero)*	→	геро́ев
Remove ь, then add ей	писа́тель *(writer)*	→	писа́телей

Care is needed if the masculine singular nominative ends in ж, ч, ш, щ. If it does, add ей, not ов: e.g. врач *(doctor)* → врачéй.

Feminine animate accusative plural:

Remove а, add nothing	актри́са	→	актри́с
Remove я, add ь:	со́ня *(dormouse)*	→	сонь
For nouns ending in ия, remove я, add й:	Мари́я	→	Мари́й
Remove ь, add ей:	ло́шадь *(horse)*	→	лошадéй

Care is needed with feminine nouns ending in а. If you are left with a cluster of consonants when you have removed the -a you usually need to insert the vowel о, е or (very occasionally) ё. Three common examples you might find in the animate accusative are:

де́вушка → де́вушек, ма́рка → ма́рок, сестра́ → сестёр

Вы зна́ете э́тих де́вушек?   *Do you know these girls?*
Нет, но я зна́ю их сестёр.   *No, but I know their sisters.*

2 Underline the plural nouns in the following sentences which would need to be in the inanimate accusative in Russian and circle those which should be in the animate accusative.

e.g. Have you ever seen these (actors) and these *plays* before?

1 We always like to watch the boats and the seagulls when we are by the sea.
2 I forgot to buy tickets for the concert.
3 Please send the customers and their purchases to the cash desk.
4 Do you prefer to read books or newspapers?
5 She says she's going to get two dogs.

3 Write sentences saying who you know, adding the correct accusative plural ending to each singular noun (they're all animate).

e.g. тури́ст → Я зна́ю тури́стов

1 инжене́р
2 медсестра́
3 футболи́ст
4 балери́на
5 врач

4 Explain who or what you're photographing by putting each singular noun in the accusative plural (animate or inanimate?).

e.g. собо́р (*cathedral*) → Я фотографи́рую собо́ры

1 коро́ва   *cow*
2 музыка́нт   *musician*
3 ло́дка   *boat*
4 магази́н   *shop*
5 пти́ца   *bird*

There are *very* few **neuter animate nouns**. A common one is лицо́ (when it means *person*). The animate accusative plural is formed simply by removing the last letter.

> ➤ **For formation of irregular animate accusative plural see Section 2.9; for genitive plural nouns see Sections 2.11 and 2.12; for use of the accusative with prepositions, see Sections 11.3, 11.4, 11.5, 11.6.**

2.9 Accusative case – irregular plurals

Some nouns do not work in the way described in Section 2.8. Fortunately, irregular accusative plural nouns fit into convenient groups (just like irregular nominative plural nouns).

Nouns which have irregular endings in the nominative plural still follow the same pattern for the accusative plural outlined in Section 2.8: if a noun is **inanimate,** the ending for the accusative plural is exactly the same as the ending for the nominative plural.

Он зна́ет все адреса́. Вы купи́ли сту́лья?
He knows all the addresses. *Did you buy the chairs?*

1 Ask about people's preferences by putting the nouns given below into the accusative plural:

e.g. лес/о́стров → Что вы лю́бите бо́льше, леса́ и́ли острова́?

1 де́рево/бе́рег
2 по́езд/тра́ктор
3 стул/цвет
4 дом/го́род

For **animate nouns:**

• those which have an irregular nominative plural ending in a stressed á take -о́в in the accusative plural: Я уже́ зна́ю профессоро́в. The irregular nominative plural учителя́ becomes учителе́й.

- those which have an irregular nominative plural ending in -ья, have the accusative plural ending -ьев (if the nominative plural is stressed on the stem) or éй (if the nominative plural is stressed on the end):

Nominative singular	Nominative plural	Accusative plural
брат *brother*	бра́тья *nom. pl. stressed on stem*	бра́тьев
друг *friend*	друзья́ *nom. pl. stressed on end*	друзе́й
сын *son*	сыновья́ *nom. pl. stressed on end*	сынове́й

- For animate nouns whose nominative singular ends in -нин, this is what happens:

Nominative singular	Nominative plural	Accusative plural
англича́нин	англича́не	англича́н
граждани́н	гра́ждане	гра́ждан

The accusative plural of the irregular feminine nouns мать and дочь are:

Nominative singular	Nominative plural	Accusative plural
дочь	до́чери	до́чере́й
мать	ма́тери	матере́й

And finally, the accusative plural for 'children' and 'people' comes from their strikingly different nominative plural form:

Nominative singular	Nominative plural	Accusative plural
ребёнок	де́ти	дете́й
челове́к	лю́ди	люде́й

2 Match the two halves of each sentence, according to the English translations in the sentences that follow.

1 Он уже́ зна́ет	**a**	англича́н в аэропорту́.
2 Вы ви́дели	**b**	учителе́й.
3 Гид встре́тил	**c**	друзе́й в рестора́н.
4 Нет, я не зна́ю	**d**	бра́тьев Влади́мира.
5 Она́ ча́сто приглаша́ет	**e**	его́ сынове́й вечера́?

1 *No, I don't know Vladimir's brothers.*
2 *She often invites friends to the restaurant.*
3 *Did you see his sons yesterday?*
4 *He already knows the teachers.*
5 *The guide met the Englishmen at the airport.*

3 Boris and Elena complete a questionnaire about their visit to England. They have made a list of what they have liked most (✓) and what they have liked least (✗). Complete the account of their visit by giving the accusative plural in Russian of their likes and dislikes (reminder бо́льше = more; ме́ньше = less).

✓	✗
towns	trains
houses	evenings
people	
hotel rooms	

Мы тури́сты в А́нглии. Что мы люби́ли бо́льше? Что мы люби́ли ме́ньше?

Мы люби́ли бо́льше_____, _____, _____, и_____.

Мы люби́ли ме́ньше_____ и_____.

➤ **For formation of irregular nominative plural, see Section 2.6; for animate accusative plural of regular nouns, see Section 2.8; for use of the accusative with prepositions, see Section 11.2.**

2.10 Genitive case – singular

The principal meaning of the genitive case is *of*, and it is also used with quantities (e.g. *a lot, a bottle, not any*, and after the numerals 2, 3 and 4):

Это паспорт студе́нта.	*It is the passport of the student (the student's passport).*
Эдесь нет телефо́на.	*Here there is no (not any) telephone.*

1 In the following sentences which nouns would be in the genitive in Russian? Underline them.

e.g. Have you seen <u>Olga's</u> book?

1 There isn't any cheese in the fridge.
2 I'd like half a kilo of ham, please.
3 Rome is the capital of Italy.
4 The tourist's passport is on the floor.
5 Igor's e-mail address is on this piece of paper.

There are two possible endings for the genitive singular of **masculine nouns**: either -a or -я.

To a consonant, add а:	лимона́д	→	лимона́да
Remove й, then add я:	Серге́й	→	Серге́я
Remove ь, then add я:	И́горь	→	И́горя

Вот буты́лка лимона́да.	*Here is a bottle of lemonade.*
Где пиджа́к Серге́я?	*Where is Sergei's (of Sergei) jacket?*
Серге́й брат и́горя.	*Sergei is Igor's (of Igor) brother.*

There are two possible endings for the genitive singular of **feminine nouns**: either -ы or -и.

Remove а, add ы:	вода́	→	воды́
Remove я, add и:	Росси́я	→	Росси́и
Remove ь, add и:	свекро́вь	→	свекро́ви

| Да́йте, пожа́луйста, буты́лку воды́. | Give me a bottle of water, please. |
| Москва́-столи́ца Росси́и. | Moscow is the capital of Russia. |

Remember: never write ы after г, к, х, ж, h, ш, щ (e.g. ко́шка→ ко́шки *of the cat*).

NB мать and дочь have irregular genitive singular forms: ма́тери and до́чери.

There are two possible endings for the genitive singular of neuter nouns: either -a or -я.

Remove o, add a:	ме́сто	→	ме́ста
Remove e, add я:	зда́ние	→	зда́ния
	по́ле	→	поля́

Neuter words which end in -мя have the irregular ending -мени: вре́мя → вре́мени, и́мя → и́мени.

| Здесь нет ме́ста. | There's no room (not any place) here. |
| У меня́ нет вре́мени! | I have no (not any) time! |

2 Look at the drawings and then make up sentences to describe who owns what:

e.g. О́льга/бага́ж
→ Э́то бага́ж О́льги.

1 Бори́с/соба́ка

2 Андре́й/автомоби́ль

3 А́нна/телефо́н

4 И́горь/ра́дио

3 Complete the phrases by putting the word in brackets into the genitive singular.

1 Бутылка (винó) *a bottle of wine*
2 Полкилó (сыр) *half a kilo of cheese*
3 Бáнка (икрá) *a jar/tin of caviar*
4 Пáчка (чáй) *a packet of tea*
5 Бутылка (вóдка) *a bottle of vodka*

....

Insight

To learn the endings of a particular case, you might find it helpful to commit to memory a couple of short phrases for each gender, e.g.:

план гóрода   *a plan of the town*
бутылка воды   *a bottle of water*
мéста нет   *there's no room*

....

4 The restaurant has run out of everything – the waiter is explaining what isn't on the menu. Complete his statements by putting the word in brackets into the genitive singular.

e.g. кýрица → У нас нет кýрицы.   *We haven't got any chicken.*

1 У нас нет_____(ветчинá).   *We haven't got any ham.*
2 У нас нет_____(пи́во).   *We haven't got any beer.*
3 У нас нет_____(хлеб).   *We haven't got any bread.*
4 У нас нет_____(говя́дина). *We haven't got any beef.*
5 У нас нет_____(шоколáд).   *We haven't got any chocolate.*

> **For use of genitive case with prepositions, see Sections 11.2, 11.3, 11.4, 11.5, 11.6; for use of genitive singular with numerals, see Sections 6.2 and 6.3, for use of genitive with comparatives, see Sections 4.4.**

2.11 Genitive case – plural

You need to use the genitive plural when you are talking about a plural quantity, for example, 'a group of tourists', 'a lot of memories', 'no photographs', 'a box of chocolates'; it is also used with numbers 5 and above (except for compounds of 1, 2, 3 and 4).

Unlike most of the cases, the genitive plural has different endings for each gender.

There are three endings for the genitive plural of **masculine** nouns: -ов, -ев, -ей.

NB If a masculine word ends in ж, ч, ш, щ, add ей, not ов: e.g. нож (*knife*) → ножéй.

Nominative singular		Genitive plural
турúст	*tourist*	турúстов
трамвáй	*tram*	трамвáев
портфéль	*briefcase*	портфéлей

There are four endings for the genitive plural of **feminine** nouns: remove a and add nothing; remove я from ия and add й; remove ь and add ей.

Nominative singular		Genitive plural
шкóла	*school*	школ
недéля	*week*	недéль
стáнция	*station*	стáнций
дверь	*door*	дверéй

NB If the feminine word ends in -a and when you remove it you are left with a consonant 'cluster' (i.e. more than one), it is sometimes necessary to insert either o, e or ё (e if the 'cluster' you are left with is жк, чк, шк). E.g.:

Nominative singular		Genitive plural
ло́жка	*spoon*	ло́жек
ма́рка	*stamp*	ма́рок
сестра́	*sister*	сестёр

1 Underline the words in the following sentences which are in the genitive plural.

e.g. Он купи́л мно́го сувени́ров. *He bought a lot of souvenirs.*

1 В кла́ссе мно́го ма́льчиков. *There are many boys in the class.*

2 Вот докуме́нты студе́нтов. *Here are the students' documents.*

3 Он дал мне мно́го книг. *He gave me a lot of books.*

4 У нас нет ма́рок. *We have no stamps.*

5 Полкило́ помидо́ров, пожа́луйста. *Half a kilo of tomatoes, please.*

There are two endings for the genitive plural of **neuter** nouns: if the word ends in o, remove it; if it ends in e, add й and if it ends in ие.

Nominative singular		Genitive plural
ме́сто	*place*	мест
по́ле	*field*	поле́й
зда́ние	*building*	зда́ний

2 Give the genitive plural of the following nominative singular nouns.

e.g. су́мка → су́мок

1	час	*hour*	**6**	мо́ре	*sea*
2	река́	*river*	**7**	гости́ница	*hotel*
3	музе́й	*museum*	**8**	ня́ня	*nanny*
4	танцо́р	*dancer*	**9**	геро́й	*hero*
5	дверь (ж)	*door*	**10**	строи́тель	*builder*

NB If the neuter word ends in -o and when you remove it you are left with a consonant 'cluster' (i.e. more than one), it is sometimes necessary to insert either o or e. Two very common examples are окно́ (*window*) → о́кон and письмо́ (*letter*) → пи́сем (notice that here the e replaces ь).

3 Complete the shopping list by putting the word in brackets into the genitive plural.

1 полкило́ _____ (апельси́н) *half a kilo of oranges.*
2 коро́бка _____ (конфе́та) *a box of sweets*
3 коробо́к _____ (спи́чка) *a box of matches.*
4 па́чка _____ (сигаре́та) *a packet of cigarettes.*
5 гроздь _____ (бана́н) *a bunch of bananas.*

Insight

Both the genitive singular and the genitive plural are useful in shopping lists – e.g. пять буты́лок воды́ *five bottles of water.* Take care if eggs are on your shopping list! The nominative singular is яйцо́, the genitive singular is яйца́ and the genitive plural яйц.

4 Put the words in column A into the genitive plural, then match them up with the words in column B in order to produce the meaning in column C.

e.g. A ма́льчик B гру́ппа C *a group of boys* → гру́ппа ма́льчиков

A	B	C	
ма́льчик	гру́ппа		*a group of boys*
докуме́нт	нет	**1**	*lots of stations*

ма́рка	гру́ппа	**2**	*a bunch of roses*
врач	мно́го	**3**	*there are no stamps*
ро́за	па́чка	**4**	*a group of doctors*
ста́нция	буке́т	**5**	*a bundle of documents*

> ➤ **For use of genitive plural with numerals, see Section 6.2.**

2.12 Genitive case – irregular plurals

The nouns which have irregular nominative plurals have irregular genitive plurals based on their nominative plural forms – so, if you know which nouns have irregular nominative plurals, then you will be well on the way to sorting out nouns with irregular genitive plurals.

This is what happens to **masculine nouns** in the genitive plural: if the nominative plural ends in stressed á, then the genitive plural ending is óв (so not strikingly irregular, just be aware of the stressed ending).

If the nominative plural ends in:

- ья and the word is stressed on the stem, the genitive plural ending is -ьев
- stressed ья́, then the genitive plural ending is -éй
- -не, then the genitive plural ending is … nothing!

Nominative singular		Nominative plural	Genitive plural
го́род	*town*	города́	городо́в
стул	*chair*	сту́лья	сту́льев
друг	*friend*	друзья́	друзе́й
англича́нин	*Englishman*	англича́не	англича́н

There are very few irregular genitive plural endings for **feminine** nouns. The most common are the words for *mother* and *daughter*:

мать → матерéй   дочь → дочерéй

1 You are showing your holiday photographs. Explain what they are of by putting each noun into the genitive plural.

e.g. друг → Вот фотогрáфии друзéй. *Here are photographs of friends.*

1	брат	**6**	англичáнин
2	стул	**7**	сын
3	ребёнок	**8**	дочь
4	пóезд	**9**	граждани́н
5	гóрод	**10**	лист

Although a number of common **neuter** nouns have irregular nominative plural forms, only a few have irregular genitive plurals, e.g.:

врéмя   (*time*)   →   времён   у́хо   (*ear*)   →   ушéй
и́мя   (*name*)   →   имён

2 If you want to buy quantities of things, you'll need the genitive plural. Make sentences by using the following words (NB a mixture of regular and irregular).

e.g. конфéта → Я хочý купи́ть мнóго конфéт. *I want to buy a lot of sweets.*

1	яйцó	*egg*
2	апельси́н	*orange*
3	откры́тка	*postcard*
4	блýзка	*blouse*
5	конвéрт	*envelope*
6	рýчка	*pen*
7	сувени́р	*souvenir*

8 дом		*house*
9 я́блоко		*apple*
10 письмо́		*letter*

And finally, the genitive plural for 'children' and 'people' comes from their strikingly different nominative plural form:

Nominative singular	Nominative plural	Genitive plural
ребёнок	де́ти	дете́й
челове́к	лю́ди	люде́й

NB After a numerals which must be followed by the genitive plural - i.e. 5 and above (aprt from compounds of 1, 2, 3 and 4), the genitive plural of челове́к is челове́к (5 челове́к, *5 people*; толпа́ люде́й *a crowd of people*).

3 The following words are in the genitive plural. Put them into the nominative singular (NB another mixture of regular and irregular).

e.g. адресо́в → а́дрес

1	дере́вьев	**6**	уше́й
2	матере́й	**7**	бу́лок
3	гости́ниц	**8**	автомоби́лей
4	англича́н	**9**	времён
5	фотогра́фий	**10**	люде́й

➤ **For irregular nominative plurals, see Section 2.6 and for use of genitive case with numerals, see Sections 6.2 and 6.3.**

2.13 Dative case – singular

The principal meaning of the dative case is *to* or *for*. It must be used for the **indirect object** in a phrase; the indirect object is the person or thing to whom/which something is given, shown told, etc., e.g.:

Subject +	Verb +	Object +	Indirect object
Vadim	*gave*	*a bunch of roses*	*to Katya*
Вади́м	дал	буке́т роз	Ка́те

The dative case must also be used following certain verbs, of which the most common are звони́ть/позвони́ть (to ring), помога́ть/помо́чь (to help) and сове́товать /посове́товать (to advise).

There are two endings for the dative singular of **masculine** nouns: -y and -ю.

Nominative singular		Dative plural
брат	*brother*	бра́ту
Серге́й	*Sergei*	Серге́ю
учи́тель	*teacher*	учи́телю

There are two endings for the dative singular of **feminine** nouns: -e and -и.

Nominative singular		Dative plural
сестра́	*sister*	сестре́
Ка́тя	*Katya*	Ка́те
Мари́я	*Maria*	Мари́и

NB The two most common irregular dative feminine forms are for *mother* and *daughter*: мать → ма́тери and дочь → до́чери.

1 Which of the words in the following passage are in the dative singular?

e.g. Она́ звони́т **инжене́ру** ка́ждый день. *She rings the engineer every day.*

Бори́с никогда́ не помога́ет дру́гу, Ви́ктору. Éсли у Ви́ктора проблéма, он звони́т тёте и́ли дя́де. Дя́дя лю́бит помога́ть племя́ннику.

Boris never helps (his) friend, Viktor. If Viktor has a problem, he rings (his) aunt or uncle. (His) uncle likes to help (his) nephew.

2 Who gave what to whom? Make sentences using the words given (the direct objects – the presents – have already been put into the accusative case for you; the meaning of your completed sentence is on the right).

e.g. Сергéй/ру́чку/Елéна → Сергéй дал ру́чку Елéне.
Sergei gave a pen to Elena.
Елéна/носки́/Сергéй → Елéна дала́ носки́ Сергéю.
Elena gave socks to Sergei.

1 Он/кни́гу/Светла́на   *He gave a book to Svetlana.*
2 Дочь/духи́/мать   *The daughter gave perfume to (her) mother.*
3 Он/цветы́/медсестра́   *He gave flowers to the nurse.*
4 А́ня/мотоци́кл/Андрéй   *Anya gave Andrei a motorbike.*
5 Она́/письмо́/дирéктор   *She gave the letter to the director.*

There are two endings for the dative singular of **neuter** nouns: -у and -ю.

Nominative singular		Dative plural
окно́	*window*	окну́
мо́ре	*sea*	мо́рю
зда́ние	*building*	зда́нию

NB The neuter words врéмя and и́мя form their dative singular as follows:
врéмя → врéмени; и́мя → и́мени.

3 Put the following words into the dative singular.

1 врач	*doctor*	**6** Ита́лия	*Italy*
2 журнали́ст	*journalist*	**7** Зо́я	*Zoya*
3 И́горь (м)	*Igor*	**8** ку́хня	*kitchen*
4 по́ле	*field*	**9** писа́тель	*writer*
5 у́лица	*street*	**10** свекро́вь (ж)	*mother-in-law*

4 Complete the passage by putting the words in brackets into the dative singular.

Вади́м звони́т _____ (мать), _____ (Татья́на), ка́ждый день в 4 часа́. Он ча́сто звони́т _____ (брат), _____ (Константи́н), и _____ (друг), _____ (Анто́н).

> ➤ **For use of dative case with prepositions, see Sections 11.3, 11.4, 11.5, 11.6; for use of dative with expressions of possibility, impossibility and necessity, see Section 10.5; for use of dative with impersonal verbs, see Section 10.5.**

2.14 Dative case – plural

The dative plural must be used if the **indirect object** of a phrase is plural; the indirect object is the person or thing to whom/which something is given, shown told, etc., e.g.:

Subject +	Verb +	Object +	Indirect object
Vadim	*gave*	*the cards*	*to his sisters*

The dative plural is straightforward, because the endings for nouns are the same for all genders. There are two possible endings (-ам, or -ям) and to determine which one should be used, look at the last letter of the nominative singular.

If the noun ends in a consonant, -a or -o in the nominative singular, then the dative plural ending is -ам. Add this ending to nouns ending in a consonant; to nouns ending in -a or -o, remove the last letter of the nominative singular, then add -ам, for example:

спортсме́н	→	Врач сове́тует спортсме́нам.	*The doctor advises the sportsmen.*
сестра́	→	Брат сове́тует сёстрам.	*The brother advises (his) sisters.*

If the noun ends in anything else in the nominative singular (i.e. -й, -ь, -я, -ия, -е, -ие), then the dative plural ending is -ям. Remove the last letter of the nominative singular and add -ям, for example:

геро́й	→	Президе́нт дал геро́ям меда́ли.	*The president gave medals to the heroes.*
строи́тель	→	Банки́р сове́тует строи́телям.	*The banker advises the builders.*

1 Match the phrases on the left with those on the right so that they accord with the English translations which follow.

1	Мини́стры сове́туют	**a**	актёрам
2	Продю́сер звони́т	**b**	ме́неджерам
3	Врач помога́ет	**c**	писа́телям
4	Программи́ст помога́ет	**d**	пацие́нтам
5	Секрета́рь советуе́т	**e**	поли́тикам

1 *The producer rings the actors.*
2 *The secretary advises the managers.*
3 *The ministers advise the politicians.*
4 *The computer programmer helps the writers.*
5 *The doctor helps the patients.*

Nouns which have irregular nominative plurals form their dative plural from the nominative plural:

Nominative singular	Nominative plural	Genitive plural
друг	друзья́	друзья́м
ребёнок	де́ти	де́тям
челове́к	лю́ди	лю́дям

The words дочь, вре́мя and и́мя form their dative plurals as follows: дочь → дочеря́м, вре́мя → времена́м, и́мя → имена́м.

2 Give the dative plural of the following nouns.

1 трамва́й	*tram*	**6** почтальо́н	*postman*
2 де́рево	*tree*	**7** преподава́тель	*teacher (in higher education)*
3 карти́на	*picture*	**8** зда́ние	*building*
4 худо́жник	*artist*	**9** ло́шадь (ж)	*horse*
5 сын	*son*	**10** официа́нтка	*waitress*

3 Build sentences from the three Russian words given in each line. The third word is in the nominative singular – you will need to put it into the dative plural.

e.g. Бабу́шка/конфе́ты/ребёнок → Бабу́шка даёт конфе́ты де́тям.

1 Касси́рша/сда́чу/клие́нт
The cashier gives change to the customers.

2 Ученики́/кни́ги/учи́тель
The pupils give the books to the teachers.

3 Медсестра́/лека́рство/ пацие́нт
The nurse gives medicine to the patients.

| 4 Гид/биле́ты/англича́нин | *The guide gives the tickets to the Englishmen.* |
| 5 Он/пода́рки/друзья́ | *He gives presents to (his) friends.* |

> ➤ **For use of dative case with prepositions, see Section 11.4; for use of dative with expressions of possibility, impossibility and necessity see Section 10.5; for use of dative with impersonal verbs, see Section 10.5; for irregular nominative plurals, see Section 2.6.**

2.15 Instrumental case – singular

The principal meaning of the instrumental case is *by* or *with* – i.e. it explains the means by which an action is achieved. In the sentence below, you would need to use the instrumental case for the words underlined:

Ivan went to Moscow by <u>train</u>. *He took photos with his* <u>camera</u>.

NB! However, if a phrase including 'with' means 'accompanied by' (e.g. 'tea with lemon', 'I'm going with my sister'), then the preposition с must be used before the noun in the instrumental: e.g. 'Я е́ду в Ло́ндон по́ездом с сестро́й' *I'm going to London with my sister.* Note that the vowel o is sometimes added to the preposition с when it is followed by a word which starts with a cluster of consonants, e.g. со внима́нием *with attention.*

The instrumental case is also used:

1 when a verb is followed by a 'complement' (which gives more information about the subject of a sentence). For example: *Ivan works as a <u>photographer</u>.*

2 in time phrases relating to seasons and parts of the day, e.g.:

ле́том	*in summer*	у́тром	*in/during the morning*
зимо́й	*in winter*	ве́чером	*in/during the evening*

1 with some common reflexive verbs, e.g. занима́ться (*to be busy, occupy oneself*) and интересова́ться (*to be interested in*): он интересу́ется рисова́нием, *he is interested in drawing.*

2 Underline the nouns in the following passage which you would need to put into the instrumental case in Russian.

In the evening I am going by train with Elena to Viktor's. Viktor works in Novgorod as an architect. Viktor's interested in sport. In the summer, he plays tennis with Sasha twice a week.

To form the instrumental case:

- **Masculine** nouns ending in a consonant add -ом, otherwise remove the last letter and add -ем: ве́чер (*evening*) → ве́чером, трамва́й → трамва́ем, учи́тель → учи́телем. Remember that you can't have unstressed о after ж, ч, ш, щ, ц! So the instrumental of муж (*husband*) → му́жем.
- **Feminine** nouns: remove last letter and add -ой to words which end in -а; add -ей to words ending in -я or -ия. If a word ends in -ь, don't remove it, just add -ю. Eg: зима́ (*winter*) → зимо́й, А́нглия → А́нглией, о́сень (*autumn*) → о́сенью (**NB** мать → ма́терью, дочь → до́черью). Remember that you can't have unstressed о after ж, ч, ш, щ, ц! So the instrumental of у́лица → у́лицей.
- **Neuter** words: just add -м! у́тро (*morning*) → у́тром, зда́ние → зда́нием (**NB** вре́мя → вре́менем).

2 Here is the passage from Exercise 1, this time in Russian. Complete it by putting the words in brackets into the instrumental singular.

Ве́чером я е́ду _____ (по́езд) с _____ (Еле́на) к Ви́ктору. Ви́ктор рабо́тает в Но́вгороде _____ (архите́ктор). Ви́ктор интересу́ется _____ (спо́рт).

44

_____ (Ле́то) он игра́ет в те́ннис с _____ (Са́ша) два ра́за в неде́лю.

3 Each customer in the restaurant wants something slightly different. Make up their requests by giving the instrumental of the following words.

a) ры́ба *fish*
e.g. рис → Мне, пожа́луйста, ры́бу с ри́сом. *For me, please, fish with rice.*

1 хлеб	*bread*
2 сала́т	*salad*
3 карто́шка	*potato*

b) чай *tea*
e.g. са́хар → Мне, пожа́луйста, чай с са́харом. *For me, please, tea with sugar.*

4 молоко́	*milk*
5 лимо́н	*lemon*
6 пече́нье	*biscuit*

Insight

In Russian, the word for 'instrumental' is твори́тельный, from the verb *to create* (твори́ть/сотвори́ть) – i.e. it is the case which shows us the person or object making something possible (*I travel to work by train*). Remember it is also often used to explain when something happens; e.g. *in the evening, in summer*.)

4 Who is going to the cinema with whom? Complete the details by putting the names in brackets into the instrumental case:

e.g. Бори́с → Мы идём в теа́тр с Бори́сом.

1 И́горь (м)
2 профе́ссор
3 Мари́я

4 друг

5 Ка́тя

> ➢ **For use of instrumental case with prepositions,**
> **see Section 11.2; for spelling rules, see Section 1.3.**

2.16 Instrumental case – plural

The instrumental plural must be used if the instrument by which an
action is performed is in the plural (e.g. *they are playing <u>with new
racquets</u>*). It will also be needed for the plural of nouns after the
preposition 'c' (e.g. *they are visiting the exhibition <u>with friends</u>*),
and after verbs which require the instrumental (e.g. занима́ться/
заня́ться *to be occupied*, and интересова́ться/заинтересова́ться
to be interested).

The instrumental plural is straightforward, because the endings
are the same for all genders, and there are just two to choose from:
-ами and -ями; to determine which one should be used, look at the
last letter of the nominative singular.

If the noun ends in a consonant, -a or -o in the nominative singular,
then the ending is -ами. Add this ending to nouns ending in a
consonant. To nouns ending in -a or -o, remove the last letter of the
nominative singular, then add -ами, for example:

гриб *(mushroom)* →	суп с гриба́ми	*soup with mushrooms*
		(i.e. mushroom soup)
ма́рка *(stamp)* →	интересова́ться	*to be interested in*
	ма́рками	*stamps*
письмо́ *(letter)* →	занима́ться	*to be busy with letters*
	пи́сьмами	

If the noun ends in anything else in the nominative singular (i.e.
-й, -ь, -я, -ия, -е, -ие), then remove the last letter of the nominative
singular and add -ями, for example:

гость (*guest*) → Он éдет в теáтр с гостя́ми. – *He is going to the theatre with guests.*

1 Who is interested in what? Make sentences by putting the singular noun into the instrumental plural:

e.g. Сергéй/кни́га (*book*) → Сергéй интересу́ется кни́гами.

1 Ири́на/симфóния (*symphony*)
2 Валенти́н/фильм (*film*)
3 Архитéктор/окнó (*window*)
4 Гитари́ст/гита́ра (*guitar*)
5 Студéнт/писáтель (*writer*)

NB! Nouns which have irregular nominative plurals form their instrumental plural from the nominative plural (but the choice is still only between the endings -ами, or -ями), for example:

Nominative singular	Nominative plural	Instrumental plural
врéмя	временá	временáми
гóрод	городá	городáми
друг	друзья́	друзья́ми
стул	сту́лья	сту́льями
у́хо	уши́	уша́ми

NB The following are exceptions and do not end in -ами, or -ями:

дочь	дóчери	дочерьми́
ребёнок	дéти	детьми́
человéк	лю́ди	людьми́

2 Put the following words into the instrumental plural.

e.g. магази́н (*shop*) → магази́нами

1	апте́ка	*chemist's*	6	де́рево	*tree*
2	зда́ние	*building*	7	друг	*friend*
3	предме́т	*subject*	8	экску́рсия	*excursion*
4	писа́тель	*writer*	9	дочь	*daughter*
5	откры́тие	*discovery*	10	компью́тер	*computer*

3 Complete the menu by putting the words in brackets into the instrumental plural.

e.g. суп с _____ (гриб) → суп с гриба́ми *mushroom soup*

МЕНЮ

1 суп с _____ (помидо́р) — *tomato soup*

2 сала́т с _____ (огуре́ц) — *cucumber salad*

ры́ба с жа́реной карто́шкой — *fish with fried potato*

бефстро́ганов — *beef stroganoff*

ку́рица с овоща́ми — *chicken with vegetables*

3 торт с _____(оре́х) — *walnut cake*

4 моро́женое с _____ (фрукт) — *ice-cream with fruits*

➤ **For uses of instrumental case, see Section 2.15; for further uses with prepositions, see Section 11.5; for nominative plurals, see Sections 2.5 and 2.6.**

2.17 Prepositional case – singular

Unlike the other cases, the prepositional case has no meaning of its own and can only be used after certain prepositions, most of which, appropriately, give information about position. The two prepositions most commonly used with the prepositional case are в (*in, at*) and на (*on, at*).

There is one regular ending for **masculine** nouns: -e.

Nom. sing.	Prep. sing.	Example	Meaning
о́фис	о́фисе	Я рабо́таю в о́фисе.	*I work in an office.*
музе́й	музе́е	Он рабо́тает в музе́е.	*He works in a museum.*
стол	столе́	Кни́га на столе́.	*The book is on the table.*

There are two regular endings for **feminine** nouns: -e and -и.

Nom. sing.	Prep. sing.	Example	Meaning
гости́ница	гостини́це	Я рабо́таю в гости́нице.	*I work in a hotel.*
дере́вня	дере́вне	Он живёт в дере́вне.	*He lives in a village.*
А́нглия	А́нглии	Я живу́ в А́нглии.	*I live in England.*
тетра́дь	тетра́ди	Упражне́ние в тетра́ди.	*The exercise is in the exercise book.*

NB *Mother* – мать → ма́тери and *daughter* – дочь → до́чери.

There are two regular endings for **neuter** nouns: -e and -и.

Nom. sing.	Prep. sing.	Example	Meaning
письмо́	письме́	Но́вости в письме́.	*The news is in the letter.*
по́ле	по́ле	Пала́тка в по́ле.	*The tent is in the field.*
зда́ние	зда́нии	О́фис в зда́нии.	*The office is in the building.*

NB Irregular forms for *time* – вре́мя (вре́мени) and *name* – и́мя (и́мени).

1 Make up sentences explaining who works where.

e.g. лабора́нт/лаборато́рия → Лабора́нт рабо́тает в лаборато́рии *the lab assistant works in the laboratory*

1	врач/в/больни́ца	*the doctor works in the hospital*
2	архите́ктор/в/зда́ние	*the architect works in the building*
3	моря́к/на/мо́ре	*the sailor works at sea*
4	официа́нт/в/рестора́н	*the waiter works in the restaurant*
5	учи́тель/шко́ла	*the teacher works in the school*

Some masculine nouns have the irregular prepositional ending -у́. The most common of these are:

аэропо́рт (*airport*)	→	аэропорту́	пол (*floor*)	→ полу́
бе́рег (*bank, shore*)	→	берегу́	сад (*garden*)	→ саду́
год (*year*)	→	году́	снег (*snow*)	→ снегу́
лёд (*ice*)	→	льду*	у́гол (*corner*)	→ углу́*
лес (*forest*)	→	лесу́	шкаф (*cupboard*)	→ шкафу́
*(Fleeting vowels)				

2 Make up sentences explaining where things are.

e.g. су́мка/на/пол → Су́мка на полу́. *The bag is on the floor*

1	самолёт/в/аэропо́рт	*The plane is at the airport*
2	ви́за/в/па́спорт	*The visa is in the passport*
3	шу́ба/в/шкаф	*The fur coat is in the cupboard*
4	компью́тер/на/стол	*The computer is on the table*
5	Мадри́д/в/Испа́ния	*Madrid is in Spain*

3 Put the following words into the prepositional case.

1	ме́сто	*place*
2	бассе́йн	*swimming pool*

3	автомоби́ль (м)	*car*
4	лаборато́рия	*laboratory*
5	сад	*garden*
6	музе́й	*museum*
7	трамва́й	*tram*
8	по́чта	*post office*
9	ку́хня	*kitchen*
10	по́ле	*field*

4 Match each question with an appropriate answer.

1	Ро́зы в шкафу́?	**a**	Нет, она́ в саду́
2	Соба́ка в университе́те?	**b**	Нет, он в теа́тре
3	Официа́нт в лаборато́рии?	**c**	Нет, они́ в буке́те
4	Актёр в о́фисе?	**d**	Нет, он на стадио́не
5	Спортсме́н на ку́хне?	**e**	Нет, он в рестора́не

> **For fleeting vowels, see Section 2.5; for more detail on prepositions used with prepositional case, see Section 11.6.**

2.18 Prepositional case – plural

The prepositional plural is needed when a plural noun follows prepositions which take the prepositional case, such as в (*in*, *at*) and на (*on*, *at*).

The prepositional plural is straightforward, because the endings are the same for all genders, and there are just two to choose from: -ах or -ях; to determine which one should be used, look at the last letter of the nominative singular.

If the noun ends in a consonant, -a or -o in the nominative singular, then the ending is -ах. Add this ending to nouns ending in a consonant. To nouns ending in -a or -o, remove the last letter of the nominative singular, then add -ах, for example:

ресторан	→	Они обедают в ресторанах.	*They have lunch in restaurants.*
квартира	→	Они живут в квартирах.	*They live in flats.*
место	→	Они сидят на местах у окна.	*They are sitting in seats by the window.*

If a noun ends in anything else in the nominative singular (i.e. -й, -ь, -я, -ия, -е, -ие), then the ending is -ях. Remove the last letter of the nominative singular and add -ях, for example:

| автомобиль | → | Водители ждут в автомобилях. | *Drivers are waiting in (their) cars.* |
| станция | → | Пассажиры ждут на станциях. | *Passengers wait at stations.* |

1 Make sentences from the words that follow.

e.g. Туристы отдыхают/пляж → Туристы отдыхают на пляжах. *Tourists rest on beaches.*

1	Продавцы работают/магазин	*Shop assistants work in shops.*
2	Студенты учатся/университет	*Students study at universities.*
3	Фермеры работают/ферма	*Farmers work on farms.*
4	Химики работают/лаборатория	*Chemists work in laboratories.*
5	Учителя работают/школа	*Teachers work in schools.*

Nouns which have irregular nominative plurals form their prepositional plural from the nominative plural (but the choice is still only between the endings -ах, or -ях), e.g.:

Nominative singular	Nominative plural	Prepositional plural
го́род	города́	города́х
друг	друзья́	друзья́х
ребёнок	де́ти	де́тях
стул	сту́лья	сту́льях
челове́к	лю́ди	лю́дях

The words мать, дочь, вре́мя and и́мя form their prepositional plurals as follows: мать → матеря́х, дочь → дочеря́х, вре́мя → времена́х, и́мя → имена́х.

2 Put the following nouns into the prepositional plural:

1 дере́вня   *village*   **6** парфюме́рия   *perfume shop*
2 го́род   *town*   **7** портфе́ль (м)   *briefcase*
3 центр   *centre*   **8** по́ле   *field*
4 страна́   *country*   **9** но́мер   *hotel room*
5 ме́сто   *place*   **10** стул   *chair*

3 Complete the passage about tourists below by putting the words in brackets into the prepositional plural. Use the English translation which follows to help you.

Тури́сты живу́т в _____ (гости́ница) и в _____ (ке́мпинг). Они́ прово́дят не́которое вре́мя в _____ (музе́й), в _____ (галере́я), в _____ (собо́р) и к концу́ дня, в _____(универма́г). Они́ то́же прово́дят не́которое вре́мя в _____ (клуб), в _____ (са́уна) и в _____ (рестора́н).

Tourists live in hotels and on campsites. They spend a certain amount of time in museums, galleries, cathedrals and, towards

the end of the day, in department stores. They also spend a
certain amount of time in clubs, saunas and restaurants.

> ➤ **For more detail on prepositions used with**
> **prepositional case, see Section 11.6; for irregular**
> **nominative plurals, see Section 2.6.**

2.19 Six-case summary

Key steps in being able to express yourself confidently in Russian
are a) understanding when each case is needed and b) knowing
the case endings of nouns in the singular and plural. Here is
a summary of the function of each case; in the examples, the
underlined word gives an example of the individual case summary.
In a typical sentence, it is necessary to use several different case
endings, so in this section, the exercises all follow the explanations,
to give you a chance to practise the key steps a) and b).

1 Nominative shows us who or what is performing the action of
a verb. The gender (masculine, feminine, neuter) of a noun is
indicated by its ending (masculine: consonant, -й,-ь, feminine:
-а, -я, -ия, neuter: -о -е, -ие). Remember that nouns are listed in
dictionaries in their nominative singular form.

<u>Мария</u> даёт бутылку вина Сергею.
<u>*Maria*</u> *gives the bottle of wine to Sergei.*

> **Insight**
>
> A soft sign ending can indicate a masculine *or* a feminine
> noun. Note that:
>
> **1** the vast majority of nouns ending in -сть are feminine; the
> only common noun to break this rule is гость (*guest*).
> **2** all months of the year ending in a soft sign are masculine.

2 **Accusative** shows us the person or thing that has an action done to it (the direct object). Also used after certain prepositions. Russian distinguishes between inanimate (a thing) and animate (a person or animal).

Мария хорошо знает <u>город</u>.
Maria knows the <u>town</u> well.

Мария хорошо понимает <u>книги</u>.
Maria understands the <u>books</u> well.

Мария хорошо знает <u>директора</u>.
Maria knows the <u>director</u> well.

Мария хорошо понимает <u>студентов</u>.
Maria understands the <u>students</u> well.

3 **Genitive** is the Russian way of saying 'of', so it indicates possession and is also used when talking about quantities (also used after certain prepositions and sometimes with the comparative):

Мария даёт бутылку <u>вина</u> Сергею.
Maria gives the bottle of <u>wine</u> to Sergei.

1 Underline the words in the following sentences which are in the accusative case (animate and inanimate).

e.g. Я люблю спорт и музыку.   *I like sport and music.*

1 Борис знает брата Ивана.   *Boris knows Ivan's brother.*
2 Вы хотите смотреть телевизор? *Do you want to watch television?*
3 Она купила стулья.   *She bought the chairs.*
4 Виктор увидел друзей в театре. *Viktor saw (his) friends at the theatre.*
5 Мы заказали курицу с рисом.   *We ordered chicken with rice.*

2a) Match the phrases on the left with those on the right, then find the matching English translation.

1 В офисе много   **a** врачей
2 В больнице много   **b** актёров

3 В шко́ле мно́го	c профессоро́ь
4 В университе́те мно́го	d компью́теров
5 В теа́тре мно́го	e учителе́й

1 *There are lots of actors in the theatre.*
2 *There are lots of professors at the university.*
3 *There are lots of computers in the office.*
4 *There are lots of teachers in the school.*
5 *There are lots of doctors in the hospital.*

2b) Look at the list of words a–e in Exercise 2a) again.

1 Which case are they all in?
2 Now put each of them back into the nominative singular.

4 **Dative** shows us the indirect object of a sentence or phrase (the person or thing that is shown, told, etc. something). Its basic meaning is 'to', 'for' (also used after certain prepositions and verbs).

Мари́я даёт буты́лку вина́ <u>Серге́ю</u>.
Maria gives the bottle of wine <u>to Sergei</u>.

5 **Instrumental** is used to describe the means by which an action is performed (e.g. 'by train', 'with a pen'), to describe accompanying circumstances (e.g. 'tea with lemon' with the preposition c), for the complement of a verb and after certain reflexive verbs.

Серге́й лю́бит е́здить <u>по́ездом</u>. *Sergei likes to travel <u>by train</u>.*
Мне сала́т с <u>помидо́рами</u>, пожа́луйста. <u>*Tomato*</u> *salad for me, please.*

6 **Prepositional**: this case has no 'meaning' of its own; it is used in phrases which indicate position and specifically with the prepositions в (in, at) and на (on, at).

Мария купила бутылку вина **в супермаркете**. *Maria bought the bottle of wine <u>at the supermarket</u>.*

3 Complete the following sentences by putting the word in brackets into the appropriate case (if the word in brackets is plural, you will need to put it into a plural case form).

1 Сергей любит _____ (дерево).
2 Мы живём в _____ (город).
3 Ольга дала _____ (Вадим) _____ (картина).
4 Я знаю _____ (студенты).
5 Я люблю ездить _____ (поезд) с _____ (друзья).
6 Он смотрит фильм с _____ (брат).
7 Анна работает _____ (медсестра) в _____ (больница).

➤ **For nominative case endings, see Sections 2.4, 2.5 and 2.6; for accusative, see Sections 2.7, 2.8 and 2.9; for genitive, see Sections 2.10, 2.11 and 2.12; for dative, see Sections 2.13 and 2.14; for instrumental, see Sections 2.15 and 2.16; for prepositional, see Sections 2.17 and 2.18. For use of cases after prepositions, see Section 11.2–11.7.**

2.20 Ten things to remember

1 In dictionaries and vocabularies nouns are given in the nominative singular.

2 A typical sentence may include several nouns which require different cases: *Yesterday I saw Ivan's* (genitive) *brother* (animate accusative) *in the supermarket* (prepositional). Don't worry! – it does get easier with practice, but to start with it's very important to work out which cases you should be using.

3 As well as working out which case of a noun to use, remember to work out the *number* of the noun (singular or plural?) and the *gender* (masculine, feminine or neuter?).

4 The two spelling rules are really important when you are applying the different case endings. If in doubt, have another look at Section 1.3!

5 The accusative case has two forms: one for inanimate nouns (things) and one for animate nouns (people and animals).

6 When you are learning and using the case endings of feminine nouns, take care to distinguish between those ending in -я and those which end in -ия, because they *decline* differently (i.e. they take different endings).

7 When you are learning and using the case endings of neuter nouns, take care to distinguish between those ending in -е and those which end in -ие, because they *decline* differently (i.e. they take different endings).

8 *Sergei rang Ivan because he wanted to help him.* Remember that the verbs *to ring* and *to help* are followed by the dative case. Ива́н позвони́л Серге́ю, потому́ что он хоте́л помо́чь ему́.

9 Some common reflexive verbs are followed by the instrumental case, e.g.: занима́ться спо́ртом *to occupy oneself with sport*, интересова́ться му́зыкой *to be interested in music*.

10 Whenever you learn a preposition (i.e. a word which comes before a noun or pronoun and which indicates position, time, method), take to learn which case must follow it (and you can check this in Unit 11).

3

Adjectives (1)

3.1 Using adjectives

An adjective is a word which describes a noun, indicating, for example, colour, size, shape, mood – a *boring* film, a *red* car, an *enormous* dog, a *round* hole. In Russian, every adjective must agree with the noun it describes in *number* (singular or plural), *gender* (masculine, feminine or neuter) and *case* (nominative, accusative, genitive, dative, instrumental, prepositional).

3.2 Cases and groups of adjectives

Like nouns, adjectives have endings for each of the six cases, singular and plural. This is not as daunting as it may sound, because with adjectives it is possible to divide them into neat groups, and each group follows the same sort of pattern.

Insight

For adjectives, as for nouns, it is vital to remember the two spelling rules:

1 Never write ы, ю, я after г, к, х, ж, ч, ш, щ; instead write и, у, а!
2 Never write an unstressed о after ж, ч, ш, щ, ц; instead write е!

3.3 Unstressed adjectives – nominative singular and plural

Adjectives are made up of a 'stem' and an 'ending' (the 'ending' is the last two letters of the adjective). The adjectives dealt with in this unit all have stressed stems (and, therefore, unstressed endings). There are different endings for masculine, feminine and neuter singular, but the nominative plural ending is the same for all genders. Dictionaries always give the masculine singular nominative form of the adjective and it is this form which tells us what sort of adjective it is (unstressed, stressed or soft).

The ending for **masculine** unstressed adjectives is -ый: но́вый телеви́зор, *new television*. Some masculine unstressed adjectives end in -ий, rather than -ый because the last letter of their 'stem' is г, к, х, ж, ч, ш, щ (first spelling rule). Two of the most common are the adjectives meaning *small* and *good*: ма́ленький ма́льчик, *small boy*; хоро́ший журна́л, *good magazine*.

NB Although some nouns with masculine meanings have feminine endings (e.g. мужчи́на (*man*), де́душка (*grandfather*)), adjectives used to describe them must be masculine: ста́рый де́душка, *old grandfather*.

1 Add the masculine adjective endings in the following phrases:

1	му́др ____ план	*a wise plan*
2	но́в ___ профе́ссор	*a new professor*
3	лёгк ___ чемода́н	*a light suitcase*
4	свёж ___ цвето́к	*a fresh flower*
5	интере́сн ___ журна́л	*an interesting magazine*

The ending for **feminine** unstressed adjectives is -ая (easy to remember, because feminine nouns usually end in -а or -я): но́вая гости́ница, *new hotel*, ста́рая ку́хня, *old kitchen*.

The ending for **neuter** unstressed adjectives is -ое (easy to remember, because neuter nouns usually end in -о or -е): но́вое окно, *new window*. Some neuter unstressed adjectives end in -ее, not -ое, because of the second spelling rule, which does not allow an unstressed о to appear after ж, ч, ш, щ, ц: свежее яйцо, *fresh egg*, хорошее место, *good place*.

The ending for all nominative **plural** adjectives of all genders is -ые. However, if the last letter of an adjective's 'stem' is г, к, х, ж, ч, ш, щ, then the ending must be -ие (in accordance with the first spelling rule): новые телевизоры, *new televisions*, старые кухни, *old kitchens*, хорошие места, *good places*.

2 Choose the appropriate adjectives from the box to describe each person – give the adjectives appropriate endings.

высокий	маленький	стройный	толстый
tall	*small*	*slim*	*fat*

женщина *woman*

мужчина *man*

1 _____ женщина *woman*
2 _____ мужчина *man*

3 Match the phrases on the left with those on the right, using the English translation as a guide.

1 хорошая	**a** лекции	*a good opera*
2 интересные	**b** фильм	*interesting lectures*
3 московское	**c** опера	*the Moscow metro*

| **4** маленький | **d** метро́ | *a small theatre* |
| **5** ску́чный | **e** теа́тр | *a boring film* |

Insight

For the nominative of masculine singular, neuter singular and for nominative plural adjectives remember that you need to be on the look out for when you need to write и rather than ы, and е rather than о.

4 The adjectives in brackets are in the masculine singular form. Make them 'agree' with their noun (e.g. make sure you put a feminine adjective ending on the adjective if it is describing a feminine noun).

e.g. (вку́сный) то́рты *delicious cakes* → вку́сные то́рты

1	_____(краси́вый) шко́ла	*a beautiful school*
2	_____(жёлтый) окно́	*a yellow window*
3	_____(све́жий) молоко́	*fresh milk*
4	_____(хоро́ший) журнали́ст	*a good journalist*
5	_____(до́брый) у́тро	*good morning*

> **For adjectival cases other than the nominative, see Sections 3.8–3.17.**

3.4 Stressed adjectives (nominative singular and plural)

A **stressed adjective** can be identified by looking at the masculine singular nominative form – it will end in -о́й: молодо́й футболи́ст, *a young football player*.

The **feminine** form of a stressed adjective is exactly the same as that of an unstressed adjective – it will end in -а́я: молода́я актри́са, *a young actress*.

The **neuter** form of a stressed adjective is exactly the same as that of an unstressed adjective – it will end in -ое: молодо́е де́рево, *a young tree*.

NB The Russian word for *big* is большо́й. Because the ending is stressed the letter ш *can* be followed by the letter о́ – this applies both to the masculine singular and to the neuter singular: Большо́й теа́тр, *Bolshoi Theatre*, большо́е окно́, *a big window*.

Plural stressed adjectives in the nominative end in -ые, whatever the gender of the noun they are describing: молоды́е лю́ди, *young people*. If the adjective's stem ends in г, к, х, ж, ч, ш, щ, then the ending must be -ие (in accordance with the first spelling rule): други́е лю́ди, *other people*.

1 Make the stressed adjectives in the following sentences agree with their nouns.

1 (плохо́й) _____ пого́да	*bad weather*
2 (прямо́й) _____ поезда́	*direct trains*
3 (молодо́й) _____ дере́вья	*young trees*
4 (родно́й) _____ язы́к	*native language*
5 (большо́й) _____ зда́ние	*a big building*
6 (передово́й) _____ статья́	*a leading article*
7 (друго́й) _____ теа́тры	*other theatres*
8 (сухо́й) _____ вино́	*dry wine*

> **For explanation of the role of adjectives in a sentence and of stems and endings, see Section 3.3; for adjectival cases other than the nominative, see Sections 3.8–3.17.**

3.5 Soft adjectives

There are only about 40 **soft adjectives**. You can recognize them because their masculine singular will end in -ний: после́дний авто́бус, *the last bus*. The feminine ending for a soft adjective is -яя; the neuter ending is -ее and the plural is -ие: вече́рняя газе́та, *evening paper*, зи́мнее у́тро, *a winter morning*, после́дние но́вости, *the latest news*.

Most soft adjectives are connected with time and seasons, as in the last examples. Others indicate location (e.g. Да́льний Восто́к *the Far East*) and two indicate colour:

си́ний дива́н   ка́рие глаза́
a navy blue sofa   *hazel eyes*

NB ка́рий is the only soft adjective whose stem does not end in н.

1 Underline the soft adjectives in the following sentences (not all the adjectives in the sentences are soft!).

1 Я чита́ю интере́сную у́треннюю газе́ту.

I'm reading an interesting morning paper.

2 Ни́жняя по́лка о́чень удо́бная.

The bottom bunk is very comfortable.

3 Вот си́няя ле́тняя ю́бка.

Here's a dark blue summer skirt.

4 Сосе́дний дом о́чень ста́рый.

The neighbouring house is very old.

5 Вот за́втрашняя програ́мма. *Here's tomorrow's programme.*

2 Match the phrases on the left with those on the right, using the English translation as a guide.

1 после́дняя   **a** у́тро   *the last station*
2 весе́ннее   **b** же́нщина   *a spring morning*
3 дре́вний   **c** кани́кулы *an ancient cathedral*
4 ле́тние   **d** собо́р   *summer holidays*
5 за́мужняя   **e** ста́нция   *a married woman*

➤ **For explanation of the role of adjectives in a sentence and of stems and endings, see Section 3.3; for adjectival cases other than the nominative, see Sections 3.8–3.17.**

3.6 Possessive adjectives (nominative singular and plural)

The possessive adjectives (my, your, etc.) indicate possession or a relationship; for example твой дом, *your house*, моя тётя, *my aunt*, Это твоё письмо? *Is this your letter?*

Possessive adjectives indicating *my, your, our* must agree in number, gender and case with the noun they qualify, rather than with the possessor:

> «Это моя сестра,» говорит Борис.
> *'This is my sister,' says Boris.*

These are the forms for the nominative singular and plural.

	Masculine	Feminine	Neuter	Plural
my (mine)	мой	моя	моё	мои
your(s), belonging to ты	твой	твоя	твоё	твои
our(s)	наш	наша	наше	наши
your(s), belonging to вы	ваш	ваша	ваше	ваши

Это твой дом?   Это моя собака.   Это ваше место?
   Вот наши внуки.
Is this your house?   This is my dog.   Is this your seat?
   Here are our grandchildren.

1 Change the English adjectives or pronouns given into their corresponding Russian forms.

   e.g. (*My*) собака в саду   →   Моя собака в саду. *My dog is in the garden.*

1 Вот (*our*) биле́ты.

2 Где (*your* (formal)) ви́зы?

3 (*My*) сестра́ прие́дет за́втра.

4 Куда́ идёт (*your* (informal)) брат?

5 (*Our*) сад о́чень большо́й.

6 (*My*) ба́бушка живёт в Ки́еве.

7 (*Your* (informal)) сын – студе́нт?

8 (*Our*) друг в Москве́.

Possessive adjectives indicating **his/hers, theirs** are invariable (i.e. never change) – this is because their literal meaning is 'of him', 'of her', 'of them':

belonging to он→	belonging to она́→	belonging to оно́→	belonging to они́→
его́	её	его́	их

Э́то его́ ме́сто?
Is this his seat?

Э́то её биле́т?
Is this her ticket?

Э́то их програ́мма?
Is this their programme?

2 Match the phrases on the right and the left, using the English translations as a guide.

1 Она́ не зна́ет,   **a** где их гости́ница.

2 Мы не зна́ем,   **b** где ва́ши кни́ги.

3 Вы не зна́ете,   **c** где её ключ.

4 Они́ не зна́ют,   **d** где на́ша соба́ка.

5 Ты не зна́ешь,   **e** где твоё письмо́.

1 *She doesn't know where her key is.*

2 *We don't know where our dog is.*

3 *You don't know where your books are.*

4 *They don't know where their hotel is.*

5 *You don't know where your letter is.*

3 Fill in the gaps by giving the appropriate form of the possessive adjective in order to complete the conversation.

1 Здра́вствуйте. Э́то _____ (*your*) бага́ж?

2 А где (*my*) _____ ключ?

3 Вот _____ (*your*) ключ. У вас есть па́спорт и ви́за?

4 Да, вот _____ (*my*) ви́за и _____ (*my*) па́спорт.

4 Complete these sentences using the appropriate possessive adjective.

e.g. Он не зна́ет, где _____ сестра́. Он не зна́ет, где его́ сестра́.
He doesn't know where his sister is.

1 Я не зна́ю, где _____ соба́ка.
2 Мы не зна́ем, где _____ друзья́.
3 Вы не зна́ете, где _____ каранда́ш?
4 Ты не зна́ешь, где _____ биле́ты?
5 Они́ не зна́ют, где _____ паспорта́.

Insight

Possessive adjectives are used less frequently in Russian than in English; for example: Я уви́дела друзе́й в теа́тре *I saw (my) friends in the theatre.* In particular, Russian tends not to use possessive adjectives when referring to parts of the body: У меня́ голова́ боли́т. *My head aches.*

> **For reflexive possessive adjectives, see Section 3.7; for possessive pronouns, see Section 7.2.**

3.7 Reflexive possessive adjectives (nominative singular and plural)

Свой is the masculine nominative singular of the reflexive possessive adjective and it indicates possession by the subject of the nearest verb; the feminine nominative singular is своя́, the neuter своё and свои́ is the nominative plural for all genders. Given that it indicates possession by the subject of the nearest verb, it can mean *my own, your (singular) own, his/her own, our own, your (polite singular, or plural) own, their own.*

As far as я, ты, мы, вы are concerned, свой is an *alternative* to мой, твой, наш, ваш (and is in fact more common in conversational Russian, especially as an alternative to твой).

So, if you want to say *I am reading my magazine*, you can say either Я читáю мой журнáл or Я читáю свой журнáл

NB! Свой is **not** an alternative to егó, её, их. If you want to say *his, her, their*, you must work out whether you mean *his own, her own, their own* or not (i.e. you must work out whether you mean that the subject of the verb is the owner). For example:

Áнна и Áндрей лю́бят свой сад means that the garden in question belongs to Anna and Andrei: *They love their (own) garden.*

Áнна и Áндрей лю́бят их сад means that Anna and Andrei love a garden – but it belongs to someone else.

They love their (friends', parents', etc.) garden.

Свой must indicate *possession* by the subject of the verb; it cannot just describe the subject of the verb. To describe the subject of the verb, you must use мой, твой, егó, её, наш, ваш, их:

Егó дéти говоря́т по-рýсски.   *His children speak Russian.*

1 Underline the words in the following passage where it would be appropriate to use the reflexive possessive (hint: there are five).

Last year we set off on holiday in our car. Unfortunately Ivan lost his passport before we reached our destination. My brother, Nikolai, tried to help him find it. Nikolai is a very impatient person and soon lost his patience with Ivan. Whilst they were arguing, I looked in his suitcase and found that his passport was right at the bottom. How I love my brothers!

Sometimes you need both an ordinary possessive and a reflexive possessive in one sentence:

Егó дочь не óчень лю́бит свой óфис.
His daughter doesn't really like her office.

In this sentence свой is needed in the second part of the sentence to indicate that the daughter doesn't like her own office (possession by the subject of любит). In the first part of the sentence the word 'his' is describing the subject of the verb and therefore the reflexive possessive cannot be used.

2 Complete the following phrases by choosing the appropriate word from the box. You will need to use one of the words in the box twice.

> её   их   мой   наши   своё   свой   свой

1 _____ сестра работает в Новгороде.
Her sister works in Novgorod.

2 Константин читает _____ письма.
Konstantin is reading his (own) letters.

3 _____ брат любит _____ велосипед.
My brother likes his own bicycle.

4 _____ друзья купили _____ дом.
Our friends have bought their own house.

5 _____ бабушка потеряла _____ письмо.
Their granny has lost her (own) letter.

3 Translate the following phrases into Russian (possessive or reflexive possessive?).

1 Their house is in the town.
2 They like their house.
3 We like your house (formal).
4 Their mother likes our house.
5 Ivan's house? I like his house!

➤ **For possessive adjectives, see Section 3.6; for possessive pronouns, see Section 7.2.**

3.8 Accusative singular of adjectives

An adjective must always agree with the noun it is describing. So, if the noun is in the accusative case, the adjective also must be in the accusative case.

If an adjective is describing a **masculine or a neuter inanimate noun** this is not a problem: the ending is just the same as it is in the nominative singular:

> Я читáю интерéсный журнáл
> *I am reading an interesting magazine*

If an adjective is describing a **masculine animate noun** (e.g. врач, *doctor*), the ending of the adjective must change; there are two possible endings, -его for soft and possessive adjectives and for unstressed adjectives whose stem ends in ж, ч, ш, щ or ц; otherwise, use -ого:

> хорóший нóвый врач   →   Я знáю хорóшего нóвого врачá
> *I know a good new doctor*

> твой прéжний учитель   →   Я знáю твоегó прéжнего учи́теля
> *I know your former teacher*

In the unlikely event of a **neuter** noun being animate, the adjective which describes it takes the same ending as in the nominative singular, for example вáжное лицó, *VIP (very important person)*.

> Вы знáете э́то вáжиое лицó?
> *Do you know this very important person?*

1 Underline all the adjectives which are in the accusative case in the passage. A translation is given to help you.

> Вчерá мы бы́ли в гóроде. В ресторáне мы ви́дели нáшего дрýга, Ивáна. Он ужé купи́л краси́вые подáрки для брáта.

Он показа́л нам но́вый сви́тер, дороги́е джи́нсы и шика́рный пиджа́к.

Yesterday we were in town. In the restaurant we saw our friend, Ivan. He had already bought some beautiful presents for his brother. He showed us a new sweater, expensive jeans and a stylish jacket.

Adjectives describing **feminine** nouns always change in the accusative, whether the noun they are describing is animate (e.g. актри́са, *actress*) or inanimate (e.g. це́рковь *church*). The four possible endings are -ую, -юю, -у or -ю, as can be seen from the following examples:

- unstressed adjective: →   я люблю́ но́вую кварти́ру.
  но́вая кьа́ртира
- stressed adjective: →   я люблю́ молоду́ю актри́су.
  молода́я актри́са
- soft adjective: →   я люблю́ дре́внюю це́рковь.
  дре́вняя це́рковь
- possessive adjective: →   я люблю́ мою́/ва́шу ю́бку.
  моя́/ва́ша ю́бка

Insight

You might find it helpful to remember that there is often a rhyming pattern between the endings of a feminine accusative adjective and its noun: я зна́ю ва́шу сестру́; вы зна́ете мою́ тётю?

2 Explain what Anya has bought by putting the phrases in the following list into the accusative case:

e.g. А́ня купи́ла _____ (краси́вая блу́за) А́ня купи́ла краси́вую блу́зу. *Anya bought a beautiful blouse.*

1 больша́я соба́ка	*big dog*
2 но́вый дива́н	*new sofa*
3 пуши́стый кро́лик	*fluffy rabbit*
4 деревя́нный стол	*wooden table*
5 но́вое окно́	*new window*
6 вку́сный торт	*delicious cake*
7 шика́рная ю́бка	*stylish skirt*
8 интере́сная кни́га	*interesting book*
9 купа́льный костю́м	*swimming costume*
10 си́няя бро́шка	*dark blue brooch*

3 Explain who Viktor met at Konstantin's yesterday evening. Put each phrase into the accusative case.

Вчера́ ве́чером Ви́ктор был у Константи́на. Там он встре́тил …

1 моя́ сестра́	*my sister*
2 молодо́й профе́ссор	*young professor*
3 дре́вний писа́тель	*ancient writer*
4 интере́сная актри́са	*interesting actress*
5 ску́чный журнали́ст	*boring journalist*

> **For nominative singular adjectives, see Sections 3.3–3.7; for accusative singular nouns, see Section 2.7.**

3.9 Accusative plural of adjectives

An adjective must always agree with the noun it is describing. So, if the noun is in the accusative plural, the adjective also must be in the accusative plural.

This is easy if the noun is **inanimate** – for all genders the ending is the same as it would be in the nominative plural, i.e. -ые or -ие.

Type of adjective	Nominative singular	Inanimate accusative plural	Example
unstressed	но́вый *new* хоро́ший *good*	но́вые хоро́шие (no unstressed о ы after ж, ч, ш, щ, ц)	Я чита́ю но́вые кни́ги. Я зна́ю хоро́шие рестора́ны.
stressed	плохо́й *bad*	плохи́е	Он переда́л плохи́е но́вости. *He passed on the bad news.*
soft	дре́вний *ancient*	дре́вние	Я люблю́ дре́вние города́.
possessive	твой *your* наш *our*	твои́ на́ши	Я ви́жу твой дом. Он чита́ет на́ши пи́сьма.

1 What does Viktor like to photograph? Complete the following sentences by choosing the correct ending for each adjective (-ые or -ие?)

Ви́ктор лю́бит фотографи́ровать ...

1 иностра́нн ___ города́	*foreign cities*
2 краси́в __ пля́жи	*beautiful beaches*
3 ле́тн ___ цветы́	*summer flowers*
4 истори́ческ ___ места́	*historical places*
5 больш ___ зда́ния	*big buildings*

If the plural object is **animate**, then the two possible endings for the adjective are -ых or -их. This applies to all genders.

Type of adjective	Nominative singular	Animate accusative plural	Example
unstressed	но́вый *new* хоро́ший *good*	но́вых хоро́ших (no unstressed o after ж, ч, ш, щ, ц)	Я зна́ю но́вых студе́нтов. Я зна́ю хоро́ших враче́й.
stressed	плохо́й *bad*	плохи́х	Он критику́ет плохи́х актёров.
soft	дре́вний *ancient*	дре́вних	Я люблю́ дре́вних писа́телей.
possessive	твой *your* наш *our*	твои́х на́ших	Я зна́ю твои́х сестёр. Он зна́ет на́ших друзе́й.

2 Meet the artist – what/whom does Katya like to paint? Put the phrases into the accusative plural (animate or inanimate?).

e.g. Ка́тя лю́бит рисова́ть _____ (высо́кий челове́к) → Ка́тя лю́бит рисова́ть высо́ких люде́й. *Katya likes to paint tall people.*

1 больша́я соба́ка   *big dog*
2 краси́вая ло́шадь   *beautiful horse*
3 зелёное де́рево   *green tree*
4 дре́вний дом   *ancient house*
5 стра́нная пти́ца   *strange bird*
6 свой брат   *her brother*
7 молода́я ко́шка   *young cat*
8 ма́ленькая кварти́ра   *small flat*
9 свой друг   *her friend*
10 изве́стный писа́тель   *famous writer*

3 Make sentences explaining what you want to buy by putting the phrases into the accusative plural.

e.g. Я хочу́ купи́ть _____ (но́вая руба́шка) → Я хочу́ купи́ть но́вые руба́шки. *I want to buy new shirts.*

1	ма́ленький соба́ка	*small dog*
2	хоро́ший костю́м	*good suit*
3	ва́ша кни́га	*your book*
4	но́вое окно́	*new window*
5	интере́сная газе́та	*interesting newspaper*

Insight

If the ending of the adjective is -ые or -ие (i.e. nominative plural or inanimate accusative plural), take care to pronounce each of the final letters; this is particularly important in order to distinguish between the masculine singular ending -ый/-ий and the masculine plural ending -ые/-ие.

> ➤ **For nominative plural adjectives, see Sections 3.3–3.7; for nominative plural nouns, see Sections 2.5 and 2.6.**

3.10 Genitive singular of adjectives

An adjective must always agree with the noun it is describing; if the noun is in the genitive singular, so must the adjective describing it. There are special genitive singular adjective endings for each gender.

The endings for **masculine and neuter adjectives** are the same: either -ого or -его (if you know the accusative adjective endings, you'll recognize that these are the same as the masculine singular animate accusative).

- All unstressed adjectives take the ending -ого unless their stem ends in ж, ч, ш, щ, ц (spelling rule number 2), in which case the ending is -его: па́спорт англи́йского (хоро́шего) актёра, *the English (good) actor's passport*; недалеко́ от ма́ленького по́ля, *not far from the small field.*

- All stressed adjectives take the ending -ого: дире́ктор Большо́го теа́тра, *the director of the Bolshoi theatre.*

- All soft adjectives take the ending -его: цена́ си́него дива́на, *the price of the dark blue sofa.*

- All possessive adjectives take the ending -его: недалеко́ от на́шего зда́ния, *not far from our building.*

1 In the following passage there are five genitive singular masculine/neuter adjectives. Underline them, using the translation to help you.

На́ша шко́ла нахо́дится недалеко́ от краси́вого па́рка. Нале́во от э́того зда́ния есть больша́я апте́ка, где рабо́тает мать моего́ дру́га, Ива́на. Друг моего́ ста́ршего бра́та тоже рабо́тает в э́той большо́й апте́ке.

Our school is situated not far from a beautiful park. To the left of this building there is a big chemist's, where the mother of my friend Ivan works. The friend of my eldest brother also works in this big chemist's.

If an adjective is describing a **feminine** noun which is in the genitive singular, then the adjective should end either in -ой or -ей.

- All unstressed adjectives take the ending -ой unless their stem ends in ж, ч, ш, щ, ц (spelling rule number 2), in which case the ending is -ей: па́спорт англи́йской (хоро́шей) актри́сы, *the English (good) actress's passport.*

- All stressed adjectives take the ending -ой: дире́ктор большо́й компа́нии, *the director of the big company.*

- All soft adjectives take the ending-ей: цена́ си́ней руба́шки, *the price of the dark blue shirt.*

- All possessive adjectives take the ending -ей: дом моéй сестры́, *the house of my sister*.

2 Explain what is not on the menu today, by using У нас нет (*we haven't any*) with the genitive singular of the following items (all feminine),

e.g. свéжая ры́ба → У нас нет свéжей ры́бы *We haven't any fresh fish*

1	ру́сская вóдка	*Russian vodka*
2	жáреная ку́рица	*roast chicken*
3	грéчиебая кáша	*buckwheat porridge*
4	вку́сная ветчинá	*delicious ham*
5	свéжая колбасá	*fresh sausage*

Insight

It is useful to remember that some adjectives are used as nouns: thus, for example морóженое *ice cream* and шампáнское *champagne* have adjectival endings:

мнóго хорóшего шампáнского — *a lot of good champagne*
мáло свéжего морóженого — *not much (little) fresh ice cream.*

3 Look at the pictures and make sentences to explain who owns what:

мáленькая стáрая бáбушка

высóкая стрóйная жéнщина

мáленький тóлстый мужчи́на

e.g. Э́то кро́лик ма́ленькой ста́рой ба́бушки.

1 Э́то соба́ка _____ _____ _____
2 Э́то ко́шка _____ _____ _____

➢ **For spelling rules, see see Section 1.3; for different categories of adjective, see Section 3.2; for genitive singular of nouns, see Section 2.10; for prepositions taking the genitive case, see Section 11.3.**

3.11 Genitive plural of adjectives

An adjective must always agree with the noun it is describing; if the noun is in the genitive plural, so must the adjective describing it. There are only two genitive plural adjective endings (irrespective of gender): -ых and -их (which are the same endings used for the animate accusative plural of adjectives). These endings apply to all three genders.

Stressed and unstressed adjectives always take the ending -ых, unless their stem ends in г, к, х, ж, ч, ш, щ (spelling rule 1).

Examples of the ending -ых
паспорта́ молоды́х тури́стов the passports of the young tourists
кни́ги совреме́нных писа́телей the books of the modern writers
фотогра́фии иностра́нных куро́ртов photographs of foreign resorts

The genitive plural adjective ending is -их if:
    the adjective's stem ends in г, к, х, ж, ч, ш, щ (spelling rule 1)
    the adjective is soft (e.g. си́ний *dark blue*)
    the adjective is possessive (e.g. мой)

Examples of the ending -их
The adjective's stem ends in г, к, х, ж, ч, ш, щ: паспортá англи́йских тури́стов passports of English tourists
The adjective is soft: кни́ги дре́вних писа́телей books of the ancient writers
The adjective is possessive: фотогра́фии на́ших друзе́й photographs of our friends

1 Using the expressions нале́во от *(to the left of)* and напра́во от *(to the right of)*, make up sentences by giving the genitive plural of each phrase.

e.g. Нале́во от/молодо́й спортсме́н → Нале́во от молоды́х спортсме́нов. *To the left of the young sportsmen.*

1 *to the left of*/у́тренняя газе́та   *morning paper*
2 *to the right of*/на́ш велосипе́д   *our bicycle*
3 *to the right of*/дорога́я ю́бка   *expensive skirt*
4 *to the left of*/деревя́нный стул   *wooden chair*
5 *to the left of*/огро́мное зда́ние   *huge building*

2 Explain which groups are visiting the museum today by using the genitive plural in the following phrases.

e.g. гру́ппа/молодо́й ма́льчик → гру́ппа молоды́х ма́льчиков. *A group of young boys.*

1 италья́нский тури́ст   *Italian tourist*
2 изве́стный врач   *famous doctor*
3 наш студе́нт   *our student*
4 пожило́й челове́к   *elderly person*
5 дре́внее зда́ние   *ancient building*

3 Match the two halves of each sentence, using the English translation as a guideline:

1	У врача мно́го	**a**	интере́сных студе́нтов
2	У профе́ссора мно́го	**b**	ле́тних блуз
3	У такси́ста мно́го	**c**	больны́х пацие́нтов
4	У банки́ра мно́го	**d**	но́вых автомоби́лей
5	У продави́щцы мно́го	**e**	серьёзных пробле́м
6	У фе́рмера мно́го	**f**	тяжёлых пи́сем
7	У президе́нта мно́го	**g**	краси́вых коро́в
8	У почтальо́на мно́го	**h**	америка́нских до́лларов

1 *The doctor has many sick patients.*
2 *The professor has many interesting students.*
3 *The taxi driver has many new cars.*
4 *The banker has many American dollars.*
5 *The shop assistant has many summer blouses.*
6 *The farmer has many beautiful cows.*
7 *The president has many serious problems.*
8 *The postman has many heavy letters.*

Insight

The genitive case is very useful when you are describing quantities – very specific ones such as 'a box of', 'a kilo of', but also more general ones such as 'a lot of', 'few', 'not any', 'enough', e.g.:

В на́шем го́роде нет роско́шных гости́ниц. *There aren't any luxurious hotels in our town.*

➤ **For spelling rules, see Section 1.3; for different categories of adjective see Section 3.2; for genitive plural of nouns, see Sections 2.11 and 2.12; for prepositions taking the genitive case, see Section 11.3.**

3.12 Dative singular of adjectives

An adjective must always agree with the noun it is describing; if the noun is in the dative singular, so must the adjective describing it. There are special dative singular adjective endings for each gender.

If an adjective is describing a **masculine** noun which is in the dative singular, then the adjective should end either in -ому or -ему.

- All unstressed adjectives take the ending -ому unless their stem ends in ж, ч, ш, щ, ц (spelling rule number 2), in which case the ending is -ему: Гид дал па́спорт англи́йскому (хоро́шему) актёру, *the guide gave the passport to the English (good) actor.*

- All stressed adjectives take the ending -ому: Он позвони́л молодо́му дире́ктору, *He rang the young director.*

- All soft adjectives take the ending -ему: Он позвони́л пре́жнему дире́ктору, *He rang the former director.*

- All possessive adjectives take the ending -ему: Он позвони́л моему́ брату́, *He rang my brother.*

If an adjective is describing a **feminine** noun which is in the dative singular, then the adjective should end either in -ой or -ей.

- All unstressed adjectives take the ending -ой unless their stem ends in ж, ч, ш, щ, ц (spelling rule number 2), in which case the ending is -ей: Гид дал па́спорт англи́йской (хоро́шей) актри́се, *The guide gave the passport to the English (good) actress.*

- All stressed adjectives take the ending -ой: Он позвони́л молодо́й англича́нке, *He rang the young Englishwoman.*

- All soft adjectives take the ending-ей: Он позвони́л пре́жней учи́тельнице, *He rang the former teacher.*

- All possessive adjectives take the ending -ей: Он позвони́л мое́й сестре́, *He rang my sister.*

1 Who is walking towards what? Make up sentences from the information given.

e.g. Еле́на/шика́рный магази́н → Еле́на идёт к шика́рному магази́ну. *Elena is walking towards a stylish shop.*

1 Татья́на/краси́вая карти́на	*beautiful picture*
2 Игорь/дре́вняя ва́за	*ancient vase*
3 Вади́м/большо́й мост	*big bridge*
4 А́ня/сосе́дний дом	*neighbouring house*
5 Па́вел/но́вая лаборато́рия	*new laboratory*

2 Look at the pictures and make sentences to explain who is giving what to whom.

пуши́стый кро́лик   больша́я соба́ка   ма́ленькая ко́шка

e.g. Ба́бушка даёт морко́вку пуши́стому кро́лику.

1 Же́нщина даёт конфе́ту _____ _____.
2 Мужчи́на даёт ры́бу _____ _____.

If an adjective is describing a **neuter** noun which is in the dative singular, then the adjective should end either in -ому or -ему (just like masculine adjectives). In the examples below the preposition к *towards/to the house* of (which must always be followed by the dative case) is used.

- All unstressed adjectives take the ending -ому unless their stem ends in ж, ч, ш, щ, ц (spelling rule number 2), in which case the ending is -ему: к нóвому (хорóшему) здáнию, *towards the new (nice) building.*

- All stressed adjectives take the ending -ому: к большóму окнý, *towards the big window.*

- All soft adjectives take the ending -ому: к сосéднему здáнию, *towards the neighbouring building.*

- All possessive adjectives take the ending -ему: к моемý мéсту, *towards my seat (place).*

3 Complete these phrases by adding the dative singular adjective endings:

1 По мо _____ мнéнию, э́то несправедлúво.
2 Мы слýшали передáчу по нóв ___ рáдио.
3 Андрéй подошёл к зелён _____ пóлю.
4 Он дóлго хóдил по сосéдн ___ магазúну.
5 Официáнт скóро подойдёт к нáш _____ столý.

4 Make sentences explaining who Ivan helps every day.

e.g. Стáрый почтáльон → Кáждый день Ивáн помогáет стáрому почтальóну. *Every day Ivan helps the old postman.*

1 рýсский студéнт   *Russian student*
2 больнáя старýшка   *sick old lady*
3 préжний мéнеджер   *former manager*

4 на́ша мать   *our mother*

5 молодо́й пиани́ст   *young pianist*

> ➤ For spelling rules, see Section 1.3; for different categories of adjective, see Section 3.2; for dative singular of nouns, see Section 2.13; for prepositions with the dative case, see Section 11.4.

3.13 Dative plural of adjectives

An adjective must always agree with the noun it is describing; if the noun is in the dative plural, so must the adjective describing it. There are only two dative plural adjective endings: -ым and -им. These endings are used for all three genders.

Stressed and unstressed adjectives always take the ending -ым (unless their stem ends in г, к, х, ж, ч, ш, щ (spelling rule 1)).

Examples of the ending -ым
гид даёт биле́ты молоды́м тури́стам the guide gives the tickets to the young tourists
гид ча́сто помога́ет иностра́нным актри́сам the guide often helps foreign actresses
фото́граф подхо́дит к зелёным поля́м the photographer is walking towards the green fields

1 Explain who sends a letter to whom by matching the two halves of each sentence, using the English translation as a guideline.

1 врач пи́шет письмо́   **a** иностра́нным поли́тикам

2 профе́ссор пи́шет письмо́   **b** больны́м пацие́нтам

3 дирижёр пи́шет письмо́   **c** потенциа́льным клие́нтам

4 журнали́ст пи́шет письмо́   **d** лени́вым студе́нтам

5 банки́р пи́шет письмо́   **e** изве́стным музыка́нтам

1 *The doctor writes a letter to the sick patients.*
2 *The professor writes a letter to the lazy students.*
3 *The conductor writes a letter to the famous musicians.*
4 *The journalist writes a letter to the foreign politicians.*
5 *The banker writes a letter to potential customers.*

The dative plural adjective ending is -им if:

- the adjective's stem ends in г, к, х, ж, ч, ш, щ (spelling rule 1)
- the adjective is soft (e.g. си́ний, *dark blue*)
- the adjective is possessive (e.g. мой)

Examples of the ending -им
The adjective's stem ends in г, к, х, ж, ч, ш, щ: гид даёт биле́ты англи́йским тури́стам the guide gives the tickets to the English tourists
The adjective is soft: мы подхо́дим к сосе́дним дома́м we are approaching the neighbouring houses
The adjective is possessive: мы помога́ем на́шим друзья́м we are helping our friends

2 Make sentences explaining who you intend to buy presents for.

e.g. мой друг → Я хочу́ купи́ть пода́рки мои́м друзья́м.

1	твоя́ дочь	*your daughter*
2	наш учи́тель	*our teacher*
3	ма́ленькая соба́ка	*small dog*
4	пре́жний дире́ктор	*former director*
5	ру́сский студе́нт	*Russian student*

Insight

There is a neat pattern to dative plural endings: -ым or -им (adjectives) and -ам or -ям (nouns). Here's a phrase to help you remember the pattern (and a useful time phrase as well!):.

По утра́м он обы́чно звони́т но́вым клие́нтам *In the mornings he usually telephones new clients.*

3 Complete the sentences by putting the adjective in brackets into the dative plural.

1 Официа́нт подхо́дит к _____(большо́й стол).
2 Архите́ктор подхо́дит к _____ (ма́ленькое окно́).
3 Татья́на подхо́дит к _____ (но́вый о́фис).
4 Ка́тя подхо́дит к _____ (свой ребёнок).
5 Ива́н подхо́дит к _____ (ста́рые друзья́).

> **For spelling rules, see Section 1.3; for different categories of adjective, see Section 3.2; for dative plural of nouns, see Section 2.14; for prepositions with the dative case, see Section 11.4.**

3.14 Instrumental singular of adjectives

An adjective must always agree with the noun it is describing; if you put the noun in the instrumental singular, you must put the adjective describing it in the instrumental singular too. There are special instrumental singular adjective endings for each gender.

The endings for **masculine and neuter** adjectives are the same: either -ым or -им:

- All unstressed and stressed adjectives take the ending -ым unless their stem ends in г, к, х, ж, ч, ш, щ (spelling rule number 1), in which case the ending is -им: посеща́ть музе́й с молоды́м иностра́нным (англи́йским) тури́стом, *to visit the museum with a young foreign (English) tourist.*

- All stressed adjectives take the ending -ым: с молоды́м тури́стом, *with a young tourist.*

- All soft adjectives take the ending -им: с пре́жним дире́ктором, *with the former director*.

- All possessive adjectives take the ending -им: с мои́м письмо́м, *with my letter*.

1 Explain what you want by putting the phrase in brackets into the instrumental singular.

1 Ко́фе с _____ (холо́дное молоко́) *coffee with cold milk*
2 Чай со _____ (све́жий лимо́н) *tea with fresh lemon*
3 Чай с _____ (бе́лый са́хар) *tea with white sugar*
4 Чай с _____ (мали́новое варе́нье) *tea with raspberry jam*

If an adjective is describing a **feminine noun** which is in the instrumental singular, then the adjective should end either in -ой or -ей (just like the instrumental singular noun ending).

- All unstressed adjectives take the ending -ой unless their stem ends in ж, ч, ш, щ, ц (spelling rule number 2), in which case the ending is -ей: фильм с хоро́шей англи́йской актри́сой, *the film with the good English actress*.

- All stressed adjectives take the ending -ой: он рабо́тает с молодо́й англича́нкой, *he works with a young Englishwoman*.

- All soft adjectives take the ending-ей: он рабо́тает с пре́жней учи́тельницей, *he works with a former teacher*.

- All possessive adjectives take the ending -ей: он рабо́тает с мое́й сестро́й, *he works with my sister*.

2 How are things done? Complete the sentence by putting the adjective in brackets into the instrumental singular (remember: because you are describing the 'instrument by which an action is performed' you don't need the preposition с).

1 Я е́ду _____ (ра́нний) по́ездом. *I travel by the early train.*

2 Я пишу́ _____ (дешёвая) ру́чкой. *I write with a cheap pen.*

3 На́до мыть посу́ду _____ (горя́чая) водо́й. *It is necessary to do the washing up with hot water.*

4 Я открыва́ю дверь _____ (мой) ключо́м. *I open the door with my key.*

5 Он гла́дит руба́шку _____ (но́вый) чтюго́м. *He irons the shirt with the new iron.*

3 Make sentences explaining who wants to go to the theatre with whom (remember: because you are describing 'in the company of' you do need the preposition c).

e.g. Зо́я/но́вый друг → Зо́я хо́чет пойти́ в теа́тр с но́вым дру́гом. *Zoya wants to go to the theatre with (her) new boyfriend.*

1 Врач/краси́вая медсестра́	*Doctor/beautiful nurse*
2 Ива́н/англи́йский тури́ст	*Ivan/English tourist*
3 Журнали́ст/изве́стный поли́тик	*Journalist/famous politician*
4 Евге́ний/моя́ сестра́	*Evgeny/my sister*
5 Муж/молода́я жена́	*Husband/young wife*

4 Explain what kind of sandwiches you want by putting each phrase into the instrumental singular.

e.g. францу́зский сыр → Я хочу́ бутербро́д с францу́зским сы́ром. *I want a sandwich with French cheese.*

1 све́жая ветчина́	*fresh ham*
2 копчёная ры́ба	*smoked fish*
3 зелёный огуре́ц	*green cucumber*
4 дорого́й майоне́з	*expensive mayonnaise*

> For spelling rules, see Section 1.3; for different categories of adjective, see Section 3.2; for instrumental singular of nouns, see Section 2.15; for prepositions with the instrumental case, see Section 11.5.

3.15 Instrumental plural of adjectives

An adjective must always agree with the noun it is describing; if the noun has to be in the instrumental plural, so must the adjective describing it. There are only two instrumental plural adjective endings: -ыми and -ими. These endings are used for all three genders.

Stressed and unstressed adjectives always take the ending -ыми (unless their stem ends in г, к, х, ж, ч, ш, щ (spelling rule 1)).

Examples of the ending -ыми
гид в музе́е с молоды́ми тури́стами the guide is at the museum with the young tourists
гид посеща́ет теа́тр с иностра́нными актри́сами the guide visits the theatre with foreign actresses
секрета́рь вошёл с ва́жными пи́сьмами the secretary came in with important letters

1 Explain who Aleksandr was at the theatre with on the different days of the week. Put the words in brackets into the instrumental plural.

1 В понеде́льник Алекса́ндр был в теа́тре с _____ (но́вый друг).

2 Во вто́рник Алекса́ндр был в теа́тре с _____ (иностра́нный гость).

3 В сре́ду Алекса́ндр был в теа́тре с _____ (ва́жный клие́нт).

4 В четве́рг Алекса́ндр был в теа́тре с _____ (молодо́й учи́тель).

5 В пя́тницу Алекса́ндр был в теа́тре с _____ (пожило́й тури́ст).

6 В суббо́ту Алекса́ндр был в теа́тре со _____ (ста́рый пенсионе́р).

7 В воскресе́нье Алекса́ндр был в теа́тре с _____ (двою́родная сестра́).

The instrumental plural adjective ending is -ими if:

- the adjective's stem ends in г, к, х, ж, ч, ш, щ (spelling rule 1)
- the adjective is soft (e.g. си́ний, *dark blue*)
- the adjective is possessive (e.g. мой)

Examples of the ending -ими
The adjective's stem ends in г, к, х, ж, ч, ш, щ: гид в музе́е с англи́йскими тури́стами the guide is in the museum with the English tourists
The adjective is soft: он рабо́тает с пре́жними поли́тиками he works with former politicans
The adjective is possessive: мы отдыха́ем с на́шими друзья́ми we are on holiday with our friends

2 What's on the menu? Match the two halves of each phrase, using the English translation as a guideline.

1 сала́т с   **a** ру́сскими гриба́ми
2 суп со   **b** вку́сными абрико́сами
3 ку́рица с   **c** све́жими овоща́ми
4 моро́женое с   **d** италья́нскими помидо́рами

Italian tomato salad
Fresh vegetable soup

Chicken with Russian mushrooms
Ice cream with delicious apricots

Insight

The instrumental case is extremely useful when talking about food – e.g. шоколад со взбитыми сливками *(hot chocolate with whipped cream)*. Note that in Russia tea is normally drunk with something sweet – including jam, which is served in a little side dish and taken by the teaspoonful – hence чай с малиновым вареньем in the first exercise of Section 3.14.

3 Who is busy with what? Give the Russian for the phrases in brackets in order to complete each sentence.

e.g. Балерина занимается _____ (new dances) → Балерина занимается новыми танцами.

1 Писатель занимается _____ *(interesting books)*.
2 Врач занимается _____ *(sick patients)*.
3 Профессор занимается _____ *(new students)*.
4 Журналист занимается _____ *(good newspapers)*.
5 Программист занимается _____ *(our computers)*.

Insight

Have you spotted that the instrumental plural endings for adjectives and nouns are exactly like the dative plural + и:

Я пишу но́вым друзья́м. *Я познако́мился/ась с э́тими друзья́ми на конце́рте.*

I am writing to some new friends. *I met these friends at a concert.*

> ➤ **For spelling rules, see Section 1.3; for different categories of adjective, see Section 3.2; for instrumental plural of nouns, see Section 2.16; for prepositions with the instrumental case, see Section 11.5.**

3.16 Prepositional singular of adjectives

An adjective must always agree with the noun it is describing; if you put the noun in the prepositional singular, you must put the adjective describing it in the prepositional singular too. There are special prepositional singular adjective endings for each gender.

If an adjective is describing a **masculine** or **neuter** noun which is in the prepositional singular, then the adjective should end either in -ом or -ем:

• All unstressed adjectives take the ending -ом unless their stem ends in ж, ч, ш, щ, ц (spelling rule number 2), in which case the ending is -ем: в но́вом (хоро́шем) рестора́не, *in a new (good) restaurant*, в краси́вом ме́сте, *in a beautiful place.*

• All stressed adjectives take the ending -ом: в Большо́м Теа́тре, *in the Bolshoi Theatre*, в плохо́м положе́нии, *in a bad position.*

• All soft adjectives take the ending-ем: в си́нем пиджаке́, *in a dark blue jacket*, в дре́внем зда́нии, *in the ancient building*

• All possessive adjectives take the ending -ем or -ём: в моём (твоём, своём, на́шем, ва́шем) до́ме, *in my (your, one's own, our, your) house*, в на́шем зда́нии, *in our building*

1 Complete the phrases by choosing the appropriate ending from the box below:

e.g. Катя рабо́тает в но́в ____ о́фисе → Катя рабо́тает в но́вом о́фисе.

> -ом   -ем

1 Ба́бушка живёт в ста́р__ до́ме.

Granny lives in an old house.

2 Зо́я рабо́тает в дре́вн___ зда́нии.

Zoya works in an ancient building.

3 Светла́на живёт в шу́мн__ го́роде.

Svetlana lives in a noisy town.

4 Андре́й живёт в краси́в___ райо́не.

Andrei lives in a beautiful region.

5 Са́ша рабо́тает на совреме́нн___ заво́де.

Sasha works in a modern factory.

If an adjective is describing a **feminine** noun which is in the prepositional singular, then the adjective should end either in -ой or -ей.

- All unstressed adjectives take the ending -ой unless their stem ends in ж, ч, ш, щ, ц (spelling rule 2), in which case the ending is -ей: в но́вой (хоро́шей) гости́нице, *in a new (good) hotel.*

- All stressed adjectives take the ending -ой: в большо́й гости́нице, *in a big hotel.*

- All soft adjectives take the ending -ей: в си́ней руба́шке, *in a dark blue shirt.*

- All possessive adjectives take the ending -ей: в мое́й кварти́ре, *in my flat.*

2 Who works where? Match the two halves of the sentences, using the English translation as a guide.

1	Мой брат рабóтает	**a**	в большóй больнѝце
2	Мой дя́дя рабóтает	**b**	в краси́вом па́рке
3	Моя́ женá рабóтает	**c**	в ма́ленькой аптéке
4	Моя́ тётя рабóтает	**d**	в сосéднем здáнии
5	Мой муж рабóтает	**e**	в хорóшей шкóле

My brother works at a good school.
My uncle works in a big hospital.
My wife works in the neighbouring building.
My aunt works in a small chemist's.
My husband works in a beautiful park.

Insight

Notice that the singular feminine adjective endings are the same for the genitive, dative, instrumental and prepositional cases: either -ой or -ей. Boris's romantic intrigues illustrate this:

Бори́с ку́пил конфéты для моéй сестры́ И́ры. Он дал цветы́ её краси́вой подру́ге Лéне. Он всё врéмя говори́т о нóвой студéнтке А́не.

3 Put the phrases that follow into the prepositional singular.

1	зелёный парк	*green park*
2	Кра́сная Плóщадь	*Red Square*
3	чёрный портфéль	*black briefcase*
4	жёлтая ю́бка	*yellow skirt*
5	си́нее нéбо	*blue sky*

➤ **For spelling rules, see Section 1.3; for different categories of adjective, see Section 3.2; for prepositional singular of nouns, see Section 2.17; for prepositions with the prepositional case, see Sections 11.2, 11.4, 11.5 and 11.6.**

3.17 Prepositional plural of adjectives

An adjective must always agree with the noun it is describing; if the noun has to be in the prepositional plural, so must the adjective describing it. There are only two prepositional plural adjective endings: -ых and -их (i.e. just like the endings for genitive plural adjectives). These endings are used for all three genders.

Stressed and unstressed adjectives always take the ending -ых (unless their stem ends in г, к, х, ж, ч, ш, щ (spelling rule 1)).

Examples of the ending -ых
карти́ны в больши́х интере́сных музе́ях the pictures are in big interesting museums
об иностра́нных шко́лах about foreign schools
в ва́жных пи́сьмах in important letters

1 Put the following phrases into the prepositional plural.

1	серьёзная проблéма	*serious problem*
2	иностра́нный город	*foreign town*
3	ночно́й клуб	*night club*
4	совреме́нный авто́бус	*modern bus*
5	плохо́е положе́ние	*bad position*

The prepositional plural adjective ending is -их if:

- the adjective's stem ends in г, к, х, ж, ч, ш, щ (spelling rule 1)
- the adjective is soft (e.g. си́ний, *dark blue*)
- the adjective is possessive (e.g. мой)

2 Describe where and how you spent your holidays by matching up the two halves of each sentence. Use the English translations as a guide.

1 мы лежа́ли	**a**	в си́них бассе́йнах
2 мы де́лали поку́пки	**b**	на жёлтых пля́жах
3 мы обе́дали	**c**	на прекра́сных ко́ртах
4 мы смотре́ли карти́ны	**d**	в больши́х музе́ях
5 мы пла́вали	**e**	в хоро́ших рестора́нах
6 мы игра́ли в те́ннис	**f**	в больши́х конце́ртных за́лах
7 мы пи́ли кокте́йли	**g**	в шика́рных магази́нах
8 мы слу́шали конце́рты	**h**	в прия́тных ба́рах

We lay on yellow beaches.
We did shopping in stylish shops.
We had lunch in good restaurants.
We looked at pictures in big museums.
We swam in blue pools.
We played tennis on splendid courts.
We drank cocktails in pleasant bars.
We listened to concerts in big concert halls.

3 Build sentences from the following vocabulary, using the prepositional plural.

e.g. Они/отдыхáть/на/приятный/курóрт → Они отдыхáют на приятных курóртах. *They holiday (rest) in pleasant resorts.*

1	Он/рабóтать/на/шýмный/завóд	*He works in noisy factories.*
2	Онá/дéлать покýпки/в/ дорогóй/магазин	*She does her shopping in expensive shops.*
3	Мы/читáть нóвости/в/ вечéрняя/газéта	*We read the news in the evening papers.*
4	Вы/обéдать/в/мáленький/ ресторáн	*You have lunch in small restaurants.*
5	Они/отдыхáть/в/красивый/ парк	*They rest in beautiful parks.*

> **For spelling rules, see Section 1.3; for different categories of adjective, see Section 3.2; for prepositional plural of nouns, see Section 2.18; for prepositions with the prepositional case, see Sections 11.2, 11.4, 11.5 and 11.6.**

3.18 Ten things to remember

1 An adjective must always agree with the noun it describes: to make sure this happens, ask yourself – is the noun singular or plural? Masculine, feminine or neuter? What case is the noun in?

2 Always ask yourself what kind of adjective you are dealing with: unstressed? Stressed? Soft? Possessive?

3 For the accusative, genitive, dative, instrumental and prepositional singular, the case endings offer you two choices: one set for stressed and unstressed adjectives, and another set for soft adjectives, possessive adjective and those with endings affected by spelling rules 1 and 2.

4 Be on the look out for when you should be writing -и not -ы (spelling rule 1), and -e not -o (spelling rule 2).

5 The possessive adjectives мой, твой, наш, ваш must agree with the noun they describe, but его (*his, its*), её (*her, its*) and их (*their*) never change.

6 Свой (the reflexive possessive adjective) indicates <u>possession by the subject of the verb,</u> so it can mean *my, your, his, hers, its, our, their*. Remember it is <u>not</u> an alternative to его, её and их: Его дочь потеряла свой паспорт – *His daughter has lost her (own) passport.*

7 The endings of feminine singular adjectives are very straightforward: *nominative*: -ая or -яя; *accusative*: -ую or -юю; *all other cases*: -ой or -ей.

8 The endings of plural adjectives are straightforward because they are the same for all genders in each case: *nominative*: -ые/-ие; *accusative*: -ые/-ие or -ых/-их; *genitive*: -ых/-их; *dative*: -ым/-им; *instrumental*: -ыми/-ими; *prepositional*: -ых/-их.

9 Take care when using the accusative plural: is the noun inanimate? (if so, the adjective ending will be -ые/-ие) or animate? (in which case the ending will be -ых/-их).

10 In the feminine instrumental singular the endings are the same for adjectives and nouns: Я интересуюсь английской историей и древней архитектурой – *I am interested in English history and ancient architecture.*

4

Adjectives (2)

4.1 Long and short forms of adjectives

Most Russian adjectives have two sorts of ending: the long form (discussed in Sections 3.1–3.18) and the short form. The short form exists in the nominative case only (when you are talking about the subject of the sentence) and is usually found at the end of a phrase or sentence. It is much less common than the long form.

The long form is used 'attributively' – i.e. in front of a noun: Известный актёр живёт в Москве. *The famous actor lives in Moscow.* The short form is used 'predicatively' – i.e. after the noun: Климат суров, *The climate is harsh.*

In modern conversational Russian, the long form is very often used everywhere and the short form hardly ever. However, sometimes the short form must be used in order to convey the correct message.

Short forms are formed by shortening the long form of the adjective.

Long form	Masculine short form	Feminine short form	Neuter short form	Plural (all genders)
красивый	красив	красива	красиво	красивы

For some adjectives, this will mean that a 'cluster of consonants' (i.e. more than one) is left together at the end of the masculine short form, and the vowel e (or sometimes o or ё) has to be inserted, for example: изве́стный, *famous, well known* – Э́тот факт изве́стен, *This fact is well known.*

1 In the following English passage underline the adjectives which are in the 'short' (predicative) position (clue: there are five).

Svetlana walks into the house and notices that all the doors and windows are open. The new curtains are blowing about in the wind. The kitchen door, however, is shut. On the table the cat lies, howling. It is clearly glad to see her. She is furious when she realizes that her son has gone out without feeding the cat. 'He is so unreliable!' she thinks.

Some Russian adjectives have no short form (e.g. colour, nationality, substance – *wooden, metal* – ordinal numerals, *first, second*, etc. and soft adjectives). But NB, the adjective рад (*glad, happy*) exists *only* in the short form.

2 The adjectives in brackets are in the masculine singular long form. Put them into the short form.

e.g. Моя́ ко́шка _____ (голо́дный) → Моя́ ко́шка голодна́. *My cat is hungry.*

1 Э́то ме́сто _____ (свобо́дный).   *This seat is free.*
2 Его́ автомоби́ль _____ (но́вый).   *His car is new.*
3 На́ши де́ти _____ (здоро́вый).   *Our children are well.*
4 Все о́кна _____ (откры́тый).   *All the windows are open.*
5 Ка́ша _____ (вку́сный).   *The porridge is delicious.*

3 Match the two halves of each sentence, using the English translations as a guide.

1 Как жаль! Рестора́н   **a** согла́сна
2 Как хорошо́! Ка́тя   **b** ра́ды
3 Как жаль! Врач   **c** откры́та

4 Он приéхал? Мы   **d** закры́т

5 Хóлодно, потомý что дверь   **e** зáнят

What a shame! The restaurant is closed.
How nice! Katya agrees (is in agreement).
What a shame! The doctor is busy.
He has arrived? We are glad.
It's cold because the door is open.

If the adjective comes before the noun or needs to be in a case other than the nominative, you must use the long form. Otherwise, in most instances you may use either the long or the short form. So *'the town is beautiful'* could be either: Гóрод краси́вый or Гóрод краси́в. However, there are some adjectives when you should always use the short form in the 'predicative' (i.e. after the noun) position, because to use the long form would imply something different (e.g. the adjective for 'ill' in the long form implies chronically sick, as opposed to the short form, which is used when you want to indicate 'not too well at the moment'). For example:

больнóй, *ill* (short form: бóлен, больнá, бóльно, больны́);

зáнятый, *occupied* (short form: зáнят, занятá, зáнято, зáняты);

свобóдный, *free, vacant* (short form: свобóден, свобóдна, свобóдно, свобóдны).

4 Look again at the adjectives a–e in Exercise 3.

1 Which is the only one you would never see in the long form?

2 Work out what the masculine singular long forms would be of the other adjectives in the right-hand column.

➤ **For comparative of long and short form adjectives, see Sections 4.2 and 4.3.**

4.2 Comparative adjectives – long form

If we say that something is 'more interesting' or 'less interesting', we are using the comparative. In English we can form the comparative by using the words *more* and *less*, or if the English adjective is very short, we can add *-er* to the end of the adjective (*it is cheaper*). Russian uses the words бо́лее (*more*) or ме́нее (*less*) in front of the long form of the adjective. This is called the compound comparative.

The words бо́лее and ме́нее never change (i.e. in their endings) but the long adjective which follows them must agree with the adjective it is describing:

Э́то бо́лее (ме́нее) интере́сный го́род.	*This is a more (less) interesting town.*
Она́ живёт в бо́лее (ме́нее) интере́сном го́роде.	*She lives in a more (less) interesting town.*

Some adjectives do not form compound comparatives. They have a long form comparative of their own. Here are the first four:

Long form adjective	Long form comparative
большо́й *big*	бо́льший (**NB** the stress is on the stem!), *bigger*
ма́ленький *small*	ме́ньший, *lesser*, *smaller*
хоро́ший *good*	лу́чший, *better*
плохо́й *bad*	ху́дший, *worse*

1 Pair up the words on the left and the right using the English translations as a guide:

1	бо́льшая	**a**	письмо́
2	ме́нее ва́жная	**b**	иде́я
3	бо́лее прия́тный	**c**	ситуа́ция
4	ме́нее интере́сное	**d**	шко́ла

5 бо́лее шика́рный	e гру́ппа
6 лу́чшая	f карти́на
7 ху́дшая	g кварти́ра
8 ме́нее краси́вая	h пиджа́к
9 бо́лее шу́мная	i дом
10 бо́льшая	j пробле́ма

1 *a bigger flat*
2 *a less important problem*
3 *a more pleasant house*
4 *a less interesting letter*
5 *a more stylish jacket*
6 *a better idea*
7 *a worse situation*
8 *a less beautiful picture*
9 *a more noisy (noisier) group*
10 *a bigger school*

The adjectives for *old* and *young* cannot form compound comparatives if you are talking about animate nouns or groups – they have their own long form comparative.

ста́рый *old*	ста́рший *older, senior*	Моя́ ста́ршая сестра́. *My older sister.*
молодо́й *young*	мла́дший *younger*	Мла́дший класс. *The junior class.*

You can, however, say э́то бо́лее ста́рое зда́ние, *it is an older building.*

2 Underline the adjectives in this passage for which you would need the compound comparative. Circle the ones which have their own long form comparative in Russian.

My younger sister, Masha, really likes shopping. Yesterday she bought a bigger bag, a newer car, a more expensive radio, a more interesting book and a smaller mobile telephone.

3 Complete a translation of this passage giving the Russian for the adjective in brackets.

Моя _____ (younger) сестра, Máша, óчень лю́бит
дéлать поку́пки. Вчерá онá купи́ла _____ (bigger)
су́мку, _____ (newer) автомоби́ль, _____ (more
expensive) рáдио, _____ (more interesting) кни́гу
и _____ (smaller) сóтовый телефóн.

The adjectives for *high and low* cannot form compound
comparatives if you are using them in the sense which means
superior and *inferior*:

высóкий *high*	вы́сший *superior, higher*	вы́сшее образовáние *higher education*
ни́зкий *low*	ни́зший *inferior, lower*	ни́зший балл *lower (bottom) mark*

You can, however, say э́то бóлее высóкое здáние, *it is a taller building*.

4 Underline all the long form comparative adjectives in the
following passage, using the English translation to help you:

Я бóлее приле́жный студе́нт, чем мой брат, Николáй,
котóрый óчень лени́вый человéк. В шкóле он всегдá получáл
ни́зшие бáллы. Он ду́мал, что футбóл бóлее интерéсное
занятие, чем урóки. Он никогдá не слу́шал, когдá пáпа
говори́л, что ему́ ну́жен бóлее серьёзный подхóд к учёбе.

*I am a more industrious student than my brother, Nikolai, who
is a very lazy person. At school he always got bottom marks.
He thought that football was a more interesting activity than
lessons. He never listened when Dad told him that he needed a
more serious approach to his studies.*

> ➤ **For short form comparatives see Section 4.3; for
> constructions with the comparative, see Section 4.4.**

4.3 Comparative adjectives – short form

If you are using a comparative adjective 'predicatively', i.e. after the noun it is describing (the book is more interesting), then you can use the short form comparative. This sort of comparative can only be used to mean more ... (interesting, beautiful, etc.)

The first really important thing to remember is that you can only use the short form comparative when the person or thing you are describing is in the nominative case.

The short comparative is formed by adding the ending -ee to the stem of the adjective; the stem of the adjective = the masculine nominative singular minus the last two letters: но́вый → нов; молодо́й → мо́лод. The short comparative -ee ending is the same for all genders and it never changes (i.e. it is invariable).

дом прия́тнее	*the house is more pleasant*
соба́ка краси́вее	*the dog is more beautiful*
письмо́ интере́снее	*the letter is more interesting*
цветы́ прекра́снее	*the flowers are more splendid*

Note that it is more common to use this form of the comparative when you are saying *A=B* (*the house=pleasant*) than it would be to say дом бо́лее прия́тный.

1 In which of the following sentences would you be able to use the short form comparative in Russian?

    1 *My brother is cleverer.*
    2 *This book is less boring.*
    3 *His car is cheaper.*
    4 *We have bought a newer car.*
    5 *Do you know where the more comfortable chair is?*
    6 *It is simpler.*
    7 *It is further to Moscow.*
    8 *We have received a more important letter.*

9 *This letter is shorter.*
10 *This radio is more expensive.*

NB! Some very common adjectives make their comparative short form irregularly. Here are some common ones:

near	бли́зкий	→	бли́же
high	высо́кий	→	вы́ше
loud	гро́мкий	→	гро́мче
hot	жа́ркий	→	жа́рче
far	далёкий	→	да́льше
cheap	дешёвый	→	деше́вле
expensive, dear	дорого́й	→	доро́же
short	коро́ткий	→	коро́че
small	ма́ленький	→	ме́ньше
young	молодо́й	→	моло́же
low	ни́зкий	→	ни́же
bad	плохо́й	→	ху́же
simple	просто́й	→	про́ще
old	ста́рый	→	ста́рше
strict	стро́гий	→	стро́же
quiet	ти́хий	→	ти́ше
fat	то́лстый	→	то́лще
good	хоро́ший	→	лу́чше
frequent	ча́стый	→	ча́ще
wide	широ́кий	→	ши́ре

2 Now complete the Russian versions of these sentences by giving the appropriate comparative form of the adjectives in brackets:

1 Мой брат _____ (у́мный).
2 Э́та кни́га _____ (ску́чный).
3 Его́ маши́на _____ (дешёвый).
4 Мы купи́ли _____ (но́вый) дом.
5 Вы не зна́ете, где _____ (удо́бный) стул?
6 Э́то _____ (просто́й).
7 До Москвы́ _____ (далёкий).

8 Мы получи́ли _____ (ва́жный) письмо́.

9 Э́то письмо́ _____ (коро́ткий).

10 Э́то ра́дио _____ (дорого́й).

Some adjectives have no short form comparative: adjectives of colour, of substance (e.g. wooden, silk).

Insight

Note the very useful phrases in which всего́ combines with a short comparative adjective:

Бо́льше всего́	*most of all*
Лу́чше всего́	*best of all*
Ху́же всего́	*worst of all*
Ча́ще всего́	*more often than not (most often)*

---

3 Look at the two pictures and then answer the questions.

ИВАН   ВАДИМ

1 Кто то́лще?

2 Кто моло́же?

> **For nominative case, see Sections 2.4–2.6 and 3.3–3.7; for long form comparative adjectives, see Section 4.2; for constructions with the comparative, see Section 4.4.**

4.4 Comparative constructions

In English we form the second part of the comparative by using the word *than* (*he has a more beautiful car than you*). In Russian this part of the sentence is formed either by using the word чем (*than*) or by using the genitive.

When we are using the long form comparative in Russian, we must form the second part of the comparative by using the word чем:

У него бо́лее краси́вый автомоби́ль, чем у вас.
He has a more beautiful car than you.

The word чем must also be used if the words его, её, их feature in the second part of the comparison:

Э́то бо́лее краси́вый автомоби́ль, чем его́.
It's a more beautiful car than his.

If you are using the short form of the comparative, there are two ways in which you can deal with the second part of your comparison (*than* …). Either use чем:

Мой дом прия́тнее, чем твой.
My house is pleasanter than yours.

Or use the genitive of the second part of your comparison:

Мой дом прия́тнее твоего́.
My house is pleasanter than yours.

1 Match the phrases on the left with those on the right, using the English translations as a guide:

1	Его́ соба́ка непослу́шнее	**a**	на́шего
2	Э́тот со́товый телефо́н бо́льше	**b**	мое́й
3	Их сад краси́вее	**c**	ва́ших

4 Ва́ше письмо́ интере́снее   **d** твоего́

5 Мои́ иде́и лу́чше   **e** моего́

1 *His dog is naughtier than mine.*

2 *This mobile phone is bigger than yours.*

3 *Their garden is more beautiful than ours.*

4 *Your letter is more interesting than mine.*

5 *My ideas are better than yours.*

Insight

Чем is actually the instrumental of что, so its literal meaning is *by/with what/that*. Notice that there is always a comma before чем when it means *than*, because it is beginning a new clause - i.e. a new part of the sentence which contains or implies a new verb: Она́ поёт лу́чше, чем я (пою́.)

If you want to 'intensify' your comparative (*it is much more interesting*), simply add the words гора́здо or намно́го:

Мой дом гора́здо прия́тнее твоего́.
My house is much pleasanter than yours.

Э́та кни́га намно́го интере́снее.
This book is much more interesting

If you want to say by how much taller/shorter, younger/older someone is, use the preposition на + accusative:

Она́ моло́же его́ на шесть лет.
She is six years younger than him.

2 Big differences! Use the comparative with намно́го and the genitive of comparison to build sentences from the following words. Use the English translation as a guide.

e.g. Вади́м/ста́рый/Ива́н → Вади́м намно́го ста́рше Ива́на.
Vadim is much older than Ivan.

1	Óльга/дóбрый/Ирúна	*Olga is much kinder than Irina.*
2	Андрéй/серьёзный/ Константúн	*Andrei is much more serious than Konstantin.*
3	Он/энергúчный/я	*He is much more energetic than me.*
4	Мой брат/ленúвый/моя́ сестра́	*My brother is much lazier than my sister.*
5	Бáбушка/молодóй/ дéдушка	*Grandmother is much younger than grandfather.*

3 Translate the following sentences into Russian (decide whether to use чем or the genitive of comparison for the second part of each sentence).

1 This is a more serious problem than his.
2 Moscow is a bigger city than Novgorod.
3 He is older than me.
4 Your television is better than mine.
5 His dog is more energetic than hers.

➤ **For genitive case, see Sections 2.10–2.12 and 3.10–3.11; for long form of comparative, see Section 4.2; for short form, see Section 4.3; for accusative case, see Sections 2.7–2.9 and 3.8–3.9.**

4.5 Superlative adjectives

If we say something is the most interesting, smallest, best we are using the superlative form of the adjective.

The superlative is very easy to form. Simply put the adjective сáмый in front of the adjective and noun you are describing. There is no short form of the superlative (so it can be used predicatively and attributively – before or after the noun):

сáмый серьёзный фильм	*the most serious film*
Э́тот фильм сáмый серьёзный	*this film is the most serious*

Make sure that the adjective **са́мый** agrees in number, gender and case with its adjective and noun:

Я изуча́ю са́мый краси́вый язы́к.	*I am studying the most beautiful language.*
Я чита́ю са́мую серьёзную кни́гу.	*I am reading the most serious book.*
Мы живём в са́мом прия́тном райо́не.	*We live in the pleasantest region.*

1 Turn the adjective in each sentence into the superlative (remember agreements).

e.g. Ири́на (лени́вый) → Ири́на са́мая лени́вая. *Irina is the laziest.*

1 Э́то _____ (краси́вый) парк. — *This is the most beautiful park.*

2 Ива́н и Андре́й _____ (тала́нтливый) футболи́сты. — *Ivan and Andrei are the most talented footballers.*

3 Вот _____ (энерги́чный) медсестра́. — *Here is the most energetic nurse.*

4 Я чита́ю _____ (интере́сный) кни́гу. — *I am reading the most interesting book.*

5 Он живёт в _____ (ма́ленький) кварти́ре. — *He lives in the smallest flat.*

2 Choose a suitable adjective from the box and then make the superlative form to complete each sentence:

жа́ркий	краси́вый	кре́пкий	холо́дный

1 Зима́ _____ вре́мя го́да. — *Winter is the coldest time of year.*

2 _____ кли́мат. — *The hottest climate.*

3 Водка _____ напиток.

Vodka is the strongest drink.

4 Это _____ квартира.

It is the most beautiful flat.

Some adjectives can form their superlative form with the ending -ейший or -айший:

Ближайшая станция метро	*The nearest metro station*
Важнейший вопрос	*The most important question*
Кратчайший путь	*A short cut* (lit. 'the shortest way')

Insight

If you want to express a firm opinion, the -ейший superlative ending is useful:

Нет ни малейшего сомнения.	*There isn't the slightest doubt.*
У меня нет ни малейшей идеи.	*I haven't the slightest idea.*
Чистейший вздор!	*Utter rubbish!*

Самый can be used with the comparatives лучший and худший to mean *best* and *worst*, or they can just be used as superlatives in their own right, so это лучшая идея and это самая лучшая идея both mean *it's the best idea*. The same applies to младший (*younger/youngest*) and старший (*older/oldest*).

To say '*the most ... of*' (e.g. *one of the most interesting books*), use the preposition из followed by the genitive case:

одна из самых интересных книг
one of the most interesting books

3 Complete the sentences with an appropriate superlative adjective, using the English translations as a guide.

1 Он оди́н из _____ гитари́стов. *He is one of the best guitarists.*

2 Э́то _____ пляж. *It is the most beautiful beach.*

3 _____ вздор! *Utter rubbish!*

4 Где _____ остано́вка авто́буса? *Where is the nearest bus stop?*

5 Э́то _____ пробле́ма. *It is the most serious problem.*

> ➤ **For long and short forms of adjective, see Section 4.1; for long and short forms of comparative adjectives, see Sections 4.2–4.4; for uses of из, see Section 11.3.**

4.6 Ten things to remember

1 Short form adjectives can only be used with nouns in the nominative.

2 The adjective for 'glad' (рад) exists only in the short form.

3 Soft adjectives and adjectives of colour, nationality and substance (e.g. wood, silk) have no short form.

4 Long form comparative adjectives: although бо́лее (*more*) and ме́нее (*less*) never change their endings, the adjective which follows must agree in number, gender and case with the noun it describes: Я хочу́ говори́ть о бо́лее серьёзных ситуа́циях (*I want to speak about more serious situations*).

5 Some common adjectives have their own long form comparative and are not used with бо́лее (*more*) and ме́нее (*less*): e.g. лу́чший (*better*), ху́дший (*worse*).

6 To say *than* in a long form comparative phrase, use чем: Я читáю бóлее интерéсный журнáл, чем ты.

7 To say *than* in a short comparative phrase, use either чем or the genitive of comparison: Он стáрше меня.

8 Many of the irregular short comparatives are very common words; they end in -же, -че, -ше, or -ще, apart from дешéвле (*cheaper*) and шúре (*wider*).

9 The superlative is formed with сáмый, which must agree in number, gender and case with its following adjective and noun: Онú рабóтали в сáмых извéстных теáтрах (*They worked in the most famous theatres*).

10 Use горáздо or намнóго in front of a comparative adjective to give it extra emphasis: Нóвый дирéктор намнóго стрóже (*The new director is much stricter*).

5

Adverbs

5.1 Adverbs of manner

Adverbs of manner describe *how* something is done; in English most adverbs which describe <u>how</u> something is done end in *-ly: she writes slowly; he runs quickly.*

Notice that in English adverbs usually follow the verb, whereas in Russian they usually precede it:

Она́ ме́дленно пи́шет.	*She writes slowly.*
Он бы́стро бе́гает.	*He runs quickly.*

Most Russian adverbs look exactly like the short form neuter adjective:

Long form neuter nominative singular	*Short form neuter singular/adverb*
Ме́дленное	ме́дленно

Most Russian adverbs, therefore, end in -o, but some end in -e because of the second spelling rule, and if an adjective is soft, its adverb will end in -e:

блестя́щий	→	блестя́ще	*brilliantly*
и́скренний	→	и́скренне	*sincerely*

The ending of an adverb is invariable (i.e. it never changes).

Look out for stress changes between some adjectives and adverbs, e.g.:

тёплый	(*warm*)	→	теплó	(*it is warm*)
плохóй	(*bad*)	→	плóхо	(*badly*)
холóдный	(*cold*)	→	хóлодно	(*it is cold*)
хорóший	(*good*)	→	хорошó	(*well*)

1 Answer using an adverb which means the opposite of the adverb in the first statement.

e.g. Ирúна плóхо поёт? Нет! Онá хорошó поёт.
Does Irina sing badly? No! She sings well.

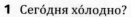

1 Сегóдня хóлодно?	(*No, today it is warm*).
2 Пианúст плóхо игрáет?	(*No, brilliantly*).
3 Студéнт бы́стро рабóтает?	(*No, slowly*).
4 Дéти шýмно игрáют?	(*No, quietly*).
5 Брат ленúво игрáет?	(*No, energetically*).

Adjectives which end in -ский have adverbs ending in -ски: практи́чески *practically (almost)*. 'Adverbial phrases' which indicate nationality are formed from по and adjectives ending in -ский: мы говори́м по-ру́сски *we speak Russian*.

2 Form adverbs from the following adjectives.

1	глу́пый	*stupid*
2	прия́тный	*pleasant*
3	хоро́ший	*good*
4	тёплый	*warm*
5	логи́ческий	*logical*
6	го́рдый	*proud*
7	впечатля́ющий	*impressive*
8	саркасти́чный	*sarcastic*
9	эгоисти́ческий	*selfish*
10	ще́дрый	*generous*
11	ти́хий	*quiet*
12	шу́мный	*noisy*

3 Work out which language is spoken by whom.

e.g. Италья́нец → Италья́нец говори́т по-италья́нски.

1	Испа́нец	*Spaniard*
2	Ру́сский	*Russian*
3	Англича́нин	*Englishman*
4	Япо́нец	*Japanese*

Insight

Sometimes English uses the word 'way' to convey 'how' something is done; in Russian, such 'how' phrases can be formed by using по- with the dative case, e.g.:

по-друго́му *in a different way*
по-но́вому *in a new way*
по-ра́зному *in various ways*

➢ **For spelling rules, see Section 1.3; for the short form of adjectives, see Section 4.1.**

5.2 Adverbs of time, place and extent

Adverbs of time, place and extent answer questions such as *where? when? to what extent?* Adverbs usually describe verbs, but they can also tell us more about an adjective or even another adverb:

Он бегает о́чень бы́стро.   *He runs very quickly.*
Как ужа́сно!   *How awful!*

All adverbs of time, place and extent are invariable (i.e. their endings never change), but notice that only a small number end in -o; however, even though давно́, по́здно and ра́но come from soft adjectives, they end in -o.

Here is a list of some common adverbs of time, place and extent:

Time (lots of these!)	Place	Extent	
e.g. вчера́ *yesterday*	верхо́м *on horseback*	вполне́	*quite*
сего́дня у́тром *this morning*	вниз *downstairs (direction)*	дово́льно	*fairly, quite, enough*
ле́том *in summer*	внизу́ *downstairs (position)*	доста́точно	*sufficiently, enough*
всегда́ *always*	где *where (position)*		
давно́ *a long time ago*	далеко́ *far*	как	*how*
до́лго *for a long time*	за грани́цу *abroad (direction)*	кра́йне	*extremely*
ещё *still, yet*	за грани́цей *abroad (position)*	немно́го/ немно́жко	*a little, a bit*
иногда́ *sometimes*	здесь *here*	неожи́данно	*unexpected(ly)*
когда́ *when*	там *there (position)*		
неда́вно *recently*	куда́ *where to (direction)*	о́чень	*very*
обы́чно *usually*		совсе́м	*quite*
по́здно *late*	наве́рх *upstairs (direction)*	соверше́нно	*quite*
пото́м *then, next*		так	*so*

ра́но *early*
сейча́с, тепе́рь
   now
ско́ро *soon*
сра́зу *at once,*
   immediately
тогда́ *then, at*
   that time
уже́ *already*
	наверху́ *upstairs*
	   (position)
	ря́дом *alongside*
	сюда́ *here (direction)*
	туда́ *there*
	   (direction)
	отку́да *from where*
	отсю́да *from here*
	отту́да *from there*
		удиви́тельно
		   surprising(ly)
		ужа́сно *terrible/*
		   terribly;
		   awful(ly)

1 Underline the adverbs in the following passage:

Yesterday we left the hotel early to meet Sofia Petrovna. We found her office easily and she immediately offered us a cup of tea. The conversation flowed smoothly and soon we were able to reach an agreement as to where the first performance would take place. Our boss was absolutely delighted with the outcome.

Insight

In Russian, adverbs which indicate where something is often distinguish between <u>position</u> and <u>direction</u>:

Direction: Куда́ он пое́дет ле́том? – За грани́цу. *Where is he going in the summer? – Abroad*

Position: Где он бу́дет отдыха́ть ле́том? – За грани́цей. Where is he spending his holidays in the summer? – Abroad

2 Match the answers on the right with the questions on the left:

1 Где вы рабо́таете?	**a** На уро́к
2 Куда́ он бежи́т?	**b** Но́вым пла́ном
3 Во ско́лько отхо́дит сле́дующий по́езд?	**c** О́чень хо́лодно
4 Кака́я сего́дня пого́да?	**d** На заво́де
5 Как лу́чше реши́ть э́ту пробле́му?	**e** В семь часо́в

> **For short forms of adjective, see Section 4.1; for use of prepositions with the accusative to express motion towards, see Section 11.2, for second spelling rule, see Section 1.3.**

5.3 Comparative adverbs

Adverbs, like adjectives, have comparative forms (e.g. *he runs more quickly* and *he runs the most quickly*).

The comparative adverb is identical to the short form comparative adjective: so, for example: быстрéе, *more quickly*, мéдленнее, *more slowly*, лýчше, *better*:

> Он всегдá рабóтает быстрéе, чем я.
> *He always works more quickly than I do.*

Adverbs ending in -и form their comparative with бóлее:

> Он всегдá рабóтает бóлее логи́чески, чем я.
> *He always works more logically than I do.*

To say, for example, *less quickly, less logically*, use мéнее with the adverb:

> Он всегдá дýмает мéнее логи́чески, чем я.
> *He always thinks less logically than I do.*

Ещё can be used with a comparative adverb to mean *even*: он рабóтает ещё быстрéе, *he works even more quickly*.

Note that дáльше (*further*) and рáньше (*earlier, previously*) come from adjectives, but are used only as comparative adverbs.

1 How are the various sportsmen performing? Build sentences using comparative adverbs.

> e.g. Андрéй бы́стро бéгает/Игорь → Андрéй бы́стро бéгает, но Йгорь бéгает ещё быстрéе. *Andrei runs quickly, but Igor runs even more quickly.*

> **1** Пиани́ст хорошó игрáет/гитари́ст
> **2** Мой брат лени́во игрáет/твой брат

3 Теннисист энергично играет/футболист
4 Баскетболист глупо играет/хоккеист
5 Игрок в гольф медленно играет/игрок в крикет

Like comparative adjectives, comparative adverbs can form constructions with both чем and with the genitive of comparison:

Виктор работает усерднее, чем Валентин.

Viktor works harder than Valentin.

Виктор работает усерднее Валентина.

Viktor works harder than Valentin.

The words гораздо or намного (*much*) can also be used with comparative adverbs:

Он работает гораздо быстрее, чем я.
He works much more quickly than I do.

2 Translate into Russian:

1 *Katya speaks more quietly than her sister.*
2 *Igor works much harder than Valentin.*
3 *Tatyana sings even worse than Zoya.*
4 *They swim more often than previously.*
5 *Louder, please!*

Insight

Some useful phrases with comparative adverbs:

Тише едешь, дальше будешь. *More haste, less speed.*
Чем больше, тем лучше. *The more, the better.*
Как можно + comparative adverb = *as ... as possible*, e.g.:
как можно скорее *as soon as possible.*
Всё + comparative = *more and more ...*, e.g.: всё чаще *more and more often.*

3 Match the phrases on the left with their translations on the right:

1	чем скорée, тем лýчше	**a**	*as cheaply as possible*
2	как мóжно прóще	**b**	*the sooner the better*
3	всё блúже	**c**	*worse and worse*
4	как мóжно дешéвле	**d**	*nearer and nearer*
5	всё хýже	**e**	*as simply as possible*

> ➤ **For the short form of comparative adjectives, see Section 4.3; for comparative constructions with adjectives, see Section 4.4.**

5.4 Superlative adverbs

Adverbs, like adjectives, have superlative forms: to make the superlative of an adverb, simply add всегó or всех after the comparative adverb.

If you want to say '*best of all*' be careful to check whether you mean '*better than anything else*' or '*better than anyone else*':

Онá игрáет на гитáре лýчше всегó.	*She plays the guitar best of all* (i.e. better than she does anything else).
Онá игрáет на гитáре лýчше всех.	*She plays the guitar best of all* (i.e. better than anyone else).

1 Complete the sentences below with either лýчше всегó or лýчше всех:

1 Мой брат говорúт по-итальянски _____ (*better than anyone else*).

2 Он игрáет в шáхматы _____ (*best of all; better than any other game*).

3 Я знáю врачá _____ (*better than I know anyone else*).

NB! The word наибо́лее can also be used to form the superlative adverb наибо́лее интере́сно *most interestingly*. If an adverb does not end in -o/-e, then the superlative adverb is formed with наибо́лее – e.g. наибо́лее логи́чески *most logically*.

> ➤ **For short forms of comparative adjective, see Section 4.3; for comparative adverbs see Section 5.3; for comparative constructions with adjectives, see Section 4.4.**

5.5 Ten things to remember

1 An adverb can indicate how (manner), when (time), where (place) or how much (to what extent).

2 In Russian, the ending of an adverb never changes (it is invariable).

3 Most adverbs of manner are identical to the neuter short form adjective: бы́стро *quickly*, шу́мно *noisily*, ти́хо *quietly/ calmly*.

4 There is a change of stress between some adjectives and their adverbs, e.g.: плохо́й → пло́хо *badly*, хоро́ший → хорошо́ *well*.

5 Adjectives ending in -ский make their adverb simply by removing the final й from the masculine nominative form: логи́ческий → логи́чески.

6 Watch out for the second spelling rule when forming the adverb from adjectives whose stem ends in ж, ч, *o*, щ, ц – e.g. masculine singular nominative – блестя́щий (*shining*; *brilliant*) → stem – блестя́щ- → adverb – блестя́ще (*brilliantly*).

7 In Russian, adverbs are usually placed before the verb: Я плохо говорю по-китайски *I speak Chinese badly*.

8 A comparative adverb looks identical to the short form adjective, except for adverbs formed from adjectives ending in -ский, where более (or менее) must be used: masculine singular nominative – логический → adverb – логически → comparative adverb – более логически.

9 Чем, the genitive of comparison, гораздо and намного are used with comparative adverbs in just the same way as with comparative adjectives.

10 With superlative adverbs, remember that you need to add всего to mean *than anything* and всех to mean *than anyone*.

6

Numerals

6.1 Cardinal numerals

Cardinal numerals answer the question *how many?* with a specific quantity: e.g. 10 days, 49 years, 2 kilos.

Here are the cardinal numerals in Russian from 1 to 20:

1	оди́н	11	оди́ннадцать
2	два	12	двена́дцать
3	три	13	трина́дцать
4	четы́ре	14	четы́рнадцать
5	пять	15	пятна́дцать
6	шесть	16	шестна́дцать
7	семь	17	семна́дцать
8	во́семь	18	восемна́дцать
9	де́вять	19	девятна́дцать
10	де́сять	20	два́дцать

Insight

There are a couple of resemblances with English numerals: 3 = три and 10 = де́сять (a little like 'decimal'). For teens of numbers, it might help you to think, for example, that the idea behind трина́дцать (13) is 'three on ten'. Take care to distinguish between 12 (двена́дцать) and 20 (два́дцать)!

Numbers above 20 are formed quite simply in Russian – just place them one after another: 24 = два́дцать четы́ре, 55 = пятьдеся́т пять, 103 = сто три.

Here are the numbers from 30 to 1000:

30	три́дцать	300	три́ста
40	со́рок	400	четы́реста
50	пятьдеся́т	500	пятьсо́т
60	шестьдеся́т	600	шестьсо́т
70	се́мьдесят	700	семьсо́т
80	во́семьдесят	800	восемьсо́т
90	девяно́сто	900	девятьсо́т
100	сто	1000	ты́сяча
200	две́сти		

1 Write out these sums as you would say them.

> + плюс   − ми́нус   = бу́дет

e.g. 46 + 6 = ? со́рок шесть плюс шесть бу́дет пятьдеся́т два

1 100 − 20 = ?
2 2 + 16 = ?
3 33 + 102 = ?
4 29 − 15 = ?
5 85 − 54 = ?

2 Match up the numbers in words on the left with the figures on the right:

1	девяно́сто два	**a**	10
2	семьсо́т два́дцать два	**b**	92
3	оди́ннадцать	**c**	722
4	де́сять	**d**	212
5	две́сти двена́дцать	**e**	11

The numeral 'one' has three forms in Russian. It behaves like an adjective: оди́н дом, *one house*; одна́ кварти́ра, *one flat*; одно́ ме́сто, *one place* (*seat*).

The numeral 'two' has two forms in Russian: два for when it is used with masculine and neuter nouns and две for when it is used with feminine nouns: У меня́ два бра́та и две сестры́, *I have two brothers and two sisters*.

3 Here are some telephone numbers. Write them out and practise saying them:

e.g. 25–27–70 два́дцать пять – два́дцать семь – се́мьдесят

1 42–93–12
2 84–53–55
3 20–30–40
4 36–62–73
5 18–11–26

Insight

Russian proverbs often feature numerals, e.g.:

Одна́ голова́ – хорошо́, а две – лу́чше. *Two heads are better than one.*

Не име́й сто рубле́й, а име́й сто друзе́й. Literally: *Don't have 100 roubles, but do have 100 friends* – i.e. *friends are more important than money.*

➤ For declension of numerals, see Section 6.2; for use of adjectives with numerals and of cases with numerals, see Section 6.3; for use of numerals in expressions with time, dates, quantities, see Sections 6.5–6.7.

6.2 Cardinal numerals – case endings

Cardinal numerals have the same six case endings as nouns and adjectives. In the tables below, the asterisk (*) indicates the animate accusative.

The **cardinal numeral** 1 works like an adjective, with adjective case endings.

	Masculine	Feminine	Neuter
Nom.	оди́н	одна́	одно́
Acc.	оди́н/одного́*	одну́	одно́/одного́*
Gen.	одного́	одно́й	одного́
Dat.	одному́	одно́й	одному́
Instr.	одни́м	одно́й	одни́м
Prep.	одно́м	одно́й	одно́м

There is one word for *one and a half*: полтора́ (for masculine and neuter nouns) and полторы́ (for feminine nouns); 1½ is followed by the genitive singular. The ending for the genitive, dative, instrumental and prepositional of both полтора́ and полторы́ is полу́тора.

2, 3 and 4 are the trickiest numerals in terms of case endings.

	2	3	4
Nom.	два/две	три	четы́ре
Acc.	два/две/двух*	три/трёх*	четы́ре/четырёх*
Gen.	двух	трёх	четырёх
Dat.	двум	трём	четырём
Instr.	двумя́	тремя́	четырьмя́
Prep.	двух	трёх	четырёх

1 Write in figures the numerals given in words below, and explain which case(s) they are in (try give all the possibles cases for those endings which could indicate more than one case).

1 двумя́
2 одному́
3 трёх
4 двух
5 четырём

Numerals which end in a soft sign (e.g. пять) are feminine nouns. Numerals with a soft sign in the middle change in the middle and at the end. 40, 90 and 100 are much more straightforward:

	40	50	90	100
Nom.	со́рок	пятьдеся́т	девяно́сто	сто
Acc.	со́рок	пятьдеся́т	девяно́сто	сто
Gen.	сорока́	пяти́десяти	девяно́ста	ста
Dat.	сорока́	пяти́десяти	девяно́ста	ста
Instr.	сорока́	пяти́десятью	девяно́ста	ста
Prep.	сорока́	пяти́десяти	девяно́ста	ста

2 Write out in Russian the genitive of the following numerals.

1 4
2 60
3 23
4 92
5 100

....
Insight

Watch out for 8 – во́семь! In the genitive, dative and prepositional во́семь becomes восьми́.

Watch out for 14 – четы́рнадцать! It comes from the word for 4 (четы́ре), but it has no 'e' in the middle.
....

The 'hundreds' base their declension on the first digit, for example:

Nom.	двéсти	пятьсóт	Dat.	двумстáм	пятистáм
Acc.	двéсти	пятьсóт	Instr.	двумястáми	пятьюстáми
Gen.	двухсóт	пятисóт	Prep.	двухстáх	пятистáх

3 Write out in Russian the dative of the following numerals.

   1 40
   2 18
   3 73
   4 300
   5 600

4 Write out in Russian the instrumental of the following numerals.

   1 3
   2 10
   3 200
   4 20
   5 5

5 Write out in Russian the prepositional of the following numerals.

   1 12
   2 86
   3 45
   4 11
   5 150

6 Buried in the following passage are six numerals written out as words, but in all sorts of different cases. Can you recognize them? A translation of the passage is given in the Key.

Борис неда́вно был в двух кни́жных магази́нах и купи́л три кни́ги. Вчера́ он чита́л свою́ но́вую кни́гу по хи́мии. Он чита́л о шестиста́х ра́зных эксперимента́х в три́дцати́ двух стра́нах. Девяно́сто шесть хи́миков получи́ли результа́ты, но в сорока́ четырёх лаборато́риях произошли́ ава́рии.

> ➤ For use of numerals in different cases, and for adjectives
> with numerals, see Section 6.3; for animate accusative, see
> Sections 2.7–2.9, 3.8 and 3.9.

6.3 Using cardinal numerals with nouns and adjectives

The number 1 works like an adjective: в одно́й но́вой шко́ле *in one new school*; в одно́м большо́м университе́те *in one big university*. However big a compound number is, if the last digit is '1', then the noun remains in the singular: Сто одна́ серьёзная пробле́ма, *101 serious problems* (and сто оди́н далмати́нец – *101 Dalmatians*!)

The numbers 2, 3 and 4 (and their compounds, e.g. 23, 34, 52) are followed by the genitive singular of nouns: У меня́ два о́фиса и два́дцать три рабо́тника. *I have 2 offices and 23 employees.*

Numbers above 5 (other than compounds of 2, 3 and 4) are followed by the genitive plural of nouns: У меня́ пять о́фисов, *I have 5 offices* (but watch out for челове́к (*person*), which behaves like this: три челове́ка, пять челове́к).

The rules for using 2, 3 and 4 + adjective + noun are different for different genders:

Masculine and neuter: when the numeral is the subject, use the genitive *plural* of the adjective and the genitive *singular* of the noun which follow it: два больши́х стола́, *2 big tables*, два больши́х о́кна, *2 big windows*.

Feminine: use *either* the nominative plural *or* the genitive plural of the adjective and the genitive singular of the noun: три краси́вые (краси́вых) сестры́ 3 *beautiful sisters*.

If numbers 5 and above are the subject (again, not compounds of 1, 2, 3 and 4, which follow their own rules) they are followed by the genitive plural of both the *noun* and the *adjective*. This applies to all genders:

пять дороги́х биле́тов	*5 expensive tickets*
два́дцать пять дороги́х биле́тов	*25 expensive tickets*
NB два́дцать два дороги́х биле́та	*22 expensive tickets*

1 Write out the numerals in words and put the nouns in brackets into the appropriate case (genitive singular or genitive plural?):

  1 Два _____ (журна́л)
  2 Шесть _____ (неде́ля)
  3 Со́рок _____ (челове́к)
  4 Два́дцать три _____ (ко́шка)
  5 Оди́ннадцать _____ (час)
  6 Сто _____ (рубль)
  7 Девятна́дцать _____ (киломе́тр)
  8 Ты́сяча _____ (кни́га)
  9 Сто четы́ре _____ (ма́льчик)
  10 Сто пять _____ (де́вушка)

2 Using the explanations above to help you, translate the following into Russian:

  1 two big dogs
  2 three small theatres
  3 one hundred and ten new students
  4 five old houses
  5 thirty two energetic boys

The rules described above apply if a numeral is in the position of subject or an inanimate object. If a numeral needs to be in a case (e.g. after a preposition), the whole numeral and its adjective and noun need to be in the same case, and the noun will be in the plural (unless it follows the numeral 1):

Я ви́жу оди́н большо́й стол и две карти́ны.	*I see one big table and two pictures.*
Биле́ты для тридцати́ пяти́ ру́сских тури́стов и одного́ англи́йского ги́да.	*Tickets for thirty five Russian tourists and one English guide.*

The animate accusative with numerals is used for 1, 2, 3, 4 on their own and for their compounds, as well as for numbers 5 and above. So, *I see 2 students, 22 professors and 5 guides* will be: Я ви́жу двух студе́нтов, два́дцать, двух профессоро́в и пять ги́дов

3 The preposition к is always followed by the dative. Explain who the policeman is walking towards by putting the following phrases into the dative.

e.g. Милиционе́р/три/англи́йский тури́ст → Милиционе́р подхо́дит к трём англи́йским тури́стам. *The policeman is walking towards three English tourists.*

1	пять/ста́рый профе́ссор	*five old professors*
2	два́дцать/серди́тый клие́нт	*twenty angry customers*
3	оди́ннадцать/шу́мный хулига́н	*eleven noisy hooligans*

4 Look at the following phrases, then look again at the explanation above and explain which endings are being used and why.

1	Он говори́л с пятью́ но́выми студе́нтами.	*He spoke with five new students.*
2	Вы не ви́дели три́дцать дву́х студе́нтоьн?	*Did you not see the 32 students?*

3 Вы не ви́дели трёх студе́нтов?   *Did you not see the three students?*

4 Он говори́л о пяти́ но́вых студе́нтах.   *He spoke about the five new students.*

5 Мы купи́ли две но́вые кни́ги.   *We bought two new books.*

Insight

Some Russian sayings with 1½ and 2:

Ни два ни полтора́ – *neither one thing nor another* (lit. *neither 2 nor 1½*)

Уби́ть двух за́йцев (одни́м вы́стрелом) – *to kill two birds* (lit. *to kill two hares with one shot*)

Похо́жи, как две ка́пли воды́ – *as like as two peas* (lit. *as two drops of water*)

➢ **For case endings of cardinal numerals, see Section 6.2.**

6.4 Ordinal numerals

Ordinal numerals (first, second, third, etc.) indicate position in an order or series. In Russian ordinal numerals are adjectives.

1st	пе́рвый	11th	оди́ннадцатый	30th	тридца́тый
2nd	второ́й	12th	двена́дцатый	40th	сороково́й
3rd	тре́тий	13th	трина́дцатый	50th	пятидеся́тый
4th	четвёртый	14th	четы́рнадцатый	60th	шестидеся́тый
5th	пя́тый	15th	пятна́дцатый	70th	семидеся́тый
6th	шесто́й	16th	шестна́дцатый	80th	восьмидеся́тый
7th	седьмо́й	17th	семна́дцатый	90th	девяно́стый
8th	восьмо́й	18th	восемна́дцатый	100th	со́тый
9th	девя́тый	19th	девятна́дцатый	1000th	ты́сячный
10th	деся́тый	20th	двадца́тый	1,000,000th	миллио́нный

All the ordinal numerals are unstressed or stressed adjectives (i.e. they behave like но́вый and большо́й) except for тре́тий (third) which is irregular.

	Masculine	Feminine	Neuter	Plural
Nom.	тре́тий	тре́тья	тре́тье	тре́тьи
Acc.	тре́тий/ тре́тьего*	тре́тью	тре́тье	тре́тьи/ тре́тьих*
Gen.	тре́тьего	тре́тьей	тре́тьего	тре́тьих
Dat.	тре́тьему	тре́тьей	тре́тьему	тре́тьим
Instr.	тре́тьим	тре́тьей	тре́тьим	тре́тьими
Prep.	тре́тьем	тре́тьей	тре́тьем	тре́тьих

(* = animate accusative).

1 Explain which month is which according to the example.

e.g. Февра́ль – второ́й ме́сяц го́да. *February is the second month of the year.*

1 апре́ль
2 ноя́брь
3 а́вгуст
4 май
5 ию́ль

When making an ordinal adjective from a compound numeral, only the last digit (the ordinal numeral) is in the form of an ordinal, so, for example:

Пятьдеся́т втора́я неде́ля го́да   *the 52nd week of the year*

If you need to put a compound numeral in a case other than the nominative, only the last digit changes its case endings:

Дни пятьдеся́т второ́й неде́ли   *the days of the 52nd week*

In abbreviations the final letter of the ordinal adjective ending is used, for example:

52-я неде́ля   *the 52nd week*

2 Who has bought which size shoes? Build sentences with the information given.

e.g. Ива́н/46   →   Ива́н купи́л ту́фли со́рок шесто́го разме́ра.

1 Вади́м/38
2 Татья́на/30
3 А́нна/32
4 Андре́й/43
5 Еле́на/36

3 Explain which floor each department is on.

e.g. Оде́жда – эта́ж 1   →   Оде́жда на пе́рвом этаже́. *Clothes are on the first floor.*

1 Бага́ж – эта́ж 2
2 Фотоаппара́ты – эта́ж 3
3 Ту́фли – эта́ж 4
4 Кни́ги – эта́ж 5
5 Сувени́ры – эта́ж 6

4 Explain which photograph is on which page (write out the numbers in words).

e.g. Фотогра́фия го́рода/стр. 14   →   Фотогра́фия го́рода на страни́це четы́рнадцатой. *The photograph of the town is on page 14 (on page the 14th).*

1 Фотогра́фия шко́лы/стр. 52
2 Фотогра́фия теа́тра/стр. 229

3 Фотогра́фия у́лицы/стр. 87
4 Фотогра́фия актёра/стр. 61
5 Фотогра́фия актри́сы/стр. 10

Note that in abbreviations the last two letters of the ordinal adjective must be used if the penultimate letter is a consonant: поку́пки сто шестьдеся́т восьмо́го клие́нта → поку́пки 168-го клие́нта.

Russian uses Roman numerals for centuries and monarchs:

XXI век   *21st century*   Пётр I   *Peter the First (the Great)*

Insight

Two Russian sayings which feature the word for 1st – пе́рвый

Любо́вь с пе́рвого взгля́да – *love at first sight*

Пе́рвый блин всегда́ ко́мом – *practice makes perfect* (lit. *the first pancake is always a lump!*)

➢ **For use of ordinal numerals in time phrases, see Section 6.5 and for dates, see Section 6.6.**

6.5 Telling the time

Both cardinal and ordinal numerals are needed when telling the time.

To answer the question *What time is it?* (Кото́рый час? or Ско́лько вре́мени?) by stating an hour: give the cardinal number followed by the word for hour (genitive singular after 2, 3, 4; genitive plural for 5 and above):

три часа́   3 o'clock
шесть часо́в   6 o'clock

To give the time on the 'right-hand side' of the clock (i.e. between the hour and the half-hour), you need to use the ordinal numbers. You also need to think ahead, because the way of saying 4.10, for example, is to say *ten minutes of the fifth hour*:

де́сять мину́т пя́того	*4.10*
два́дцать пять мину́т пя́того	*4.25*

To express the half hour, use either полови́на or its abbreviation пол-:

полови́на пя́того	*4.30*
полпя́того	*4.30*

To give the time on the left-hand side of the clock (i.e. after the half-hour), the preposition без (*without*) is needed. This preposition is followed by the genitive case.

без десяти́ (мину́т) шесть	*5.50 (without ten minutes six;*
	the word мину́т *is optional)*
без че́тверти шесть	*5.45 (without quarter six)*

По́лдень means *mid-day* and по́лночь means *midnight*; в по́лночь means *at midnight*.

1 Say what time it is using the twelve-hour clock:

e.g. Кото́рый час? 2.10 → де́сять мину́т тре́тьего

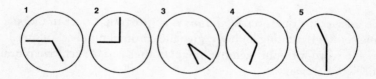

To answer the question *At what time?* (В кото́ром часу́? Во ско́лько?), use the preposition в + *accusative* for the right-hand side of the clock:

в де́сять мину́т пя́того   *at 4.10*

For the half hour, use either в + *prepositional*:

в полови́не пя́того   *at 4.30*

or the shorter form, without в: полпя́того

For the left-hand side of the clock, в is not needed:

без че́тверти шесть   *at 5.45*

You can also state the time by just using cardinal numerals (i.e. by using the twenty-four hour clock):

Ско́лько вре́мени? Оди́ннадцать три́дцать   *What time is it? 11.30*

В кото́ром часу́? В восемна́дцать пятна́дцать   *At what time? At 18.15*

2 Say when the trains leave using the twenty-four hour clock.

e.g. Пермь 18.30 → По́езд в Пермь отхо́дит в восемна́дцать три́дцать. *The train for Perm leaves at 18.30.*

1 Новосиби́рск — 07.15
2 Тверь — 14.55
3 Я́лта — 21.35
4 Воро́неж — 19.30
5 Ки́ров — 17.10

3 Complete the statements on the left by inserting the appropriate times in words, using the information given on the right. Use the twelve-hour clock.

1 Он встаёт в _____   *He gets up at 7.00.*
2 Он за́втракает в _____   *He has breakfast at 7.15.*

3 Его рабочий день _____ начинается в	*His working day begins at 8.45.*
4 Он обедает в _____	*He has lunch at 1.35.*
5 Его рабочий день _____ кончается в	*His working day finishes at 5.30.*

Insight

Here are two simple ways to deal with approximate times:

To say *between four and five o'clock*, you can simply say в пятом часу (lit. in the fifth hour). Take care to distinguish between this and в пять часов *at five pm*).

To say at *approximately five o'clock*, put часов at the beginning of the phrase – часов в пять.

> **For genitive singular, see Section 2.10; for без, see Section 11.5; for declension of третий, see Section 6.4.**

6.6 Dealing with dates

The months of the year are written with a small initial letter (unless they are at the beginning of a sentence). They are all masculine.

январь	апрель	июль	октябрь
февраль	май	август	ноябрь
март	июнь	сентябрь	декабрь

To answer the question Какое сегодня число? (*What is the date today?*), the neuter form of the ordinal numeral is used (to agree with число, *date*) followed by the genitive case of the month:

Сегодня первое мая.   *Today it is the 1st of May.*

Note that in the case of compound numerals, only the last digit is in the ordinal form:

Сего́дня два́дцать седьмо́е февраля́.   *Today it is the 27th of February.*

1 Write out the dates in words.

e.g. 2/5 → Сего́дня второ́е ма́я.

1	6/11	**4**	3/10	**7**	25/6
2	25/8	**5**	29/2	**8**	1/9
3	7/1	**6**	16/4	**9**	31/12

To answer the question Како́го числа́? (*On which date?*), the ordinal numeral must be put into the genitive case: День рожде́ния моего́ му́жа тре́тьего октября́. *My husband's birthday is on the 3rd of October.*

2 Explain where you will be on which dates.

e.g. 01/8 Пари́ж → Пе́рвого а́вгуста я бу́ду в Пари́же. *On the 1st of August I will be in Paris.*

1 10/8 Вене́ция
2 16/8 Берли́н
3 20/8 Москва́
4 25/8 Ки́ров
5 30/8 Но́вгород

3 Complete the sentences on the left and match them with their meanings on the right.

1 Я пое́ду во Фра́нцию _____.

2 Мы получи́ли письмо́ _____.

3 Он позвони́л мне _____.

4 Её день рожде́ния _____.

a *Her birthday is on 7th March.*

b *I am going to France on 18th August.*

c *They left Germany on 22nd November.*

d *We received the letter on 3rd April.*

5 Они уе́хали из Герма́нии _____.   **e** *He rang me on 30th January.*

To answer the question Како́й год? (*Which year?*), Russian uses the following formula:

1999 = *the one thousand nine hundred and ninety-ninth year*

ты́сяча девятьсо́т девяно́сто девя́тый год = 1999г.

i.e. the last digit is an ordinal numeral.

2000 = *the 2000th year* = двухты́сячный год = 2000г.

2010 = *the two thousand and tenth year* = две ты́сячи деся́тый год = 2010г.

Note that the letter г. (for год) usually follows the year when it is written in figures.

To answer the question В како́м году́? (*in which year?*), the ordinal numeral must be put into the prepositional case:

Ста́лин у́мер в ты́сяча девятьсо́т пятьдеся́т тре́тьем году́.   *Stalin died in 1953.*

If details of dates and months are given before the year, then the ordinal numeral must be put into the genitive case:

Она́ родила́сь три́дцать пе́рвого ма́рта ты́сяча девятьсо́т четы́рнадцатого го́да.   *She was born on 31st March 1914.*

4 Write out in words the years in which these Russian poets were born.

1 Пу́шкин роди́лся в 1799г.
2 Ле́рмонтов роди́лся в 1814г.
3 Блок роди́лся в 1880г.

4 Ахма́това родила́сь в 1889г.

5 Пастерна́к роди́лся в 1890г.

6 Цвета́ева родила́сь в 1892г.

> ➤ **For the prepositional singular of adjectives, see Section 3.16; for ordinal numerals and abbreviation of ordinal numerals, see Section 6.4.**

6.7 Quantities, age and distance

The Russian unit of currency is the rouble (= one rouble) and this is divided into 100 kopeks (одна́ копе́йка = one kopek). Here is a summary of what happens to the endings of these words after numerals:

1 and compounds of 1 (21, 101, etc.)	2, 3, 4 and their compounds (24, 52, etc.)	5 and above (except for compounds of 1, 2, 3, 4)
1 (одна́) копе́йка 51 копе́йка 1 рубль 101 рубль	4 копе́йки 32 копе́йки 3 рубля́ 464 рубля́	5 копе́ек 40 копе́ек 5 рубле́й 1000 рубле́й

Note that the abbreviations for рубль and копе́йка are: р. and к.:

11р.22к. *11 roubles 22 kopeks*

1 Ask the question and give the answer, indicating the price of each item.

e.g. зубна́я па́ста/11р. → Ско́лько сто́ит зубна́я па́ста? Оди́ннадцать рубле́й. *How much is the toothpaste? Eleven roubles.*

1 деревя́нный стол/1250р.   *wooden table*

2 япо́нский телеви́зор/3000р.   *Japanese television*

3 конве́рт/3р.20к   *envelope*
4 кра́сная ру́чка/15р.50к.   *red pen*
5 буты́лка кра́сного вина́/40р.   *bottle of red wine*

The words *litre*, *gram* and *kilogram* have passed straight into Russian as литр, грамм, килогра́мм (often shortened to кило́). The prefix пол- is used to indicate half a litre or half a kilogram. Note that the word грамм has two acceptable forms of the genitive plural: either грамм or гра́ммов:

его́ вес – се́мьдесят килогра́ммов	his weight is 70 kilos
полкило́ апельси́нов	half a kilo of oranges
две́сти гра́мм(ов) сы́ра	200 grams of cheese
литр молока́	a litre of milk

The abbreviation for килогра́мм is кг.

2 What quantities have been bought?

e.g. Два килогра́мма бана́нов

2кг.

1 хлеб/4кг.   *bread*
2 мя́со/1/2кг.   *meat*
3 са́хар/5кг.   *sugar*
4 помидо́р/3кг.   *tomato*
5 апельси́н/6кг.   *orange*

Age: the dative case is used to express age, with the word for year (год), which has the genitive plural лет: Ско́лько ему́ лет? (literally: *how many to him of years?*): Ему́ 15 лет (21 год, 22 го́да, 25 лет), *He is 15 (21, 22, 25).*

3 Explain how old each member of the family is.

e.g. Дéдушка /88 → Дéдушке вóсемьдесят вóсемь лет.
Grandfather is 88 years old.

1 Бáбушка/81   *grandmother*
2 Мать/55   *mother*
3 Отéц/54   *father*
4 Сын/32   *son*
5 Дочь/30   *daughter*
6 Внук/12   *grandson*

Distance in Russian is measured in metres and kilometres (метр and киломéтр).

Егó рост в– два мéтра.	*His height is 2 metres.*	Note the need for в + acc. (lit. *his height is at 2 metres*).
От гóрода до дáчи – двáдцать киломéтров.	*From the town to the dacha it is 20 kilometres.*	Note the need for o + gen. and до + gen. (*lit.away from the town as far as the dacha*).
Мы живём в двадцати киломéтрах от дáчи.	*We live 20 kilometres from the dacha.*	Note that both the numeral and kilometres must be in the prepositional plural (*lit. We live at 20 kilometres*) and that you must then use от + gen. (*lit. away from the dacha*).

The abbreviation for киломéтр is км.

> ➤ **For use of cardinal numerals, see Sections 6.1–6.3; for dative case see Sections 2.13, 2.14, 3.12, 3.13; for genitive case, see Sections 2.10–2.12; for prepositional plural of nouns see Section 2.18.**

6.8 Ten things to remember

1 Cardinal numerals express a definite quantity – 6, 400, etc; cardinal numerals which end in a soft sign are feminine nouns.

2 Numerals which have a soft sign in the middle change in the middle and at the end in the genitive, dative, instrumental and prepositional cases.

3 One (1) works like an adjective and must agree with its following noun (or noun and adjectives) in gender and case.

4 Two (2) has two forms: два for masculine and neuter nouns and две for feminine.

5 2, 3 and 4 and their compounds (i.e. 24, 92, 103, etc.) are followed by the genitive singular of nouns.

6 Ordinal numerals (first, fifteenth, etc.) indicate position in an order or series. The ordinal numeral трётий *third* is irregular.

7 Watch out in particular for the genitive case: e.g. полтретьего (*at*) *2.30.*

8 Russian dates (just like English dates) use the ordinal numeral, so 12th April = двенáдцатое апрéля.

9 When talking about the age of someone, use год after 1 and its compounds, гóда after 2, 3, 4 and their compounds, and лет after all other numbers.

10 The genitive singular and plural of *rouble* and *kopek* are vital when dealing with Russian currency – 24 копéйки, 55 копéек, 4 рубля́, 600 рублéй.

7

Pronouns

7.1 Personal pronouns

Personal pronouns (I, you, he, she, it, etc.) can stand in place of a noun to indicate who or what is involved in an action.

In the following table the personal pronouns are in the nominative case.

Singular	Grammatical name	Plural	Grammatical name
я, *I*	first person singular	мы, *we*	first person plural
ты, *you*	second person singular	вы, *you*	second person plural
он, *he, it*	third person singular	они, *they*	third person plural
она, *she, it*	third person singular		
оно, *it*	third person singular		

In the nominative case, the personal pronoun stands in front of the verb in both statement and question:

Вы работаете в Москве?   *Do you work in Moscow?*
Да, я работаю в Москве.   *Yes, I work in Moscow.*

You: The second person singular ты is used to address people you know very well and for children and pets. Вы is the formal way of addressing one person and it is also the only way of addressing more than one person (whether you know them well or not). Вы is usually written with a capital letter if you are writing to someone.

1 Which of the following people would you address as вы and which as ты?

1	муж	*husband*
2	сын	*son*
3	собáка	*dog*
4	начáльник	*boss*
5	нóвый клиéнт	*new customer*

He, she, it, they: Он is used when you are dealing with a masculine singular noun:

Телевúзор не рабóтает → Он не рабóтает *
The television isn't working → It isn't working
Врач не рабóтает → Он не рабóтает
The doctor isn't working → He isn't working

Онá is used in the place of feminine nouns (*she, it*) and онó with neuter nouns (*it*):

Óльга рабóтает? → Онá рабóтает?
Is Olga working? → Is she working?
Рáдио рабóтает? → Онó рабóтает?
Is the radio working? → Is it working?
Онú is the only word for *they*, irrespective of gender:
Óльга и Ворúс рабóтают? → Онú рабóтают?
Are Olga and Boris working? Are they working?

2 Replace the people in italics with a personal pronoun.

e.g. *Татья́на* в шкóле → Онá в шкóле. *Tatyana is in school → She is in school.*

1 *Мой брат* в óфисе.
2 *Медсестра и врач* в больнице.
3 *Бабушка и ты* в театре.
4 *Сестра и я* в Москве.
5 *Вадим и Андрей* в Сибири.

3 Replace the nouns in italics with a personal pronoun.

e.g. *Радио на столе* → Онó на столé. *The radio is on the table* → *It is on the table.*

1 *Нож* на столé.	*The knife is on the table.*
2 *Метрó* в Москвé.	*The metro is in Moscow.*
3 *Виза* в сýмке.	*The visa is in the bag.*
4 *Велосипéд и мотоцикл* на ýлице.	*The bicycle and the motorbike are in the street.*
5 *Яблоки* в магазине.	*The apples are in the shop.*

Insight

The personal pronoun is not left out in written Russian, but is sometimes omitted in conversational language:

Хóчешь чай? Да, хочý.   *Do you want some tea? Yes, I do (want some).*

4 Match the sentences on the left with those on the right.

1 Я не знáю, где они живýт.	**a**	*You live in town.*
2 Мы живём в деревне.	**b**	*They know where he is.*
3 Они знáют, где он.	**c**	*She doesn't know where you are.*
4 Ты живёшь в гóроде.	**d**	*We live in a village.*
5 Онá не знáет, где вы.	**e**	*I don't know where they live.*

There is no special word order for pronouns within a sentence, but they do have different forms for the accusative, genitive, dative, instrumental and prepositional cases.

Nom.	я	ты	он/онó	онá	мы	вы	они́
Acc.	меня́	тебя́	его́	её	нас	вас	их
Gen.	меня́	тебя́	его́	её	нас	вас	их
Dat.	мне	тебé	емý	ей	нам	вам	им
Instr.	мной	тобóй	им	ей	на́ми	ва́ми	и́ми
Prep.	мне	тебé	нём	ней	нас	вас	них

Insight

Some tips about personal pronouns:

the cases of он are identical to those of онó.

the accusative/genitive form of он/онó (его́) is pronounced *yevo* (i.e. the letter г is pronounced as a v).

If you are using the nominative, genitive, dative, instrumental or prepositional case of он/онó/онá/они́ after a preposition, add an н to the front of the pronoun:

Я игра́ю в те́ннис с ним.   *I play tennis with him.*

(The prepositional case always involves the use of a preposition and this is why the prepositional case of он/онó/онá/они́ in the table above starts with the letter н).

Note that о becomes обо in the phrase обо мне *about me*; and с becomes со in the phrase со мной *with me*.

5 Match the phrases on the left and the right, using the English translations as a guide.

1 Я рабо́таю   **a** с ней
2 Он рабо́тает   **b** с ним
3 Ты рабо́таешь   **c** с ва́ми
4 Они́ рабо́тают   **d** с на́ми
5 Вы рабо́таете   **e** со мной

1 *I work with him.*
2 *He works with you (polite).*
3 *You (familiar) work with me.*
4 *They work with her.*
5 *You (formal) work with us.*

6 The verb звони́ть *(to ring, telephone)* takes the dative case. Explain who is ringing whom today.

   e.g. Ива́н/я → Сего́дня Ива́н звони́т мне

   1 я/ты
   2 О́льга/мы
   3 Он/вы
   4 Са́ша/она́
   5 Ты/он

7 Explain who is invited to your party by putting the personal pronouns in brackets into the accusative case.

   e.g. Я приглаша́ю _____ (ты) на вечери́нку →
   Я приглаша́ю тебя́ на вечери́нку. *I invite you to a party.*

   1 Я приглаша́ю _____ (он) на вечери́нку.
   2 Я приглаша́ю _____ (они́) на вечери́нку.
   3 Я приглаша́ю _____ (вы) на вечери́нку.

Russian prefers to use the personal pronoun (rather than the possessive adjective) when talking about parts of the body:

У меня́ боли́т голова́. *My head aches.*

Russian can use the personal pronoun instead of the possessive adjective when talking about place:

У меня́ в ко́мнате *In my room*

8 Who has a headache? Complete the following sentences by giving the genitive of the personal pronouns in brackets.

У него́ боли́т голова́

1 У _____ (ты) боли́т голова́

2 У _____ (она́) боли́т голова́

3 У _____ (вы) боли́т голова́

Insight

Be careful to distinguish between меня́ (*me* – accusative; *of me* – genitive) and мне (*to, for me* – dative; обо мне *about me* – prepositional).

Phrases which include ... *and I* (e.g. *you and I*) start with мы in Russian: мы с ва́ми *you and I* (lit.: *we with you*).

> **For use of prepositions, see Unit 11.**

7.2 Possessive pronouns

The possessive pronoun (mine, yours, his, etc.) is formed in exactly the same way as the possessive adjective, but remember that it replaces the adjective and the noun: *Is this your book? Yes, it's mine.*

If you are indicating possession by *me, you, us* then the possessive pronoun must agree in number, gender and case with what is possessed (not with the possessor). Here are the forms of the possessive pronouns *mine, yours, ours* in the nominative case:

	Masculine	Feminine	Neuter	Plural
mine	мой	моя́	моё	мои́
yours *belonging to* ты	твой	твоя́	твоё	твои́
ours	наш	на́ша	на́ше	на́ши
yours *belonging to* вы	ваш	ва́ша	ва́ше	ва́ши

Э́то твоя́ кни́га Вади́м? Да, моя́.
Is this your book, Vadim? Yes, it's mine.
Э́то твой журна́л, Ка́тя? Да, мой.
Is this your magazine, Katya? Yes it's mine.

1 A mix-up! Explain to Vadim that he's giving lost property out to the wrong people. Use the English translations as a guideline.

e.g. Па́вел/ру́чка/*mine* → Па́вел, вот твоя́ ру́чка. Нет, э́то не моя́. *Pavel, here's your pen. No, it's not mine.*

1 Ка́тя/письмо́/*mine*   *Katya, here's your letter. No, it's not mine*

2 Ви́ктор/сви́тер/*mine*   *Viktor, here's your sweater. No, it's not mine.*

3 Са́ша и Аня/кни́ги/*ours* *Sasha and Anya, here are your books. No, they're not ours.*

4 Светла́на и Та́ня/
фотогра́фии/*ours*   *Svetlana and Tanya, here are your photographs. No, they're not ours.*

5 Андре́й/руба́шка/*mine* *Andrei, here's your shirt. No, it's not mine.*

The possessive pronouns for *his, hers, its, theirs* are invariable (i.e. they never change):

belonging to он: его́	belonging to она́: её	belonging to оно́: его́	belonging to они́: их

Это кни́га Вади́ма? Да, его́.
Is this Vadim's book? Yes, it's his.
Это журна́л Ка́ти? Да, её.
Is this Katya's magazine? Yes, it's hers.

2 Make questions from the following items and give the answer using possessive pronouns.

e.g. она́/маши́на → Это её маши́на? Да, её. *Is it her car? Yes, it's hers.*

1 он/дом   *house*
2 они́/соба́ка   *dog*
3 вы/па́спорт   *passport*
4 я/письмо́   *letter*
5 мы/фотогра́фия   *photograph*

3 Match the phrases on the right and left, using the English translation as a guide.

1 Паспорта́ в тво́ей су́мке?   **a** Да, твоё.
2 Ключи́ в её маши́не?   **b** Да, их.
3 Письмо́ о на́ших биле́тах?   **c** Да, веё.
4 Это моё вино́?   **d** Да, в мое́й.
5 Это их а́дрес?   **e** Да, о на́ших.

1 *Are the passports in your bag? Yes, they're in mine.*
2 *Are the keys in her car? Yes, they're in hers.*
3 *Is the letter about our tickets? Yes, ours.*
4 *Is this my wine? Yes, it's yours.*
5 *Is this their address? Yes, it's theirs.*

> **For possessive adjectives, see Section 3.6.**

7.3 Interrogative pronouns

If you want to ask the questions *What? Who? Which/what sort of? Whose?* then you need to use interrogative pronouns.

Что (*what*) is needed when you are asking about the identity of something:

Что э́то? Рису́нок и́ли фотогра́фия? *What is it? A drawing or a photograh?*

The phrase что э́то тако́е? means *what is that?*
Что can also be used in its different case forms to make questions:

Nom.	что	Dat.	чему́
Acc.	что	Instr.	чем
Gen.	чего́	Prep.	чём

e.g. О чём вы говори́те? *What are you talking about?*

Кто is used when you want to find out the identity of a person:

Кто э́то? Э́то но́вый дире́ктор? *Who is that? Is it the new director?*

Кто can also be used in its different case forms to make questions:

Nom.	кто	Dat.	кому́
Acc.	кого́	Instr.	кем
Gen.	кого́	Prep.	ком

e.g. О ком вы говори́те? *Who are you talking about?*

Note that Russian always uses кто when referring to people, unlike English which sometimes uses what, for example:

Кем вы хоти́те быть? *What do you want to be? (lit.: As whom do you want to be?)*

1 Match the phrases on the left with the translations on the right:

1 О чём она́ ду́мает?	**a** Who is he going to the theatre with?
2 Чем он занима́ется?	**b** Who do you know?
3 С кем он идёт в теа́тр?	**c** What is she thinking about?
4 Кем ты хо́чешь быть?	**d** What do you want to be?
5 Кого́ вы зна́ете?	**e** What is he busy with?

Како́й means *which/what/what sort of* when you are requesting specific detail about something. It is a stressed adjective (and so works in the same way, for example, as молодо́й – *young*):

Како́й у них дом?	*What sort of house have they got?*
В каки́х города́х вы бы́ли?	*Which cities did you visit? (lit.: were you in?)*

2 Find out about someone's purchases by making questions from the information below and using the interrogative pronoun како́й.

e.g. газе́та → Каку́ю газе́ту вы покупа́ете? *Which/what sort of newspaper are you buying?*

1 кварти́ра	*flat*
2 автомоби́ль	*car*
3 зда́ние	*building*
4 велосипе́д	*bicycle*
5 кни́ги	*books*

Чей means *whose*, used when you are trying to find out what belongs to whom. It must agree with the noun it precedes:

Masculine singular	Чей э́то па́спорт?	*Whose passport is this?*
Feminine singular	Чья э́то ви́за?	*Whose visa is this?*
Neuter singular	Чьё э́то ме́сто?	*Whose place is this?*
Plural	Чьи э́то биле́ты?	*Whose tickets are these?*

3 Ask what belongs to whom, using the interrogative pronoun чей.

e.g. тýфли → Чьи э́то тýфли? *Whose are these shoes?*

1 гáлстук *tie*
2 чемодáн *suitcase*
3 ю́бка *skirt*
4 плáтье *dress*
5 носки́ *socks*

4 Translate these sentences into Russian.

1 *Which newspaper are you reading?*
2 *What are you thinking about?*
3 *Who are you going to the shop with?*
4 *What is this? A book or a magazine?*
5 *Whose are these children?*

➤ **For stressed adjectives, see Section 3.4.**

7.4 Demonstrative pronouns

Demonstrative pronouns indicate *which one* – i.e. they give the answer *this, that, such*.

Э́тот means *this* (something close by) and тот means *that* (something not so close):

Вы предпочитáете э́тот   *Do your prefer this*
гáлстук и́ли тот?   *tie or that one?*

Э́тот and тот have case endings which are very similar to those of adjectives:

	Masculine and Neuter	Feminine	Plural
Nom.	э́тот/тот	э́та/та	э́ти/те
Acc.	э́тот (э́того*)/тот (того́*)	э́ту/ту	э́ти (э́тих*)/те (тех*)
Gen.	э́того/того́	э́той/той	э́тих/тех
Dat.	э́тому/тому́	э́той/той	э́тим/тем
Instr.	э́тим/тем	э́той/той	э́тими/те́ми
Prep.	э́том/том	э́той/той	э́тих/тех

* = animate accusative

1 Ask about preference by using the demonstrative pronouns э́тот and тот.

e.g. дом → Вы предпочита́ете э́тот дом и́ли тот дом, вон там? *Do you prefer this house or that house over there?*

1 пальто́   *coat*
2 ша́пка   *hat*
3 шарф   *scarf*
4 руба́шка   *shirt*
5 ту́фли   *shoes*

....

Insight

NB! Э́то also has the meanings *this is, that is, these are, those are*. In these meanings, its ending never changes:

Э́то мой муж   *This is my husband.*
Э́то мой де́ти   *These are my children.*

....

As well as meaning *that*, **тот** also has the meaning of *the same* (when used with же):

Она́ получи́ла тот же пода́рок от меня́.
She received the same present from me.

The phrase **тот же** can also be used with **са́мый** to mean *the very same*:

Она́ получи́ла те же са́мые духи́ от меня́.
She received the very same perfume from me.

2 Complete the sentences by giving the Russian for the word in brackets.

1 Кто _____ (*is it*)? _____ (*it is*) наш врач.
2 Они́ живу́т в _____ (*this*) до́ме.
3 Вчера́ мы бы́ли в теа́тре с Бори́сом и Серге́ем. _____ (*the latter*) рабо́тает врачо́м.
4 Вы уже́ зна́ете об _____ (*this*) пробле́ме?
5 Вот _____ (*the same*) кни́га!
6 Он получи́л _____ (*the very same*) га́лстук.
7 Мы чита́ем _____ (*the same*) газе́ту.
8 Они́ рабо́тают на _____ (*these*) заво́дах.
9 Я иду́ в теа́тр с _____ (*such*) интере́сными друзья́ми.
10 Лу́чшие магази́ны на _____ (*this*) у́лице.

The demonstrative pronoun **тако́й** means *such* and is used in combination with long adjectives. It declines like stressed adjectives such as **молодо́й**, *young*:

Така́я краси́вая карти́на в тако́м интере́сном музе́е.
Such a beautiful picture in such an interesting museum.

....

Insight
Useful phrases using **какой** and **такой** in the instrumental singular with the word **о́браз** *way*:

Каки́м о́бразом?	*In what way?/how?*
Каки́м о́бразом вы реши́ли пробле́му?	*In what way did you solve the problem?*

Таки́м о́бразом — *in such a way/in this way/ thus*

Таки́м о́бразом всё бы́ло хорошо́. — *Thus everything was OK.*

3 Choose the appropriate word from the box to complete the following sentences.

> э́то   каку́ю   така́я   како́м

1 В _____ го́роде ты живёшь?
2 Кто _____?
3 Э́то _____ краси́вая фотогра́фия.
4 _____ ша́пку ты предпочита́ешь?

> ➤ **For stressed adjectives, see Section 3.4.**

7.5 Determinative pronouns

Determinative pronouns make it clear **who** or **what** is involved; in Russian the following words are determinative pronouns:

весь	*all*
ка́ждый	*every*
любо́й	*any*
сам	*self*
са́мый	*the very*

The pronoun **весь** indicates *all, the whole*:

Он рабо́тал весь день. — *He worked all day.*
Мы приглаша́ем всю гру́ппу. — *We invite the whole group.*

Весь declines as follows:

	Masculine	Feminine	Neuter	Plural
Nom.	весь	вся	весь	все
Acc.	весь/ всего*	всю	весь/всего*	все/всех*
Gen.	всего	всей	всего	всех
Dat.	всему	всей	всему	всем
Instr.	всем	всей	всем	всёми
Prep.	всём	всей	всём	всех

* = animate accusative

Insight

The prepositions в in/at and с with acquire an -o when they occur before весь, whilst о about becomes обо:

во весь рост	at full-length; (to sit up) straight; in its full magnitude
во всех странах	in all countries
со всей группой	with the whole group
обо всём	about everything

1 Match the phrases on the left with the translation on the right.

1 Расскажи мне обо всём!
2 Во всех больших оркестрах.

3 Больше всего я люблю петь.
4 Не всем нравится рок-музыка.
5 К сожалению, гид потерял всю группу!

a *In all big orchestras.*
b *Unfrotunately, the guide lost the whole (all the) group!*
c *Tell me about everything!*
d *Most of all I like singing.*
e *Not everyone likes rock music.*

Другой means *other* and works like a stressed adjective; it is often found in combination with **некоторый** *some*, e.g.:
Некоторым понравился концерт, но другие сказали, что

програ́мма неинтере́сная. *Some (people) liked the concert, but others said the programme wasn't interesting.*

Ка́ждый means *every* and declines like an unstressed adjective (i.e. it declines like но́вый):

Он рабо́тает ка́ждое у́тро.   *He works every morning.*

Любо́й means *any* and declines like a stressed adjective (i.e. it declines like молодо́й, *young*):

Позвони́те мне в любо́е вре́мя   *Ring me at any time.*

2 Answer the questions according to the instruction in English.

1 Где мо́жно купи́ть чай?   *in any shop*
2 Где мо́жно купи́ть ко́фе?   *in every shop*
3 Где мо́жно купи́ть молоко́?   *in all shops*
4 Где мо́жно купи́ть вино́?   *in some shops*

Сам (*himself*) declines like э́тот (so, for example сама́ means *herself*) and it must agree with the noun it defines:

Мы пригласи́ли самого́   *We invited the president*
президе́нта.   *himself.*

Са́мый declines like an unstressed adjective (i.e. it declines like но́вый). It makes the location of something very specific:

В са́мом це́нтре го́рода.   *Right in the centre (in the very centre) of town.*

3 Choose the appropriate word from the box below to complete each sentence. Use the English translations which follow as a guide.

> всей ка́ждого любо́м сам самому́

1 Мо́жно купи́ть ма́рки в _____ магази́не.
2 _____ компози́тор идёт на конце́рт.

3 Есть таки́е города́ по _____ А́нглии.

4 У меня́ пода́рки для _____ ребёнка.

5 Он идёт к_____ дире́ктору.

1 *It is possible to buy stamps in any shop.*

2 *The composer himself is going to the concert.*

3 *There are such towns throughout England.*

4 *I have presents for every child.*

5 *He is going to see the director himself.*

4 Translate into Russian.

1 *We work every day.*

2 *The actress herself is going to the theatre.*

3 *I will wait right by the library.*

4 *All our friends are going to the concert.*

5 *Which tickets do you want? Any.*

Insight

There are lots of useful phrases based on весь. Here are a few examples:

Всё в поря́дке	*Everything's in order/OK*
Всё равно́	*It's all the same/makes no difference*
Всего́ хоро́шего	*All the best*
От всей души́	*With all (from the bottom of) one's heart.*

5 Match the phrases on the left with their translations on the right:

1 Я пишу́ ей ка́ждый день.

2 Приходи́ в любо́й день.

3 Мы бы́ли в о́фисе весь ве́чер.

4 Сам учи́тель сказа́л э́то.

5 Я подожду́ тебя́ у са́мого вхо́да.

a *The teacher himself said this.*

b *I write to her every day.*

c *Come on any day.*

d *I will wait for you right by the entrance.*

e *We were in the office all evening.*

> **For unstressed adjectives, see Section 3.3, for stressed adjectives, see Section 3.4.**

7.6 Reflexive pronouns

The reflexive pronoun себя means *self* and it must refer back to the subject of the verb; it is used when *self* would be either stated or implied. In English we might say *He is bringing the camera with him (in other words, we don't actually say with himself,* but this is what is implied). In Russian this would require the use of the reflexive pronoun себя: Он берёт с собой фотоаппара́т.

1 Put an asterisk by the words which would have to be followed by a reflexive pronoun in Russian (hint: there are five).

The tourist came into his room and shut the door behind him. He saw in front of him a large room with a bed, a chair and a washbasin, but no towels. He was glad he had brought some with him. As he was feeling rather tired, he decided to have a wash and a sleep, although he imagined that the bed would not be very comfortable.

The pronoun себя declines as follows:

Accusative	себя
Genitive	себя
Dative	себе
Instrumental	собо́й
Prepositional	себе́

Note that it is used for all persons (*myself, yourself, himself, herself, itself, ourselves, yourselves, themselves*) and that it does not exist in the nominative.

Себя is often required after prepositions in contexts where we would not state the word *self* in English, for example, compare.

Он ви́дит пе́ред собо́й большу́ю соба́ку.	*He sees a big dog in front of him (self)*
Мы закры́ли за собо́й дверь. and	*We closed the door behind us (ourselves)*
Он купи́л шокола́д для себя́.	*He bought the chocolate for himself.*

2 Translate into Russian.

1 *What did you buy for yourself?*
2 *He thinks only about himself.*
3 *I am bringing the wine with me.*
4 *We are bringing the dog with us.*

Insight

The reflexive pronoun occurs in certain common verbs, e.g.:

вести́ себя́	*to behave*
представля́ть себе́	*to imagine*
чу́вствовать себя́	*to feel*

Sometimes a preposition is also involved, as in вы́йти из себя́ *to lose one's temper* – literally (and rather alarmingly!) *to walk out of oneself.*

3 Choose the appropriate word from the box in order to complete the following sentences, using the English translation as a guide.

себя́   себе́   собо́й

1 Он хорошо ведёт _____.
2 Я представляю _____, что это трудно.
3 Закрой за _____ дверь!
4 Я плохо чувствую _____.
5 Мы купили шампанское для _____.

1 *He is behaving well.*
2 *I imagine that it is difficult.*
3 *Close the door behind you!*
4 *I feel ill.*
5 *We bought the champagne for ourselves.*

4 Match the phrases on the left with their translations on the right.

1 Как вы себя чувствуете?
2 Как он ведёт себя?

a *How is he behaving?*
b *Are you bringing the money with you?*

3 Вы берёте с собой деньги?

c *You only think about yourself!*

4 Что вы видите перед собой?
5 Вы думаете только о себе!

d *How are you feeling?*
e *What can you see in front of you?*

➤ **For use of prepositions, see Unit 11.**

7.7 Relative pronouns

A relative pronoun relates to the noun which it follows and thus links parts of a sentence. In Russian, the relative pronoun means *who*, *which*, *that*, and it can refer to both people and things.

Молодой человек, который катается на лыжах, экс-чемпион мира.

The young man is skiing. The young man is the former world champion. → *The young man who is skiing is the former world champion.*

Молодóй человéк, котóрый катáется на лы́жах, экс-чемпиóн ми́ра.

Котóрый is an adjective, so it has masculine, feminine, neuter and plural endings for all six cases. In order to work out the gender and the number, first look at the noun which it follows; in order to work out the case, work out what 'job' котóрый is doing in the second part of the sentence. For example, is it a subject or an object?

Актри́са, котóрая (*subject*) игрáет роль Óльги, óчень талáнтливая.
The actress who is playing the role of Olga is very talented.
Актри́са, котóрую (*object, therefore accusative*) вы лю́бите, óчень талáнтливая.
The actress whom you like is very talented.

1 Make sentences about the following people's jobs, with котóрый referring to the subject in the nominative case.

e.g. Влади́мир/Ки́ев/врач → Влади́мир, котóрый живёт в Ки́еве, врач.

1 Óльга/Ки́ров/продавщи́ца
2 Нáши друзья́/Можáйск/учителя́
3 Ви́ктор/Москвá/перевóдчик
4 Сáша/Ворóнеж/юри́ст
5 Áня/Я́лта/медсестрá
6 Вади́м/Óбнинск/гид

2 Describe what Olga has just bought, with котóрый referring to the object in the accusative case:

e.g. апельси́ны/вку́сные → Апельси́ны, котóрые Óльга купи́ла, вку́сные.

1 велосипéд/большóй   *bicycle/big*
2 джи́нсы/мóдные   *jeans/fashionable*

3 цветы/красивые   *flowers/beautiful*
4 юбка/короткая   *skirt/short*

If the который part of the sentence involves a preposition, that preposition must always come in front of который.

Офис, в котором мы работаем, не очень большой.
The office in which (prepositional case after в) we work is not very big.
Друзья, с которыми мы отдыхали, живут в Лондоне.
The friends with whom (instrumental case after с) we were on holiday live in London.

NB Который is only for use after nouns; to say *'that'* after verbs, don't use который, use что:

Я думаю, что они приедут.   *I think that they will come.*

3 Complete the sentences using the preposition and the relative pronoun который. The case is given in brackets at the end of the sentence.

e.g. Стол, под _____ сидит кошка, в углу. (под + *instr.*) →
Стол, под которым сидит кошка, в углу. *The chair, under which the cat is sitting, is in the corner.*

1 Друг, к _____ мы идём, музыкант.

(к + *dat.*)
2 Здания, в _____ они работают, очень большие.

(в + *prep.*)
3 Врач, с _____ она говорила, очень добрый.

(с + *instr.*)
4 Фильм, о _____ вы говорите, не очень хороший.

(о + *prep.*)
5 Студенты, от _____ мы получили письмо, работают в Африке.

(от + *gen.*)

4 Use кото́рый to make one sentence in Russian out of two using the English sentence as a guide:

e.g. Мой дя́дя инжене́р. Ты говори́л с ним вчера́. *My uncle, with whom you spoke yesterday, is an engineer.* → Мой дя́дя, с кото́рым вы говори́ли вчера́, инжене́р.

1 Соба́ка о́чень ста́рая. Ты сфотографи́ровал её.

The dog which you photographed is very old.

2 Шко́ла о́чень хоро́шая. Ты говори́шь о ней.

The school about which you are speaking is very good.

Insight

There is always a comma before a кото́рый phrase! – Ты зна́ешь футболи́ста, кото́рый заби́л гол? *Do you know the footballer who scored the goal?*

In longer sentences, the кото́рый phrase must be enclosed by commas – Футболи́ст, кото́рого удали́ли с по́ля, гро́мко протесту́ет. *The footballer who has been sent off is protesting loudly.*

As well as being used as an interrogative pronoun meaning *what*, **что** is also used as a relative pronoun:

- with всё (*all, everything*): У меня́ всё, что на́до. *I have everything (that) I need.*
- with то (*that*) to link two parts of a sentence.

Notice that both то and что must decline according to the context:

Я расскажу́ вам о том, что я зна́ю.
I'll tell you about (that which) what I know.
Мы начнём с того́, чем мы занима́лись вчера́.
We'll start with what (literally 'from that which') we were busy with yesterday.

- to 'sum up' a previous part of the sentence (i.e. it links up to the whole of the preceding clause):

Он расска́зывал нам о свое́й пое́здке в А́фрику, что бы́ло о́чень интере́сно.

He told us about his trip to Africa, which was very interesting.

Кто is used as a relative pronoun:
- after тот (*the one ...*)

Тот, кто хо́чет прийти́ на вечери́нку.

Whoever (literally 'the one who') wants to come to the party.

- after все (*everyone*)

Я приглаша́ю всех, кто хо́чет прийти́ на вечери́нку.

I invite all who want to come to the party.

Notice that, when used with тот and все, кто is always followed by a singular verb.

5 Match each Russian phrase with its translation.

1 Я дам вам всё, что на́до.
2 Мы интересу́емся тем, что вы говори́те.
3 Тот, кто не хо́чет танцева́ть, мо́жет отдыха́ть.
4 Э́ти места́ для тех, кто уже́ купи́л биле́ты.
5 Я расскажу́ вам обо всём, что случи́лось.

a *These places are for those who have already bought their tickets.*
b *Whoever (the one who) does not want to dance can rest.*
c *I will tell you about everything that (all that which) happened.*
d *I will give you everything (all that) you need.*
e *We are interested in what (that which) you say.*

6 Choose the appropriate word from the box below to complete each sentence. English translations are given as a guide:

$$\boxed{\text{кто \quad что}}$$

1 Все, _____ смотре́л фильм, говоря́т, что хоро́ший.
2 Он зна́ет всех, _____ придёт на вечери́нку.
3 Они́ забы́ли биле́ты, _____ бы́ло о́чень пло́хо.
4 Я начну́ с того́, _____ он сказа́л мне.
5 Он сказа́л мне всё, _____ он знал.
6 Они́ смо́трят телеви́зор ка́ждый ве́чер, _____ о́чень пло́хо.

1 *Everyone (all) who watched the film says that it is good.*
2 *He knows everyone (all) who is (are) coming to the party.*
3 *They have forgotten the tickets, which is very bad.*
4 *I will start with what (that which) he told me.*
5 *He told me everything (that) he knows.*
6 *They watch television every evening, which is bad.*

➢ **For use of что and кто as interrogative pronouns, see Section 7.3.**

7.8 Indefinite pronouns

An indefinite pronoun gives an answer to the questions *who, what, where, when, how, why,* but the answer is not a definite one:
When will you ring? I'll ring you sometime.
Who is this letter for? Please give it to someone/anyone in the office.

In Russian, an indefinite pronoun is made by adding **-то** or **-нибудь** to question words such as кто *who,* где *where,* что *what.* The particle **-то** indicates something rather more specific than **-нибудь**, e.g.:

Кто́-то = someone in the sense of a particular person, definitely involved in an action, but whose identity is not known: Бори́с сказа́л, что кто-то в гру́ппе хо́чет би́лет. *Boris said that someone in the group wants the ticket.*

Кто́-нибудь = someone in the sense of *anyone at all* (i.e. someone hypothetical – кто́-нибудь implies *whoever it may be*): Да́йте билéт комý-нибудь в грýппе. *Give the ticket to someone/anyone in the group.*

So, -то is more specific, and -нибудь more vague:

гдé-то	*somewhere*	гдé-нибудь	*somewhere/anywhere*
кáк-то	*somehow*	как-нибудь	*somehow/anyhow*
какóй-то	*some sort of*	какóй-нибудь	*some/any sort of*
когдá-то	*sometime*	когдá-нибудь	*sometime/anytime*
ктó-то	*someone*	ктó-нибудь	*someone/anyone*
кудá-то	*(to) somewhere*	кудá-нибудь	*(to) somewhere*
почемý-то	*for some reason*	почемý-нибудь	*for some/any reason*
чтó-то	*something*	чтó-нибудь	*something/anything*

1 Underline the words in the following passage where you would choose to use the particle -то and put a circle round the words where you would choose to use the particle -нибудь in Russian.

Someone called you this morning. He said something about a meeting tomorrow. For some reason he didn't want to talk to me. He just said that if you can't be on time you should ring anyone in the office.

2 Now complete the Russian version of this passage with the appropriate phrases:

_____ позвонúл тебé сегóдня ýтром. Он сказáл _____ о совещáнии зáвтра. Он _____ не хотéл говорúть со мной. Он сказáл тóлько, что éсли вы не смóжете приéхать вó-время, нáдо позвонúть _____ в óфис.

Remember that you use the appropriate case of какóй, кто and что when you use them with -то with or -нибудь:

Купúте какóе-нибудь   *Buy some/any sort*
   винó.   *of wine.*

Он сейча́с за́нят	He's busy with
чем-то ва́жным.	something important at the moment.
Вы зна́ете кого́-нибудь в	Do you know
Новосиби́рске?	anyone in Novosibirsk?

3 Complete each sentence by choosing the appropriate phrase from the box, using the English translations as a guide.

> где́-нибудь како́м-то когда́-нибудь кого́-то
> что́-нибудь что́-то

1 Гид _____ сказа́л об экску́рсии в музе́й.
2 Вы бы́ли _____ в Москве́?
3 Напиши́те _____ о ва́шей семье́!
4 Они́ хотя́т отдыха́ть _____ на ю́ге.
5 Она́ уже́ зна́ет _____ в орке́стре.
6 Я ра́ньше рабо́тал в _____ о́фисе в Ки́рове.

1 *The guide said something about an excursion to a museum.*
2 *Have you ever been to Moscow?*
3 *Write something (anything at all) about your family!*
4 *They want to go on holiday somewhere or other in the south.*
5 *She already knows someone in the orchestra.*
6 *Previously I worked in some office or other in Kirov.*

> ➤ **For declensions of кто and что see Section 7.3.**

7.9 Ten things to remember

1 Мы с сестро́й – *my sister and I*: use мы с + instrumental for phrases indicating ... *and I.*

2 Use у + genitive of the personal pronoun when talking about parts of the body: У меня́ боли́т го́рло. *I have a sore throat.*

3 Его́ *his*, *its*, её *hers*, их *theirs* are invariable (they never change), but мой *my*, твой *yours*, наш *ours*, ваш *yours* work like adjectives and must agree in number, gender and case with the noun they replace.

4 Кто and что have six case forms, so take care to choose the case required by the particular question you ask: Комý он позвони́л? *Who did he ring?* (dative case after the verb позвони́ть).

5 Это doesn't change its ending if it means *it is* or *these are*, but the word for *this* works like an adjective (э́тот, э́та, э́то, э́ти).

6 The way to say *the same* before a noun is to use тот же; же never changes, but тот must agree with the noun it describes.

7 Весь *all* works like an adjective and most of its case forms start with вс-, so some prepositions need an -o to be added (to make pronunciation easier); e.g.: со все́ми *with everyone (all)*.

8 When using кото́рый look <u>back</u> to the noun to work out the number and gender of it and <u>forward</u> to what happens next in the sentence to decide on the case for кото́рый.

9 When asking *what* someone does, Russian asks *as whom do you work?* – Кем вы рабо́таете?

10 To say *someone*, choose between кто́-то (more specific) and кто́-нибудь (less specific – *someone* in the sense of *anyone at all*).

8

....

Verbs (1)

8.1 Using verbs: the infinitive and the present tense

A **verb** describes actions, feelings and states:

I wash the car.
He hates cold weather.
She is very ill.

The **infinitive** is the *to do* part of the verb – e.g. *to wash, to hate, to be.*

The **present tense** is the form of the verb which tells us that the action/feeling/state the verb describes is happening <u>now</u>, in the present, or that it is <u>ongoing</u>.

1 Identify the words in the following passage which are in the infinitive and those which are in the present tense (hint: there are three infinitives and seven present tense verbs).

Tatyana's daughter, Anya, is a doctor and she works at the other side of the city. It is really hard for her to arrive at work on time, as she has so much to do at home each morning and her two children are not always ready for school on time. But she really loves her job at the hospital and does not want to change it.

➤ **For formation of the present tense, see Sections 8.2–8.6.**

8.2 Regular present tense

To make the present tense in Russian, we must first of all look at the infinitive (the *to do* part of the verb). Verbs whose infinitive ends in the letters -ать usually belong to the 'first conjugation' – i.e. a group of verbs that form their present tense according to the same pattern.

In order to make the present tense of a verb ending in -ать the first thing to do is to remove the last two letters (ть), and then add the endings, which are different for each *person* of the verb. Here is the verb for *to work* (рабóтать); the endings added to make the present tense are in bold upper case:

я рабóта**Ю**	*I work*
ты рабóта**ЕШЬ**	*you work*
он, онá, онó рабóта**ЕТ**	*he, she, it works*
мы рабóта**ЕМ**	*we work*
вы рабóта**ЕТЕ**	*you work*
онú рабóта**ЮТ**	*they work*

Insight

In English there are three ways of expressing the present tense: *I work*, *I am working*, *I do work*. In Russian there is only one form of the present tense: я рабóтаю

1 Complete the sentences by filling in the correct verb endings.

e.g. Он _____ (читáть) газéту → Он читáет газéту. *He is reading a newspaper.*

1 Вы _____ (слýшать) рáдио.   *You are listening to the radio.*
2 Мы _____ (игрáть) в тéннис. *We are playing tennis.*
3 Ты _____ (покупáть) чай.   *You are buying tea.*
4 Онá _____ (понимáть) вопрóс? *Does she understand the question?*
5 Я _____ (знать) дирéктора. *I know the director.*

Occasionally, first conjugation infinitives end in -ять, as in the case of the verbs *to cough* (кáшлять) and *to stroll* (гуля́ть). Their present tense is made in just the same way as for verbs ending in -ать:

я гуля́**Ю**	*I stroll*
ты гуля́**ЕШЬ**	*you stroll*
он, онá, онó гуля́**ЕТ**	*he, she, it strolls*
мы гуля́**ЕМ**	*we stroll*
вы гуля́**ЕТЕ**	*you stroll*
онú гуля́**ЮТ**	*they stroll*

2 Complete each sentence with an appropriate verb from the box.

> гуля́ют игрáешь отвечáет покупáю понимáем

1 Я _____ нóвый компью́тер.
2 Он _____ на вопрóс.
3 Мы _____ вáшу проблéму.
4 Ты _____ в футбóл?
5 Онú чáсто _____ в пáрке.

Occasionally first conjugation infinitives end in -еть, as in the case of the verbs *to know how to* (умéть). Their present tense is made in just the same way as for verbs ending in -ать:

я умé**Ю**	*I know how to*
ты умé**ЕШЬ**	*you know how to*
он, онá, онó умé**ЕТ**	*he, she, it knows how to*
мы умé**ЕМ**	*we know how to*
вы умé**ЕТЕ**	*you know how to*
онú умé**ЮТ**	*they know how to*

3 Put the infinitives of these first conjugation verbs into the present tense to agree with their subject.

e.g. игра́ть/он → он игра́ет, *he is playing*

1 знать/вы   *to know*
2 понима́ть/ты   *to understand*
3 ка́шлять/я   *to cough*
4 рабо́тать/она́   *to work*
5 отвеча́ть/они́   *to answer*
6 спра́шивать/мы   *to ask*
7 покупа́ть/он   *to buy*
8 гуля́ть/мы   *to stroll*
9 слу́шать/вы   *to listen*
10 уме́ть/ты   *to know how to*

Verbs whose infinitive ends in the letters -ить belong to the **'second conjugation'** – i.e. a group of verbs which all form their present tense according to the same pattern.

In order to make the present tense of a verb ending in -ить the first thing to do is to remove the last three letters (ить) to give the *stem*, and then add the endings, which are different for each *person* of the verb. Here is the verb *to speak* (говори́ть) with the endings added to make the present tense in bold upper case:

я говор**Ю**	*I speak*	мы говор**И**М	*we speak*
ты говор**И**ШЬ	*you speak*	вы говор**И**ТЕ	*you speak*
он, она́, оно́ говор**И**Т	*he, she, it speaks*	они́ говор**Я**Т	*they speak*

Occasionally second conjugation infinitives end in -ать, as in the case of the verbs *to shout* (крича́ть). Their present tense is made in just the same way as for verbs ending in -ить:

я кричу́	*I shout*	мы крич**И**М	*we shout*
ты крич**И**ШЬ	*you shout*	вы крич**И**ТЕ	*you shout*
он, она́, оно́ крич**И**Т	*he, she, it shouts*	они́ крич**А**Т	*they shout*

Insight

Remember the first spelling rule and watch out for verbs like лежа́ть *to be lying down*, молча́ть *to be silent*, слы́шать *to hear*;

you will need to add -y (not -ю) and -a (not -я) to make the present tense, e.g.: я слы́шу *I hear*, они́ молча́т *they are silent*.

4 Put the infinitives of these second conjugation verbs into the present tense to agree with their subject.

e.g. говори́ть/мы → мы говори́м *we are speaking*

1	молча́ть/я	*to be silent*
2	стро́ить/ты	*to build*
3	сто́ить/оно́	*to cost*
4	кури́ть/вы	*to smoke*
5	ва́рить/они́	*to cook*
6	гото́вить/мы	*to prepare*
7	лежа́ть/я	*to lie (be lying down)*
8	крича́ть/вы	*to shout*
9	слы́шать/вы	*to hear*
10	говори́ть/ты	*to speak*

Sometimes second conjugation infinitives end in -ять or -еть as in the case of the verbs *to stand* (стоя́ть) and *to look/watch* (смотре́ть). Their present tense is made in just the same way as for verbs ending in -ить:

я сто**Ю**	*I stand*
ты сто**И́ШЬ**	*you stand*
он, она́, оно́ сто**И́Т**	*he, she, it stands*
мы сто**И́Т**	*we stand*
вы сто**И́ТЕ**	*you stand*
они́ сто**Я́Т**	*they stand*

я смотр**Ю́**	*I look*
ты смо́тр**ИШЬ**	*you look*
он, она́, оно́ смо́тр**ИТ**	*he, she it looks*
мы смо́тр**ИМ**	*we look*
вы смо́тр**ИТЕ**	*you look*
они́ смо́тр**ЯТ**	*they look*

5 Complete the sentences by filling in the correct verb endings.
e.g. Он _____ (готóвить) обéд → Он готóвит обéд.
He is preparing lunch.

1	Вы _____ (слы́шать) рáдио.	*You (can) hear the radio.*
2	Мы _____ (стоя́ть) у окнá.	*We stand by the window.*
3	Они́ _____ (стрóить) дом.	*They are building a house.*
4	Онá _____ (смотрéть) фильм?	*Is she watching the film?*
5	Ты _____ (звони́ть) дирéктору.	*You are ringing the director.*

Insight

Be careful to distinguish between стóить *to cost* and стоя́ть *to stand*. Notice in particular that стóить is stressed on the beginning and стоя́ть on the end: Он стои́т в óчереди *He is standing in a queue.* Билéт стóит 10р. *The ticket costs 10 roubles.*

6 Complete each sentence with an appropriate verb from the box.

> звоню́ слы́шите смóтришь стóит стоя́т

1 Я чáсто _____ мои́м друзья́м.
2 Вы _____ звонóк телефóна?
3 Кóфе _____ 10 рублéй.
4 Ты _____ футбóл?
5 Они́ _____ у вхóда.

➤ **For personal pronouns and persons of the verb, see Section 7.1; for first spelling rule, Section 1.3.**

8.3 Consonant changes in the present tense

Some second conjugation verbs change the final consonant of their stem in the first person singular only (i.e. in the

I form of the present tense) before adding the present tense endings.

If the stem of a second conjugation verb ends in -д, in the first person singular the д changes to ж, as in the verb *to see*:
ви́деть: я ви́жу ты ви́дишь он ви́дит мы ви́дим вы ви́дите они́ ви́дят

If the stem of a second conjugation verb ends in -з, in the first person singular the з changes to ж, as in the verb *to take (by transport)*:
вози́ть: я вожу́ ты во́зишь он во́зит мы во́зим вы во́зите они́ во́зят

If the stem of a second conjugation verb ends in -с, in the first person singular the с changes to ш, as in the verb *to carry*:
носи́ть: я ношу́ ты но́сишь он но́сит мы но́сим вы но́сите они́ но́сят

If the stem of a second conjugation verb ends in -ст, in the first person singular the ст changes to щ, as in the verb *to whistle*:
свисте́ть: я свищу́ ты свисти́шь он свисти́т мы свисти́м вы свисти́те они́ свистя́т

If the stem of a second conjugation verb ends in -т, in the first person singular the т changes to ч, as in the verb *to fly*:
лете́ть: я лечу́ ты лети́шь он лети́т мы лети́м вы лети́те они́ летя́т

1 Complete the sentences with an appropriate verb from the box.

> во́зит гла́жу лети́те ношу́ сиди́т

1 Óльга _____ у телеви́зора.
2 Я _____ руба́шки.
3 Авто́бус _____ пассажи́ров.
4 Я _____ пи́сьма на по́чту.
5 Сего́дня вы _____ на самолёте.

If the stem of a second conjugation verb ends in б, в, м, п, or ф, then in the first person singular an extra л is added, as in the verb *to prepare*:

гото́вить: я гото́влю ты гото́вишь он гото́вит мы гото́вим вы гото́вите они́ гото́вят

2 All the verbs in the following list are second conjugation. Give the first person singular (я form) of the present tense of each one. (Hint: some need a consonant change and some don't.)

1	люби́ть	*to like/love*
2	спать	*to sleep*
3	говори́ть	*to speak*
4	сиде́ть	*to sit*
5	ла́зить	*to climb*
6	стоя́ть	*to stand*
7	проси́ть	*to ask*
8	смотре́ть	*to look/watch*
9	корми́ть	*to feed*
10	звони́ть	*to ring/telephone*

3 Match the phrases on the left and right, using the English translation as a guide.

1	Фе́рмер	**a**	сиди́м у са́мого экра́на.
2	Вы	**b**	ко́рмит свои́х коро́в.
3	Мы	**c**	гото́влю у́жин на ку́хне.
4	Я	**d**	кричи́т он.
5	Ура́!	**e**	спи́те всю ночь.

1 *The farmer feeds his cows.*
2 *You sleep all night.*
3 *We sit right by the screen.*
4 *I prepare supper in the kitchen.*
5 *Hurrah! He shouts.*

The key is to remember that consonant changes apply **only to the я form of the present tense** (i.e. the first person singular). Here is a summary of the changes:

Д → Ж   С → Ш   Т → Ч   З → Ж   СТ → Щ
Б, В, М, П, Ф → БЛ, ВЛ, МЛ, ПЛ, ФЛ

➢ **For stem of verb and present tense of second conjugation verbs, see Section 8.2.**

8.4 Irregular present tense

Not all verbs follow the regular patterns of the first and second conjugations as described in Section 8.2, but most have infinitives which end in -ть; a few end in -ти or -чь.

The key to using the present tense of irregular verbs is to learn the stem, because this is not formed simply by removing the end of the infinitive. Once you know the irregular stem, the endings follow regular patterns.

Here are some common examples of irregular verbs which take the following pattern of endings:

-у	-ём
-ёшь	-ёте
-ёт	-ут

i.e. the я and они forms both feature the letter у and all the other forms have the letter ё.

These endings are added to the *stem* of the verb. Look carefully at the irregular stem of each verb:

Infin.	Stem	я	ты	он, она́, оно́	мы	вы	они́
брать to take	бер-	беру́	берёшь	берёт	берём	берёте	беру́т
ждать to wait	жд-	жду	ждёшь	ждёт	ждём	ждёте	ждут
жить to live	жив-	живу́	живёшь	живёт	живём	живёте	живу́т
идти́* to walk, go on foot	ид-	иду́	идёшь	идёт	идём	идёте	иду́т
класть to put	клад-	кладу́	кладёшь	кладёт	кладём	кладёте	кладу́т

* Note that other verbs ending in -ти follow this pattern (e.g. расти́, *to grow*).

Some other irregular verbs work in almost the same way, but have -ю and -ют as their first person singular and third person plural endings:

Infin.	Stem	я	ты	он, она́, оно́	мы	вы	они́
лить to pour	ль-	лью	льёшь	льёт	льём	льёте	льют
петь to sing	по-	пою́	поёшь	поёт	поём	поёте	пою́т
пить to drink	пь-	пью	пьёшь	пьёт	пьём	пьёте	пьют

1 Make the present tense by choosing the appropriate ending from the box.

-у	-ю	-ёшь	-ёт	-ём	-ёте	-ут	-ют

e.g. ждать/ты → ты ждёшь
1 брать/мы
2 жить/я
3 пить/вы

4 класть/они́
5 идти́/он
6 петь/ты
7 лить/я
8 ждать/они́
9 пить/я
10 жить/мы

2 Insert the correct subject to match the verb.

1 _____ жду
2 _____ иду́т
3 _____ поём
4 _____ живёшь
5 _____ пьют
6 _____ берёте
7 _____ кладёт

Insight

For most irregular verbs, when you learn the stem, the я and
ты forms of the present tense, you have all the information
you need for the rest of the present tense, because the я and
они́ forms feature the same final vowel and the ты form tells
you what the final vowel will be for the он, она́, оно́, мы and
вы forms.

3 Look at the pictures of Ivan and Vadim and answer the
question.

Кто поёт и кто пьёт?

ВАДИМ

ИВАН

4 Translate into Russian.

1 *Ivan drinks vodka.*
2 *Olga lives in a flat.*
3 *He is waiting at the theatre.*
4 *We are taking the tickets.*
5 *They are singing this evening.*

Here are some common examples of verbs which take the endings:

-у (or -ю)	-ем
-ешь	-ете
-ет	-ут (or -ют)

i.e. the я and они forms both feature the letter у (or -ю) and all the other forms have the letter е.

Infin.	Stem	я	ты	он, она́, оно́	мы	вы	они́
е́хать *to go by transport travel, drive*	éд-	е́ду	е́дешь	е́дет	е́дем	е́дете	е́дут
иска́ть *to look for*	ищ-	ищу́	и́щешь	и́щет	и́щем	и́щете	и́щут
мыть *to wash*	мó-	мо́ю	мо́ешь	мо́ет	мо́ем	мо́ете	мо́ют
писа́ть *to write*	пиш-	пишу́	пи́шешь	пи́шет	пи́шем	пи́шете	пи́шут
пла́кать *to cry*	плач-	плачу́	пла́чешь	пла́чет	пла́чем	пла́чете	пла́чут

5 Complete the following sentences with the present tense of the appropriate verb. Use the English translations as a guide.

e.g. Он _____ в Сара́тов → Он е́дет в Сара́тов. *He is going (by transport) to Saratov.*

1 Я ча́сто _____ моему́ дру́гу.
2 Сего́дня мы _____ в центр го́рода.
3 Вы не о́чень ча́сто _____ посу́ду.
4 Почему́ ты _____?
5 Они́ _____ свой паспорта́.

1 *I often write to my friend.*
2 *Today we are travelling into the centre of town.*
3 *You don't very often wash the dishes.*
4 *Why are you crying?*
5 *They are looking for their passports.*

6 Choose the appropriate personal pronoun from the box to complete each sentence.

я	ты	он	мы	они́

1 _____ и́щут ги́да.
2 _____ почему́-то пла́чет.
3 _____ е́дешь в го́род.
4 _____ мо́ю посу́ду.
5 _____ е́дем в Москву́.

Verbs whose infinitives end in -авать, -овать or -евать all form their stems in a similar way:
Verbs which end in **-авать**

Дава́ть, the verb for *to give*, is an example of a present tense of verbs whose infinitive ends in -авать. Its present tense is formed like this:

я да**Ю**	*I give*	мы да**ЁМ**	*we give*
ты да**ЁШЬ**	*you give*	вы да**ЁТЕ**	*you give*
он да**ЁТ**	*he gives*	они́ да**ЮТ**	*they give*

NB the verb *to swim*, пла́вать, has the present tense пла́ваю, пла́ваешь (i.e. like a regular first conjugation verb).

Verbs which end in **–овать** and **-евать**

Путеше́ствовать, the verb *to travel*, is an example of a verb whose infinitive ends in -овать, and танцева́ть, the verb *to dance*, is an example of the -евать infinitive ending. The present tense of these verbs is:

я путеше́ств**У́Ю**	*I travel*
ты путеше́ств**УЕШЬ**	*you travel*
он путеше́ств**УЕТ**	*he travels*
мы путеше́ств**УЕМ**	*we travel*
вы путеше́ств**УЕТЕ**	*you travel*
они́ путеше́ств**УЮТ**	*they travel*

я танц**У́Ю**	*I dance*
ты танц**У́ЕШЬ**	*you dance*
он танц**У́ЕТ**	*he dances*
мы танц**У́ЕМ**	*we dance*
вы танц**У́ЕТЕ**	*you dance*
они́ танц**У́ЮТ**	*they dance*

7 Put the infinitive into the correct form of the present tense.

1	я/танцева́ть	*to dance*
2	ты/дать	*to give*
3	он/рекомендова́ть	*to recommend*
4	мы/встава́ть	*to get up*
5	вы/сове́товать	*to advise*
6	они́/рискова́ть	*to risk*
7	она́/узнава́ть	*to find out, recognize*
8	я/испо́льзовать	*to use*
9	мы/тре́бовать	*to demand, require*
10	они́/путеше́ствовать	*to travel*

> ➤ **For present tense of first conjugation verbs, see Section 8.2.**

8.5 The present tense of *to be, to have, to be able, to want*

The verbs *to be, to have, to be able* and *to want* have more irregularities than other verbs and, as they are such common verbs, they need special care.

Russian has an infinitive for the verb *to be* (**быть**), but there is no present tense. So, if you want to make a statement using the present tense of the verb *to be*, you need to use one of the following methods:

- use a dash if you are defining a noun: Áня – врач, *Anya is a doctor*.
- use nothing at all, other than the word (usually an adverb) you wish to state: Хóлодно, *it is cold*, интерéсно, *it is interesting*.
- use the word есть: В гóроде есть аптéка, *There is a chemist's in town*.
- or, if you want to say *there isn't, there aren't*, use нет followed by the genitive case: Здесь нет киóска, *There's no kiosk here*.

To express the verb *to have* Russian uses the preposition **у** with the genitive case of the 'owner' and the nominative of the thing owned: У нас дом, *We have a house* (lit.: *by us house*); у Áни собáка, *Anya has a dog* (lit.: *by Anya dog*). Есть can be used to give added emphasis: У вас есть дом?, *Do you have a house?* To use this construction in the negative, use нет and the genitive of the thing not owned: У нас нет дóма, *We haven't got a house*.

1 Translate into Russian.

   1 *My brother is an engineer.*
   2 *It is cold today.*
   3 *There is a key on the table.*
   4 *There aren't any shops in the village.*

2 Explain who has got what.

e.g. Ка́тя/сы́н ✓ → У Ка́ти есть сын.
Áня /сын ✗ → У Áни нет сы́на.

Вади́м	дом	✓
Бори́с	автомоби́ль (м)	✗
Та́ня	телеви́зор	✓
Зо́я	кварти́ра	✓
И́горь	ко́шка	✗
Серге́й	компью́тер	✗

3 Match the phrases.

1 У врача́	**a**	мно́го книг
2 У профе́ссора	**b**	мно́го раке́ток
3 У библиоте́каря	**c**	мно́го пи́сем
4 У почтальо́на	**d**	мно́го студе́нтов
5 У теннис́иста	**e**	мно́го пацие́нтов

The verbs *to be able* and *to want* have stems which change during the present tense:

мочь *to be able (can)*	хоте́ть *to want*
я могу́	я хочу́
ты мо́жешь	ты хо́чешь
он мо́жет	он хо́чет
мы мо́жем	мы хоти́м
вы мо́жете	вы хоти́те
они́ мо́гут	они́ хотя́т

4 Complete the following sentences with the present tense of either мочь or хоте́ть, using the English translations as a guide.

e.g. Он _____ отдыхать в Крыму. → Он хочет отдыхать в Крыму. *He wants to have a holiday in the Crimea.*

1 Он _____ прийти в театр.
2 Турист не _____ посмотреть фильм.
3 Нет, спасибо, я не _____ кофе.
4 Ты не _____ плавать сегодня, если горло болит.
5 Костя и Лена _____ купить новую квартиру.

1 *He can come to the theatre.*
2 *The tourist doesn't want to watch the film.*
3 *No, thank you, I don't want any coffee.*
4 *You can't swim today if you have a sore throat.*
5 *Kostya and Lena want to buy a new flat.*

Insight

NB! Уметь *to know how to/can*: уметь means *can* only in the sense of *can = knows how to*:

Я не могу петь – у меня горло болит. *I can't sing – my throat's sore.*
Я не умею играть на инструменте, но люблю слушать музыку. *I can't play an instrument, but I like listening to music.*

> **For genitive case, see Sections 2.10–2.12 and 3.10–3.11.**

8.6 The present tense of reflexive verbs

A reflexive verb expresses an action that 'reflects' back to the subject; it is the sort of verb which in English is followed by … *self* or where … *self* can be understood, for example *to wash* (*oneself*). The ending -ся (or sometimes -сь) is what identifies a reflexive verb in the infinitive and these endings appear in the present tense as follows:

умыва́ться *to wash oneself, get washed*	
я умыва́юсь	мы умыва́емся
ты умыва́ешься	вы умыва́етесь
он умыва́ется	они́ умыва́ются

So, the ending is -сь for the я and вы forms of the present tense, and -ся for all the other parts of the present tense.

Some common examples of reflexive verbs where ... *self* is stated or implied are:

гото́виться	*to prepare oneself, get ready*
купа́ться	*to bathe, take a bath*
ложи́ться спать	*to go to bed* (lit.: *to lie down to sleep*)
одева́ться	*to dress oneself, get dressed*
причёсываться	*to do one's hair*
раздева́ться	*to get undressed, take one's coat off*

1 Fill in the missing words.

1 Я _____ в 8 часо́в.

2 Он _____ пе́ред зе́ркалом.

Some verbs which are reflexive in Russian would not state or even imply the word ... *self* in English; these reflexive verbs often involve the idea of 'to be ...' and are *intransitive* verbs (i.e. they have no object). For example, the Russian verb *to be situated* is находи́ться: Наш дом нахо́дится в го́роде. *Our house is situated in the town.* Other common 'intransitive' reflexive verbs are *to begin* (i.e. *to be started*) and *to end* (i.e. *to be finished*).

to begin, start:

начина́ться   Фильм начина́ется в 9 часо́в   *the film starts at 9 o'clock*

to end, finish:

конча́ться   Фильм конча́ется в 11 часо́в   *the film ends at 11 o'clock*

2 Translate into Russian.

1 *I get dressed at 8 o'clock.*
2 *He gets washed at 7 o'clock.*
3 *They get undressed at 10 o'clock.*
4 *The concert ends at 10 o'clock.*
5 *You go to bed at 11 o'clock.*

Another group of reflexive verbs whose English versions would not state or imply ... *self* are concerned with feelings. Here are some common examples:

беспоко́иться	*to worry, be anxious*
боя́ться	*to fear, be afraid*
горди́ться	*to be proud*
наде́яться	*to hope*
смея́ться	*to laugh*
улыба́ться	*to smile*

3 Match the phrases on the left with their translations on the right.

1 Врач беспоко́ится о пацие́нте. **a** *The concert starts at seven.*

2 Конце́рт начина́ется в 7 часо́в. **b** *At what time do you get washed?*

3 Он всегда́ ра́но ложи́тся спать. **c** *The doctor is worried about the patient.*

4 Я наде́юсь, что всё бу́дет хорошо́. **d** *He often bathes in the river.*

5 Он ча́сто купа́ется в реке́.	**e** *When does the film start?*
6 Во ско́лько вы умыва́етесь?	**f** *He always goes to bed early.*
7 Архите́ктор горди́тся но́вым зда́нием.	**g** *What are you worried about?*
8 Когда́ начина́ется фильм?	**h** *The architect is proud of the new building.*
9 Мы мно́го смеёмся.	**i** *We laugh a lot.*
10 О чём ты беспоко́ишься?	**j** *I hope everything will be all right.*

> ➤ **For telling the time, see Section 6.5.**

8.7 Ten things to remember

1 The infinitive is the 'to do' form of the verb; in Russian the infinitive usually ends in -ть, and occasionally -ти or -чь.

2 Although most verbs with an infinitive ending in -ать are first conjugation, watch out for those which are second conjugation, especially: крича́ть, лежа́ть, молча́ть, слы́шать.

3 You will sometimes need to apply the second spelling rule with verbs of the second conjugation: after г, к, х, ж, ч, ш, щ never write ю or я but always у and а.

4 For the present tense of irregular verbs, be sure to learn the stem, **я** and **ты** forms.

5 Some second conjugation verbs change the last consonant of the stem in the **я** form only; be sure to learn the very common verbs where this happens: я ви́жу *I see*, я гото́влю *I prepare/cook*, я куплю́ *I will buy*, я люблю́ *I like/love*, я прошу́ *I ask/request/beg*, я сижу́ *I sit*, я сплю *I sleep*.

6 Watch out for the differences between петь *to sing* and пить *to drink*.

7 Мочь means *can, to be able* in the sense of something being physically possible; уметь means *can* in the sense of *knowing how*.

8 There is no present tense of the verb *to be*.

9 English often misses out the *self* which must be there in Russian reflexive verbs (e.g. одеваться – *to get dressed/dress oneself*).

10 To express the verb *to have*, use y + genitive case of the 'owner': У Саши много денег. *Sasha has a lot of money.*

9

Verbs (2)

9.1 Using verbs: the future and past tenses; imperfective and perfective aspects

The future tense is used to talk about what actions, feelings and states which *will* or *are going to* happen. The past tense describes actions, feelings and states which happened in the past: in English there are various forms of the past tense: *was/were doing, used to do, has/have done, did, had done*. Russian has just two ways of expressing the future tense, and two ways of expressing the past; nevertheless, it can express all the different versions of English future and past tenses thanks to something called the *imperfective and perfective aspects* – English has no equivalent of this system.

A small minority of verbs have only one infinitive, while verbs of motion (to run, to swim, etc.) have three.

When you look up a Russian verb in a dictionary you will usually be given two infinitives, for example писáть/написáть (*to write*). The first of these is called the *imperfective* and the second is the *perfective*. The imperfective infinitive is used to make:

- the present tense
- the compound future
- the imperfective past.

The imperfective is always associated with the process of an incomplete, unspecific, ongoing action or a frequently occurring action.

The perfective infinitive is used to make:

- the simple future
- the perfective past tense.

The perfective is always associated with result, successful completion.

Imperfective and perfective *'pairs'* are usually related to each other in one of the following ways:

- писáть/написáть (*to write*), i.e. the perfective = imperfective +prefix (i.e. small addition to the front of the infinitive). Other common examples of this sort of pair are: вúдеть/увúдеть (*to see*); читáть/прочитáть (*to read*).
- решáть/решúть (*to decide*), i.e. the imperfective is 1st conjugation and the perfective is 2nd conjugation. Another common example of this sort is: получáть/получúть (*to receive*).
- Sometimes there is a really striking difference between the two infinitives: говорúть/сказáть (*to talk, speak, say*); возвращáться/вернýться (*to return*); садúться/сесть (*to sit down*).

Insight
Unfortunately, there is no simple way of predicting what the perfective infinitive might be, so it is really important, every time you come across a new verb, to make sure you learn both infinitives – then you have everything you need to make all the future and past tenses!

1 Match the imperfective infinitive on the left with its perfective infinitive on the right.

1 говори́ть	**a** написа́ть
2 ви́деть	**b** верну́ться
3 сади́ться	**c** уви́деть
4 писа́ть	**d** сесть
5 возвраща́ться	**e** сказа́ть

Even when using the infinitive itself, we must be careful to select either the imperfective or the perfective according to the golden rule of: *imperfective = process/frequent/unspecific* and *perfective = result/completion*. For example: Я уме́ю писа́ть, *I know how to write*. Here the imperfective for *to write* has been chosen because we are describing an ongoing situation, a habitual state of affairs. In contrast, Он обеща́л написа́ть письмо́ дире́ктору сего́дня (*He promised to write a letter to the director today*) requires the perfective of *to write*, since it refers to a specific occasion.

Certain verbs are always followed by an imperfective infinitive in Russian: конча́ть/ко́нчить, *to finish*, начина́ть/нача́ть, *to begin*, продолжа́ть, *to continue*, перестава́ть/переста́ть, *to cease, stop* (e.g. *He stopped playing*).

2 Complete the translations of these sentences by filling in the appropriate infinitive in Russian; use the English translations as a guide.

1 Гид продолжа́л _____ .
2 Я хочу́ _____ письмо́ Бори́су за́втра.
3 Я предпочита́ю _____ газе́ты.
4 Они́ переста́ли _____ в де́вять часо́в.
5 Он реши́л _____ во вто́рник.

1 *The guide continued speaking.*
2 *I want to write the letter to Boris tomorrow.*
3 *I prefer to read newspapers.*
4 *They stopped playing at 9 o'clock.*
5 *He decided to return on Tuesday*

3 Translate the following sentences and phrases into Russian; the imperfective/perfective pair of infinitives is given on the right.

1 He prefers to read newspapers.	читáть/прочитáть
2 I want to send this letter today.	посылáть/послáть
3 The actor starts speaking at 7.	говорúть/сказáть
4 We continue watching television.	смотрéть/посмотрéть
5 They like to relax on the beach.	отдыхáть/отдохнýть
6 I want to take the book now.	брать/взять
7 We want to buy this dog.	покупáть/купúть
8 Do you prefer to listen to the radio?	слýшать/прослýшать
9 Do you want to return today?	возвращáться/ вернýться

> ➤ **For present tense see Unit 8; for compound future see Section 9.2; for simple future see Section 9.3; for imperfective past, see Section 9.4; for perfective past see Section 9.5.**

9.2 Compound future

In Russian, the **compound future** is used to describe actions in the future which are incomplete, unspecific, repeated or continuing: e.g. *I will write to you every day; tomorrow I will write a few letters and do some gardening.*

1 Which verbs in the following passage which would be in the compound future in Russian? (Hint: there are four.)

*On Saturday I fly to Saint Petersburg at 10 a.m. While I am
there I will have meetings with Russian representatives of the
company, but I hope that I will also visit some museums and
theatres. I promise that I will ring you as regularly as I can
during my stay, or else I will use e-mail at the hotel.*

As its name suggests, the compound future is made up of two
parts, the future tense of the verb *to be* + an imperfective
infinitive; although the *verb to be*, быть, has no present tense of
its own, it does have a future:

я бу́ду	*I will be*	мы бу́дем	*we will be*
ты бу́дешь	*you will be*	вы бу́дете	*you will be*
он бу́дет	*he will be*	они́ бу́дут	*they will be*

This can be used in its own right, as well as being part of the
compound future, for example: За́втра мы бу́дем в Москве́,
Tomorrow we will be in Moscow.

The second component of the compound future is the
imperfective infinitive or aspect, because the compound
future is associated with the process of an incomplete,
unspecific, ongoing action or a frequently occurring action in
the future.

Here is an example of the compound future being used to
describe a repeated action in the future:

Я буду́ писа́ть тебе́ ка́ждый день. *I will write to you every day.*

And here is an example of the compound future being used to
describe an action which is not concerned with any result or
completion and there is no specific time at which the events will
happen:

Завтра мы бу́дем смотре́ть телеви́зор и рабо́тать в саду́.
Tomorrow we will watch (a bit of) television and (do some) work in the garden.

2 Build sentences using the compound future, to give the meanings indicated on the right.

e.g. Я/де́лать/поку́пки на ры́нке → Я бу́ду де́лать поку́пки на ры́нке. *I will do the shopping at the market.*

1 Он ча́сто/звони́ть/дру́гу.   *He will ring his friend often.*
2 Ба́бушка/отдыха́ть/до́ма.   *Granny will be resting at home.*
3 Мы/игра́ть/в гольф ка́ждый день.   *We will play golf every day.*
4 За́втра я/занима́ться/ уро́ками.   *I will be busy with lessons tomorrow.*
5 В университе́те он/ изуча́ть/ исто́рию.   *At university he will study history.*

3 Match the phrases on the left with those on the right, using the English translation as a guide.

1 За́втра мы   **a** бу́дете в Росси́и, вы бу́дете звони́ть мне ка́ждый день?
2 Сего́дня вечером ты   **b** бу́дем игра́ть в кри́кет.
3 В ма́е они́   **c** бу́дут отдыха́ть в Ита́лии.
4 Когда́ вы   **d** бу́ду рабо́тать в саду́.
5 По́сле обе́да я   **e** бу́дешь писа́ть мно́го пи́сем.

1 *Tomorrow we will play cricket.*
2 *This evening you will write a lot of letters.*
3 *In May they will go on holiday (rest) in Italy.*
4 *When you are (will be) in Russia, will you ring me every day?*
5 *After lunch I will work in the garden*

➤ **For simple future, see Section 9.3; for imperfective and
   perfective aspects, see Section 9.1.**

9.3 Simple future

In Russian, the simple future is used to describe actions in the
future which are single, specific, complete; they are concerned with
result and successful completion (rather than process).

1 Which verbs in the following passage would be in the simple
future in Russian? (Hint: there are four.)

*I will ring you tomorrow at 10 a.m., then I will write a letter to
the director. As far as I know, he will be visiting lots of offices
in England, but he has promised that he will visit our office on
Tuesday. He will be considering all our proposals before his
departure. Hopefully, he will sign the contract on Tuesday.*

The simple future is formed from the perfective infinitive. There
are no new endings to learn, since it is formed in exactly the
same way as the present tense, but from the perfective infinitive.
So, for example, the difference between *I am doing* and *I will
do*: я де́лаю (*I am doing*) is formed from the imperfective
infinitive де́лать and я сде́лаю (*I will do*) is formed from the
perfective infinitive сде́лать.

| написа́ть | я напишу́ | *I will write* |
| пообе́дать | ты пообе́даешь | *you will have lunch* |

объяснить	он объяснит	*he will explain*
получить	мы получим	*we will receive*
решить	вы решите	*you will decide*

Although the perfective infinitive for most verbs is formed by the addition of a prefix to the imperfective or a change to the second conjugation for the perfective, some common verbs have irregular verbs for their perfective:

Meaning	Imperfective infin.	Perfective infin.	Simple future
to get up	вставать	встать	я встану, ты встанешь, он встанет, мы встанем, вы встанете, они встанут
to give	давать	дать	я дам, ты дашь, он даст, мы дадим, вы дадите, они дадут
to lie down	ложиться	лечь	я лягу, ты ляжешь, он ляжет, мы ляжем, вы ляжете, они лягут
to sit down	садиться	сесть	я сяду, ты сядешь, он сядет, мы сядем, вы сядете, они сядут
to say	говорить	сказать	я скажу, ты скажешь, он скажет, мы скажем, вы скажете, они скажут (**NB** other verbs ending in –казать conjugate in the same way)
to be able, can	мочь	смочь	я смогу, ты сможешь, он сможет, мы сможем, вы сможете, они смогут

2 What will you achieve while your friend is watching television? Build sentences using the simple future:

e.g. Пока́ ты смо́тришь телеви́зор/написа́ть письмо́ →
я напишу́ письмо́ Бори́су. *While you're watching television I'll write the letter to Boris.*

1 позвони́ть дру́гу	*I'll ring a friend.*
2 накорми́ть соба́ку	*I'll feed the dog.*
3 пообе́дать на ку́хне	*I'll have lunch in the kitchen.*
4 купи́ть молоко́	*I'll buy some milk.*
5 вы́учить но́вые слова́	*I'll learn some new words.*

3 Here is a page from your diary, with just the briefest of notes. Make up sentences to describe your plans for each day. Monday has been done for you:

e.g. В понеде́льник я встре́чу Са́шу.

ПОНЕДЕЛЬНИК	встре́тить Са́шу	*meet Sasha*
ВТОРНИК	купи́ть пода́рки	*buy presents*
СРЕДА	позвони́ть ма́ме	*ring Mother*
ЧЕТВЕРГ	написа́ть письмо́ бра́ту	*write letter to brother*
ПЯТНИЦА	вы́учить грамма́тику	*learn the grammar*
СУББОТА	отремонти́ровать маши́ну	*repair the car*
ВОСКРЕСЕНЬЕ	заказа́ть биле́ты	*book tickets*

Insight

English sometimes uses the present tense when the future is implied, e.g.: *If Boris arrives on time, we'll give him the present.* In Russian, both verbs in this sentence (*arrives* and *ask*) must be in the simple future: Е́сли Бори́с придёт во́время, мы дади́м ему́ пода́рок.

➤ **For compound future, see Section 9.2; for imperfective and perfective aspects, see Section 9.1; for formation of present tense verbs, see Unit 8.**

9.4 Imperfective past

The imperfective past is used to describe actions/feelings/states in the past which were repeated, continuing or incomplete/interrupted. It is made from the imperfective infinitive, e.g.:

I always used to play squash on Saturdays; He was playing squash when he fell; We played squash yesterday; We played squash for two hours yesterday.

The final example includes the length of time the activity continued and when this is the case the imperfective will always be required. The imperfective past is also used when describing weather, colour, mood, appearance, etc.: *It was cold when we were playing squash.*

1 Which verbs in the passage below which would be in the imperfective in past tense in Russian? (Hint: there are six.)

When we used to live in a flat it was impossible to have a dog, but when we moved into a house with a garden, we bought one. He was a large black mongrel and he loved to play in the garden. One day he was barking by the gate when the postman arrived. He thought the dog was aggressive and refused to come in.

To form the imperfective past tense, remove the last two letters (ть) from the imperfective infinitive, then add the endings (reflexive endings on the right):

- if the subject of the verb is masculine singular   add -л   -лся
- if the subject of the verb is feminine singular   add -ла   -лась
- if the subject of the verb is neuter singular   add -ло   -лось
- if the subject is plural (any gender)   add -ли   -лись

In other words, the endings have to agree in number and gender in the singular with the subject of the verb. For вы, the past tense ending will always be -ли whether вы is being used to refer politely to one person or in the plural to apply to more than one person; for я and ты the ending will depend on the identity of the person (Игорь, ты за́втракал? Ка́тя, ты за́втракала? *Igor/Katya, were you having breakfast?*)

игра́ть	→	Вчера́ мы игра́ли в сквош	*Yesterday we played squash.*
одева́ться	→	Они́ всегда́ одева́лись в шесть часо́в	*They always used to get dressed at 6 o'clock.*

2 Police enquiry: explain who was doing what when the telephone rang.

e.g. Когда́ зазвони́л телефо́н/Вади́м/спать → Вади́м спал.
When the telephone rang Vadim was sleeping.

1	О́льга/за́втракать	*Olga was having breakfast.*
2	Меня́ зову́т Еле́на, я/мыть посу́ду	*I (Elena) was washing up.*
3	Он/игра́ть в ка́рты	*He was playing cards.*
4	Мы смотре́ть/телеви́зор	*We were watching television.*
5	Вы/возвраща́ться в о́фис	*You were returning to the office.*
6	Они́/писа́ть пи́сьма	*They were writing letters.*
7	Бори́с и Светла́на/гото́вить обе́д	*Boris and Svetlana were preparing lunch.*

Irregular verbs form their past tense in the same way (e.g. жить → мы жи́ли *we lived*), apart from verbs whose infinitive does not end in -ть:

везти (*to take by transport*)	→	вёз, везла́, везло́, везли́
вести (*to take on foot, lead*)	→	вёл, вела́, вело́, вели́
есть (*to eat*)	→	ел, е́ла, е́ло, е́ли
идти (*to go on foot, walk*)	→	шёл, шла, шло, шли
мочь (*to be able, can*)	→	мог, могла́, могло́, могли́
нести (*to carry*)	→	нёс, несла́, несло́, несли́

The verb *to be* (быть) exists only in the imperfective. This occurs very frequently in descriptions of weather, colour, mood, appearance, etc.: e.g. Вчера́ он был в плохо́м настрое́нии. *Yesterday he was in a bad mood.*

3 Explain which verbs in the following sentences are in the imperfective past tense, and give reasons.

1 Вчера́ он рабо́тал в библиоте́ке два часа́.
Yesterday he worked in the library for two hours.

2 Она́ игра́ла в те́ннис, когда́ она́ уви́дела Бори́са.
She was playing tennis when she saw Boris.

3 В ма́рте мы бы́ли в Ита́лии.
In March we were in Italy.

4 Они́ шли в центр, когда́ заме́тили авто́бус.
They were walking to the centre when they noticed the bus.

5 Вы всегда́ де́лали поку́пки в на́шем магази́не.
You always used to do your shopping in our shop.

> **For the present tense of reflexive verbs, see Section 8.6; for imperfective past tense, see Section 9.3.**

9.5 Perfective past

The perfective past is used to describe completed actions in the past; the emphasis is on result (not process).

The perfective past tense would be needed in Russian to express ideas such as:

Вчера́ он купи́л автомоби́ль.
Она́ позвони́ла Вади́му в
  де́сять часо́в.

Yesterday he bought a car.
She rang Vadim at
  10 o'clock

1 Which verbs in the following passage which you would translate
by the perfective past? (Hint: there are 10.)

*She had already finished the book when the phone rang. It was
Boris, inviting her to the theatre. She refused politely, because
she had already agreed to go to the cinema with Sergei. While
she was speaking to Boris, her brother rang the doorbell. She
hung up quickly and rushed to the door. Her brother was
looking tired. 'I have brought the plants you asked for,' he said.*

The perfective past tense is very simple to form. Remove the last
two letters (ть) from the imperfective infinitive. The endings are
just the same as for the imperfective past (reflexive endings on
the right):

- if the subject of the verb is masculine   add -л   -лся
  singular:
- if the subject of the verb is feminine   add -ла   -лась
  singular:
- if the subject of the verb is neuter singular: add -ло   -лось
- if the subject is plural (any gender):   add -ли   -лись

Just as for the imperfective past, the endings are rather like
those of an adjective, and they must agree in number and gender
in the singular with the subject of the verb. If the subject of the
verb is вы, then the past tense ending will always be -ли whether
вы is being used to refer politely to one person or in the plural
to apply to more than one person; for я and ты the ending will
depend on the identity of the person (И́горь, ты поза́втракал?
Ка́тя, ты поза́втракала? *Igor/Katya, have you had breakfast?*)

написа́ть → Вчера́ вы написа́ли   *Yesterday you wrote an*
              ва́жное письмо́.   *important letter.*
сказа́ть → «Да,» сказа́л он.   *'Yes,' he said.*

| одéться | → | Сегóдня онú одéлись в семь часóв. | *Today they got dressed at 7 o'clock.* |

2 What has already been done? Look at the rota below and explain who has done what. The first one has been done for you:

e.g. Хорошó! Óльга ужé пропылесóсила. *Good! Olga has already done the hoovering.*

Óльга	пропылесóсить	*to hoover*	✓
Вадúм	вы́мыть посýду	*to do the washing up*	✓
Вы	приготóвить обéд	*to prepare the lunch*	✓
Онú	сдéлать покýпки	*to do the shopping*	✓
Нáдя	накормúть собáку	*to feed the dog*	✓
Игорь	вы́стирать бельё	*to do the washing*	✓

Irregular verbs form their perfective past tense in the same way; here are some examples of those whose infinitives do not end in -ть:

лечь (*to lie down*)	→	лёг, леглá, леглó, леглú
пойтú (*to go on foot, walk*)	→	пошёл, пошлá, пошлó, пошлú
смочь (*to be able, can*)	→	смог, смоглá, смоглó, смоглú
понестú (*to carry*)	→	понёс, понеслá, понеслó, понеслú

Notice that the perfective infinitive of to *eat* loses the **three** letters of its infinitive:

| съесть (*to eat*) | → | съел, съéла, съéло, съéли |

3 Igor and Zoya have had a lot of interruptions. Explain what they were doing by translating the following sentences into Russian. NB! Some of the past tenses will be imperfective and some perfective. The vocabulary you need is in brackets.

1 *Igor and Zoya were repairing the car when Boris rang.* (ремонтúровать/отремонтúровать автомобúль, звонúть/позвонúть)

2 *Igor and Zoya were doing the washing when the washing machine broke down.*

(стира́ть/вы́стирать бельё, стира́льная маши́на лома́ться/
слома́ться)

3 *Igor and Zoya were planting trees in the garden when their
son returned.*

(сажа́ть/посади́ть дере́вья в саду́, их сын возвраща́ться/
верну́ться)

4 *Igor and Zoya were doing the shopping when Zoya lost the
money.*

(де́лать/сде́лать поку́пки, теря́ть/потеря́ть де́ньги)

Russian has no *pluperfect* tense (*I <u>had</u> written the letter*); the
perfective past is used for all of the following: *I wrote, I have
written, I had written*. The golden rule is that if the action was
completed in the past, the perfective must be used:

Он пообе́дал в два часа́.	*He had lunch at 2 o'clock.*
Да, он уже́ пообе́дал.	*Yes, he has already had lunch.*
Он уже́ пообе́дал, когда́	*He had already had lunch when*
Ве́ра верну́лась.	*Vera returned.*

Insight

Checklist to help you use perfective past tense:

- Use it to talk about result/completion in the past.
- Remove -ть from the infinitive.
- Check the gender if subject is singular, and add -л(ся),
  -ла(сь), -ло(с), -ли(сь), as appropriate (always plural
  ending for вы!)

➤ **For imperfective and perfective aspects, see Section 9.1;
for imperfective past, see Section 9.4.**

9.6 Ten things to remember

1 The imperfective aspect deals with **process** – incomplete,
ongoing, unspecific, repeated.

2 The perfective aspect deals with **result** – specific, successful completion.

3 Most verbs have two infinitives: imperfective and perfective.

4 The verbs for *to begin/start, to continue, to finish, to stop/end* can only be followed by an imperfective infinitive.

5 The present tense is formed from the imperfective infinitive.

6 The compound future is made up of two parts: the future of быть + an imperfective infinitive.

7 The simple future is formed from the perfective infinitive (exactly the same endings as for the present tense!)

8 The imperfective past and the perfective past are formed from different infinitives, but have the same endings.

9 Verbs whose infinitives do not end in -ть form their past tense with the same endings but not simply by removing the last two letters from the infinitive.

10 Russian has no pluperfect tense (*had done*): the perfective past covers this.

10

Verbs (3)

10.1 Verbs of motion

Verbs of motion have two imperfective and one perfective infinitive; this means that there are two ways of forming the present tense and the imperfective past tense.

	A Imperfective (indefinite)	B Imperfective (definite)	C Perfective
to run	бе́гать	бежа́ть (бегу́, бежи́шь)	побежа́ть
to take, lead (on foot)	води́ть	вести́ (веду́, ведёшь)	повести́
to transport	вози́ть	везти́ (везу́, везёшь)	повезти́
to travel, drive, go by transport	е́здить (е́зжу, е́здишь)	е́хать (е́ду, е́дешь)	пое́хать
to fly	лета́ть	лете́ть (лечу́, лети́шь)	полете́ть
to carry	носи́ть	нести́ (несу́, несёшь)	понести́
to swim, sail	пла́вать	плыть (плыву́, плывёшь)	поплы́ть
to go/walk	ходи́ть	идти́ (иду́, идёшь)	пойти́

From column A we make:

- the present tense which deals with habits and generalizations: Ему́ два го́да и он уже́ хо́дит везде́. *He is 2 and he already walks everywhere.*
- the past tense which deals with habits, generalizations *and* return journeys. Он всегда́ ходи́л по го́роду по́сле обе́да, *He always walked around town after lunch.* Он уже́ ходи́л в го́род, *He has already been to town (i.e. there and back).*

1 Practise using the Column A verbs in order to complete these sentences.

1 Он ча́сто _____ за грани́цу.	*He often travelled (went) abroad.*
2 Ка́ждый день она́ _____ в па́рке.	*Every day she runs in the park.*
3 Когда́ он жил на берегу́ мо́ря, он _____ в мо́ре.	*When he lived at the seaside he used to swim in the sea.*
4 Мы обы́чно _____ из Хитро́у.	*We usually fly from Heathrow.*
5 Она́ ча́сто _____ дочь в шко́лу.	*She often takes her daughter to school (by car).*

Insight

From column A, the verb носи́ть features in some useful phrases, eg.:

Носи́ть костю́м/бо́роду/очки́	*to wear a suit/beard/glasses*
Носи́ть свою́ деви́чью фами́лию	*to use one's maiden name.*

NB! нести́/понести́ from columns B and C cannot be used in these contexts.

From column B we make:

- The present tense which deals with actions in progress, that are happening now: Он идёт в кварти́ру. *He is walking into the flat.*
- The past tense which deals with an action in progress, in one direction: Он шёл в го́род, когда́ он упа́л. *He was walking into town when he fell.*

Insight

In practice, the compound future of verbs of motion is not often used, but can be made from the future of быть with *either* the indefinite *or* definite imperfective infinitive, depending on whether the action being described is general (indefinite) or whether it implies one direction (definite).

2 Practise using the Column B verbs in order to complete these sentences.

1 Сегóдня он _____ за грани́цу.
He is travelling (going) abroad today.

2 Кудá онá _____ тепéрь?
Where is she running to now?

3 Он _____ к фи́нишу.
He is swimming towards the finishing line.

4 Мы _____ из Хитрóу, когдá самолёт сломáлся.
We were flying out of Heathrow when the 'plane broke down.

5 Онá _____ дочь в шкóлу, когдá потеря́ла ключ.
She was taking her daughter to school (by car) when she lost her key.

From column C we make:

- The simple future: Зáвтра он пойдёт в гóрод. *Tomorrow he will walk into town.*
- The past tense which means a single completed action (in one direction): Он пошёл в гóрод в 4 часá. *He went to (set off for) town at 4 o'clock.*

3 Practise using the Column C verbs in order to complete these sentences.

1 Зáвтра он _____ в Грéцию.
Tomorrow he will go to Greece,

2 Я сейчáс _____ за врачóм.
I will run for the doctor now.

3 Он _____ до фи́ниша.
He will swim as far as the finishing line.

4 Мы _____ в Москву́ в 3 часá.
We flew to Moscow at 3 o'clock.

5 Она _____ дочь в школу
  в 9 часов.

*She took her daughter to
school (by car) at 9 o'clock.*

4 Choose the correct verb from the box to complete the sentences.

> нёс   понёс   несёт

1 Почтальон _____ (*is carrying*) письма на почту.
2 Почтальон уже _____ (*has carried*) письма на почту.
3 Почтальон_____ (*was carrying*) письма на почту.

Insight

Some useful phrases based on verbs of motion:

Вести дневник	*To keep a diary.*
Мне везёт/повезло	*I'm lucky/was lucky.*
Идёт снег/пошёл дождь	*It is snowing/it started to rain.*
Идёт новый фильм	*There's a new film on.*
Это платье тебе идёт	*This dress suits you.*

A prefix is something added ('fixed') to the beginning of a
word which gives it added meaning. *Prefixed verbs of motion*
are a very useful group of verbs, indicating specific direction;
they have only one imperfective and one perfective form. It is
important to know:

the meaning of each prefix;
the imperfective and perfective infinitives to which these prefixes
are added
which preposition + case to use after the prefixed verb.

The following table gives the most common prefixes and
meanings of their use with the imperfective and perfective

> ➤ **For irregular past tense verbs, see Section 9.4; for
> prepositions see Unit 11; for case endings of nouns and
> adjectives, see Units 2 and 3.**

infinitive forms for the verbs meaning *to go on foot* and *to go by transport*:

-ходи́ть/-йти́   (*on foot*)
-ездить/-ехать   (*by transport*)

Prefix	Preposition + case	Prefixed verb of motion	Meaning
в-	в/на + acc.	входи́ть/войти́ *въезжа́ть/ въе́хать	*To enter, walk into* *To enter, drive into*
вы-	из/с + gen.	выходи́ть/вы́йти выезжа́ть/ вы́ехать	*To exit, walk out of* *To exit, drive out of*
до-	до + gen.	доходи́ть/дойти́ доезжа́ть/ дое́хать	*To walk as far as* *To drive as far as*
за-	в + acc. (place) к + dat. (to see a person)	заходи́ть/зайти́ заезжа́ть/зае́хать	*To call in at/pop into* (*on foot*) *To call in at/pop into* (*by transport*)
от-	от + gen.	отходи́ть/отойти́ *отъезжа́ть/ отъе́хать	*To move away from* (*on foot*) *To go/drive away from*
пере-	че́рез + acc.	переходи́ть/ перейти́ переезжа́ть/ перее́хать	*To cross (on foot)* *To cross, drive across*
под-	к + dat.	подходи́ть/ подойти́ *подъезжа́ть/ подъе́хать	*To approach, walk up to* *To approach, drive towards*

при-	в/на + acc.	приходи́ть/ прийти́ NB *perfective drops letter* й – я приду́ приезжа́ть/ прие́хать	*To arrive (on foot)* *To arrive (by transport)*
про-	ми́мо + gen.	проходи́ть/ пройти́ проезжа́ть/ прое́хать	*To pass, walk past* *To pass, drive past*
с-	с + gen.	сходи́ть/сойти́ *съезжа́ть/ съе́хать	*To get down from, get off* *To go down, drive down/off*
у-	из/с + gen.	уходи́ть/уйти́ уезжа́ть/уе́хать	*To leave, go away (on foot)* *To leave, go away (by transport)*

* Note that -езжа́ть/-е́хать (*travel, drive*) starts with a vowel, and a hard sign must be added to prefixes which end in a consonant.

5 Complete the passage with the appropriate prefixed verbs of motion. They are all in the present tense and are forms of -ходи́ть/-йти́ or -езжа́ть/-е́хать.

Ка́ждое у́тро я **1**_____ (*go out of*) из до́ма в во́семь часо́в. Я **2**_____ (*approach*) к остано́вке авто́буса. Когда́ авто́бус **3**_____ (*arrives*), я **4**_____ (*get in*). Когда́ я **5**_____ (*arrive*) в го́род, я **6**_____ (*get off*) и **7**_____ (*walk past*) ми́мо библиоте́ки и **8**_____ (*go into*) в о́фис.

The prefixes used with -ходи́ть/–йти́ and -е́здить/-е́хать are also used with the following pairs:

-бе́гать/-бежа́ть	*run*	-вози́ть/-везти́	*transport*
-води́ть/-вести́	*lead*	-лета́ть/-лете́ть	*fly*
-носи́ть/-нести́	*carry*	-пла́вать/-плыть	*swim, sail*

So, for example, выбега́ть/вы́бехать means *to run out* and
приноси́ть/принести́ means *to bring* (lit. *to arrive carrying*).
The prepositions which follow prefixed forms of these pairs are
exactly the same as for the prefixed forms of -ходи́ть/-йти́ and
-е́здить/-е́хать, e.g.: Она́ вбежа́ла в ко́мнату. *She ran into the
room.*

Insight

Prefixes can help work out what Russian words mean (not just
verbs of motion!). E.g.: удаля́ть means *to remove*; it is based on
the prefix у- + далёкий *distant*. Включа́ть *to switch on, turn on*
is based on the prefix в- *into* and ключ *key* (so, literally, *to put
the key into*).

6 Choose the appropriate preposition from the box to complete
each sentence according to the sense of the English translations.

> в из к до с ми́мо от че́рез на

1	О́льга вбежа́ла __ ко́мнату.	*Olga ran into the room.*
2	Авто́бус подъезжа́ет __ остано́вке.	*The bus is approaching the stop.*
3	Бори́с доплы́л __ фи́ниша.	*Boris swam as far as the finishing line.*
4	Тури́сты вы́шли __ музе́я.	*The tourists went out of the museum.*
5	Макси́м придёт __ конце́рт за́втра.	*Maksim will (come to) arrive at the concert tomorrow.*
6	Бизнесме́ны вылета́ют __ Хитроу сего́дня.	*The businessmen are flying out of Heathrow today.*
7	Студе́нты прохо́дят __ университе́та.	*The students are walking past the university.*
8	Ба́бушка сошла́ __ авто́буса.	*Grandmother got off the bus.*

9 Актёр отошёл ___ неё. *The actor moved away from her.*

10 Он всегда́ перехо́дит ___ у́лицу здесь. *He always crosses the road here.*

7 Translate into Russian.

1 *I am walking into the theatre.*
2 *He is carrying the books into the room.*
3 *We are running out of the park.*
4 *They are leading the dog across the street.*

> ➢ **For restrictions on use of в, see Section 11.2; for consonant changes in present tense, see Section 8.3.**

10.2 Conditions

In English, the 'conditional mood' deals with conditions and hypotheses, and it often involves the word 'if'. In Russian, there are two ways of dealing with conditions, depending on whether they are 'open' or 'closed'.

An 'open' condition is one which still has a chance of occurring: *If it is fine tomorrow we will go to the beach.* If the condition refers to the future, Russian uses the future tense in both parts of the sentence.

If it will be fine tomorrow we will go to the beach.
Е́сли за́втра пого́да бу́дет хоро́шая, мы пойдём на пляж.

If you will get up on time, we will be able to catch the bus.
Е́сли ты вста́нешь во́время, мы смо́жем успе́ть иа авто́бус.

The future tense of to be is needed to give the future with words such as на́до (*it is necessary*) and нельзя́ (*it is not possible, one may not*):

Завтра нельзя будет смотреть телевизор.
It won't be possible to watch the television tomorrow.

1 Boris won't be allowed to go out tonight unless … Complete the conditions imposed on him by using the future tense.

e.g. Борис сможет пойти на дискотеку, но только если он …
Boris will be able to go to the disco tonight, but only if he …
убирать/убрать в доме → уберёт в доме *(will tidy) tidies up in the house.*

1	писать/написать письмо дедушке	*to write a letter to grandfather*
2	пылесосить/пропылесосить ковёр	*to hoover the carpet*
3	стирать/выстирать бельё	*to do the washing*
4	рано вставать/встать	*to get up early*
5	чистить/почистить машину	*to wash the car*

2 More practice with the future! Give ten variations on the beginning of a theme by translating the phrases into Russian; the imperfective/perfective verb pair is given for you on the right.

Я буду рад (рада), если он … *I will be glad if he …*

1	*arrives on time*	приезжать/приехать
2	*doesn't forget his money*	забывать/забыть
3	*rings the professor*	звонить/позвонить
4	*writes a letter to his brother*	писать/написать
5	*sells his motorbike*	продавать/продать
6	*gives me a present*	давать/дать
7	*books the tickets*	заказывать/заказать
8	*buys a dog*	покупать/купить
9	*does the shopping*	делать/сделать
10	*returns early*	возвращаться/вернуться

If the open condition refers to an ongoing situation in the present, then the present tense must appear in both parts of the sentence:

If you like the food, I am pleased.
Éсли вам нра́вится éда, я рад (ра́да).

3 Tick the sentences where you would use the present tense in both parts and put a cross against the sentences where you use the future in both parts.

  1 *We are always glad if they send us a card.*
  2 *They will not be pleased if you don't send them a card.*
  3 *You are never satisfied if the food is cold.*
  4 *If you don't ring me tonight I will be furious.*

Insight

Open conditions – some tips:

- Is it still possible in the future? or an ongoing situation in the present?
- Ongoing situations in the present: present tense in both parts of the sentence!
- About the future? – future tense in both parts of the sentence!
- Don't mix your tenses!

A **closed condition** is one which is no longer possible, or could never happen, or a general assumption (hypothesis), e.g.: *If it had been fine we could have gone to the seaside today. If I knew how to play chess properly, I might occasionally win a game.*

To express this kind of condition, Russian uses the phrase **éсли бы** (*if*) followed by a verb in the 'conditional mood'. The conditional is really easy to form! – first put the verb in the past tense (from either the imperfective or perfective infinitive, depending on the usual rules determining choice of aspect) and follow it by the invariable (i.e. never changes) word бы.

Éсли бы он знал пра́вду, он рассерди́лся бы.
If he knew the truth he would be very angry.

Alternatively, the *if* clause comes second:

Он о́чень рассерди́лся бы, е́сли бы он знал пра́вду.

The implication in this type of condition is that *'he doesn't, so he won't'*. **NB!** The two parts of the sentence must both include бы and be separated by a comma.

4 Match up the two halves of each sentence. Hint: make sure the subject of the verb in one half is the same as the subject in the other (or that it matches the pronoun in the y construction).

e.g. у меня́ → я пошла́ бы

1 Е́сли бы у меня́ бы́ло вре́мя,
2 А́ня купи́ла бы дом,
3 Они́ пла́вали бы в бассе́йне,

4 Вади́м отдыха́л бы в Япо́нии,
5 Е́сли бы у нас бы́ли биле́ты,

a е́сли бы у них бы́ло вре́мя.
b я пошла́ бы на о́перу.
c е́сли бы он говори́л по-япо́нски.
d мы пошли́ бы в теа́тр.
e е́сли бы у неё бы́ли де́ньги.

5 Е́сли бы бы́ли де́ньги … What would they do if they had the money? Build sentences from the information given.

e.g. Та́ня/путеше́ствовать за грани́цей → Е́сли бы у неё бы́ли де́ньги, Та́ня путеше́ствовала бы за грани́цей. *If she had the money, Tanya would travel abroad.*

1 Они́/постро́ить да́чу
2 Мы/купи́ть пода́рки для друзе́й
3 Па́вел/сиде́ть до́ма
4 Ка́тя/купи́ть но́вую оде́жду
5 Вы/доста́ть биле́ты в Большо́й теа́тр

to build a house in the country
to buy presents for friends

to stay (sit) at home
to buy new clothes
to get tickets for the Bolshoi Theatre

The good news is that there is no conditional perfect in Russian. *He would have been very angry if he had known the truth* would simply be, as above: Он о́чень рассерди́лся бы, е́сли бы он знал пра́вду; i.e. the same form covers *would, would have*.

6 Е́сли бы то́лько! *If only!* Complete the sentences by making a main clause from the information given.

e.g. Е́сли бы то́лько он позвони́л, я/переда́ть ему́ но́вости. →
Е́сли бы то́лько он позвони́л, я переда́л(а) бы ему́ но́вости.
If only he had rung, I would have given him the news.

1 Е́сли бы то́лько мы не забы́ли, А́ня не/рассерди́ться на нас.
If only we hadn't forgotten, Anya would not be (would not have been) cross with us.

2 Е́сли бы то́лько она́ зна́ла об э́том, она́/позвони́ть ему́.
If only she had known about this, she would have rung him.

3 Е́сли бы то́лько мы пришли́ во́время, мы/уви́деть их.
If only we had arrived on time, we would have seen them.

Insight

Some tips about бы:

Although бы usually follows the verb, it can follow any word in the sentence which requires special emphasis: Е́сли бы она́ узна́ла об э́том, она́ бы засмея́лась. *If she had found out about this, **she** would have laughed.*

Conditions do not always include a е́сли clause; sometimes they simply express a desire: Я о́чень хоте́л(а) бы отдыха́ть в Ита́лии! *I would really like to have a holiday in Italy!*

---

7 Бы́ло бы лу́чше, е́сли бы … *It would be better if …* Complete the phrase using the information given.

e.g. мы/написа́ть письмо́ ему́ → Бы́ло бы лу́чше, е́сли бы мы написа́ли ему́ письмо́. *It would be better if we wrote him a letter.*

1 она́/согласи́ться на э́то   *to agree to this*
2 у него́/быть лэпто́п   *to have a laptop computer*
3 я/знать его́ а́дрес   *to know his address*

> ➤ **For formation of imperfective and perfective aspects, and the past and future tense, see Unit 8.**

10.3 Imperatives (commands)

The **imperative** or **command** form is used to tell people what to do, to make requests and suggestions.

The imperative can be made from either the present tense (imperfective) or the simple future (perfective):

- Commands made from the imperfective present refer to things that need to be done habitually and they tend to be more friendly than those made from the perfective future.

- Negative commands are usually made from the imperfective, but the perfective is used for warnings.

- Commands with a very specific element are formed from the perfective. Here are some examples:

Commands	Make the imperative from
Do sit down and make yourself comfortable!	imperfective
Sit down at once!	perfective
Don't open the window!	imperfective
Don't slip!	perfective
Shut the door now!	perfective

1 Match the Russian commands with their English versions.

1 Подождите минуточку!		**a** *Ring me tomorrow!*
2 Передайте мне воду!		**b** *Let's go for a walk!*
3 Иди сюда!		**c** *Pass me the water!*
4 Позвони мне завтра!		**d** *Listen carefully!*
5 Садись!		**e** *Sign, please!*
6 Давай погуляем!		**f** *Do sit down!*
7 Откройте окно!		**g** *Go through to the sitting room!*
8 Проходите в гостиную!		**h** *Wait a moment!*
9 Слушайте внимательно!		**i** *Open the window!*
10 Подпишите, пожалуйста!		**j** *Come here!*

If you want to give a command to someone you address as ты or вы, then for most verbs, first of all take the ты form of the present tense or simple future and remove the last three letters. If you're left with a vowel, add й (if you're commanding ты) or йте (if you're commanding вы); if you're left with a consonant add и (if you're commanding ты) or ите (if you're commanding вы).

Type of verb	Infinitive	Present: ты form	Command form (ты)	Command form (вы)
1st conjugation	играть	играешь	играй! *play!*	играйте! *play!*
2nd conjugation	смотреть	смотришь	смотри! *look!*	смотрите! *look!*
Irregular present	писать	пишешь	пиши! *write!*	пишите! *write!*
Reflexive	садиться	садишься	садись! *sit down!*	садитесь! *sit down!*

Some common irregular imperatives: есть *to eat* → ешь! ешьте! пить *to drink* → пей! пейте! быть *to be* → будь!

бу́дьте! помо́чь *to help* → помоги́! помоги́те! встава́ть, *to get up* → встава́й! встава́йте!

2 Make the ты form of the imperative from the infinitives.

1 спать		*to sleep*
2 написа́ть		*to write*
3 брать		*to take*
4 купи́ть		*to buy*
5 поблагодари́ть		*to thank*

3 Make the вы form of the imperative from the infinitives.

1 забы́ть		*to forget*
2 отдыха́ть		*to rest*
3 слу́шать		*to listen*
4 рабо́тать		*to work*
5 улыба́ться		*to smile*

Insight

In formal/official notices, you will see the infinitive instead of the imperative. Here are some common examples:

Не кури́ть! *No smoking!*
По газо́нам не ходи́ть! *Keep off the grass!*
Про́сьба не говори́ть! *Quiet, please do not disturb!*
(lit. *request not to talk*).

To make a command/suggestion for *us*, use дава́й (if *us* = я + ты) or дава́йте (if *us* = я + вы) and the мы form of the simple future: Дава́й(те) посмо́трим телеви́зор! *Let's watch the television!*

4 Translate into Russian.

1 Don't forget the tickets. (warning)
2 No smoking!

3 Pass me the key, please.

4 Let's ring Tanya.

> ➤ **For formation of the present tense, see Unit 8; for formation of the simple future, see Section 9.3.**

10.4 Negatives

If you want to explain what is not being done, happening, etc., you need the negative. In Russian negatives occur a) with conjugated verbs (i.e. a verb in a tense) and b) with infinitives.

a) negatives with a conjugated verb

This is formed by placing не immediately before the verb:

Он не работает.	*He isn't working.*
Мы не знаем, когда она придёт.	*We don't know when she will arrive.*

As the verb *to be* has no present tense, the word нет is used to mean *there is/are not*; this is always used with the genitive of the thing which is lacking:

У меня нет времени.	*I have no time (lit.: by me there is not any time).*
Его нет дома.	*He is not at home (lit.: of him there is not at home).*

1 Match the negative sentences on the left with the English translations on the right.

1 У меня нет времени!   **a** *We don't have any money for the ticket.*

2 Её нет дома.   **b** *I don't know why he isn't here.*

3 Я не знаю, почему его здесь нет.   **c** *I haven't got any time!*

4 У нас нет де́нег на биле́т. **d** *They don't understand what you're saying.*

5 Они́ не понима́ют, что вы говори́те. **e** *She's not at home.*

As well as being used with conjugated verbs to mean *not*, не must be used in other negative phrases, such as *never, nothing, nowhere, no one*. The following negative words must always include не and a conjugated verb; in English we can say, eg, *nowhere* or *not anywhere*, but Russian has only one way of making such negative phrases:

ничего́ не	*nothing, not … anything*
никогда́ не	*never, not … ever*
нигде́ не	*nowhere, not … anywhere* (of position, location)
никуда́ не	*nowhere, not … anywhere* (of direction, movement towards)
никто́ не	*no one, not anyone*

Negative word	Example
ничего́ *nothing*	Я ничего́ не понима́ю. *I don't understand anything.*
никогда́ *never*	Я никогда́ не смотрю́ телеви́зор. *I never watch television.*
нигде́ *nowhere* (*of position*)	Я нигде́ не ви́жу ключи́. *I can't see the keys anywhere.*
никуда́ *nowhere* (*of direction*)	Вы никуда́ не идёте сего́дня? *Aren't you going anywhere today?*
никто́ *no one*	Никто́ не понима́ет её. *No one understands her.*

The negatives ничего́ and никто́ decline like что and кто. If they are used with a preposition, then the preposition must follow the ни part of the word:

Я никого́ не зна́ю.	*I don't know anyone.*
Я ни о ком не ду́маю.	*I'm not thinking about anyone.*

Я ничего́ не зна́ю. *I don't know anything.*
Я ни о чём не ду́маю. *I'm not thinking about anything.*

2 Build negative sentences using the following components.

e.g. Ви́ктор/не/люби́ть/слу́шать му́зыку → Ви́ктор не лю́бит слу́шать му́зыку. *Viktor doesn't like listening to music.*

1 Ви́ктор/никогда́ не/петь пе́сни
2 Ви́ктор/нигде́ не/слу́шать поп-му́зыку
3 Ви́ктор/никто́ не/слу́шать поп-му́зыку с
4 Ви́ктор/ничего́ не/знать о му́зыке

Viktor never sings songs.
Viktor never listens to pop music anywhere.
Viktor doesn't listen to pop music with anyone.
Viktor knows nothing about music.

3 Complete the following conversation by giving a negative answer to each question, according to the prompts.

e.g. Вы хоти́те вино́? *I never drink wine* → Я никогда́ не пью вино́.

1 Вы лю́бите фи́льмы?
2 Здесь есть кинотеа́тр?
3 Чем вы занима́етесь в свобо́дное вре́мя?

I don't like watching films.
There isn't a cinema here.
I don't do anything (am not busy with anything) in my spare time.

4 Где вы лю́бите отдыха́ть?   *I don't like to go on*
                                   holiday (rest) anywhere.

4 Match the following sentence halves to make full sentences.

1 Я ничего́   **a** не ду́маешь
2 Мы никогда́   **b** не понима́ю
3 Вы нигде́   **c** не посеща́ем теа́тр
4 Они́ нико́му   **d** не отдыха́ете
5 Ты ни о ком   **e** не пи́шут

Insight

Tips about using ничего́:

- Remember to stress ничего́ on the final syllable.
- As well as being used in constructions meaning *nothing*,
  ничего́ also means *never mind!* and *all right, not bad*
  (e.g. *how do you feel? I'm all right*)
- ничего́ подо́бного! means *nothing of the kind!*

b) negatives with an infinitive

In expressions such as *there is nothing for me to do; there was
no one for us to ask; there's no time to rest!* the verb being
negated is in the infinitive *(nothing to do; no one to ask; no time
to rest)*. In Russian, this is expressed by using a negative word
which starts with the stressed syllable не.

The key negative words used with infinitives (with very literal
translations into English) are:

не́где	*not where*	не́где стоя́ть	*There's nowhere to stand.*
не́куда	*not to where*	не́куда идти́	*There's nowhere to go.*
не́кто	*not who*	не́кого спроси́ть	*There's no one to ask.*
не́когда	*not when*	не́когда отдыха́ть	*There's no time to rest.*
не́что	*not what*	не́чего есть	*There's nothing to eat.*

The negatives не́что and не́кто decline like что and кто; if they are used with a preposition, then the preposition must follow the не́ part of the word:

Не́чем писа́ть.	*There's nothing to write with.*
Не́ на что жа́ловаться.	*There's nothing to complain about.*

If you want to indicate who has nothing to eat, nowhere to rest, etc., then you must use the dative case of that person:

Вам не́ на что жа́ловаться.	*You've got nothing to complain about.*
Мне не́чем писа́ть.	*I've got nothing to write with.*

5 Match the Russian phrases with their English translations.

1	Не́когда чита́ть.	**a**	*I have nothing to wear.*
2	Мне не́чего носи́ть.	**b**	*You will have nowhere to go.*
3	Нам не́чего бы́ло пить.	**c**	*Boris has no one to talk to.*
4	Вам не́куда бу́дет идти́.	**d**	*The children will have no one to play with.*
5	Здесь не́чего чита́ть.	**e**	*There is no time to read.*
6	Тебе́ не́ о чём беспоко́иться.	**f**	*There is no point worrying.*
7	Не́кого спроси́ть.	**g**	*There is nothing to read here.*
8	Не́чего беспоко́иться.	**h**	*We had nothing to drink.*
9	Бори́су не́ с кем говори́ть.	**i**	*There is no one to ask.*
10	Де́тям не́ с кем бу́дет игра́ть.	**j**	*You have nothing to worry about.*

6 Build sentences about the problems of Ivan and Maria.

e.g. Ива́н и Мари́я/идти́ в теа́тр/не́кто/с → Ива́ну и Мари́и не́ с кем идти́ в теа́тр. *Ivan and Maria have no one to go to the theatre with.*

1	Ива́н и Мари́я/смотре́ть телеви́зор/не́когда	*no time to watch television*
2	Ива́н и Мари́я/писа́ть пи́сьма/не́что	*nothing to write letters with*

3 Ивáн и Марáя/приглашáть на обéд/нéкто	*no one to invite to lunch*
4 Ивáн и Марáя/пить/нéчто	*nothing to drink*
5 Ивáн и Марáя/звонúть/нéкто	*no one to ring*

These negative and infinitive phrases can be put into a past or future context by using the past and future tenses of быть:

Мне нéчем бы́ло писáть.	*I had nothing to write with.*
Вам нé на что бýдет жáловаться.	*You will have nothing to complain about.*

Insight

Tips about using нéчего:

- Remember that it is stressed on the first syllable.
- Нéчего can be used to mean *there's no point*.
- Нéчего сказáть! means *indeed! Well, I declare!*
- Нé за что can be used to mean *don't mention it*.

7 Translate into Russian.

1 *You will have nothing to do.*
2 *Don't mention it.*
3 *There's nothing to eat.*
4 *The doctor had no time to rest.*
5 *We had nothing to read.*

➤ **For declension of что and кто, see Section 7.3; for use of prepositions, see Unit 11; for formation of dative cases, see Sections 2.13, 2.14, 3.12, 3.13.**

10.5 Impersonal constructions

An impersonal construction is one which does not follow the usual pattern of a subject in the nominative + verb in a tense. In Russian, verbs are used in impersonal constructions in both the infinitive and in tenses, and the dative case is often involved. Three groups of impersonal constructions are explained in this Section: a) with the verb *to be* and adverbs; b) with expressions of possibility, impossibility, necessity; c) with verbs in the third personal singular; d) expressing pity, feeling sorry for.

a) impersonal constructions with *to be* and **adverbs**

As быть (*to be*) does not exist in the present tense, many impersonal constructions consist only of the dative case and an adverb. Many expressions of *feeling* are made in this way:

Мне хóлодно.	*I am cold/I feel cold.*
	(lit.: *to me it is cold*)
Борúсу лýчше.	*Boris is/feels better.*
	(lit.: *to Boris it is better*)
Как тебé не сты́дно!	*You should be ashamed of yourself!*
	(lit.: *how to you is it not shameful?*)

In this sort of expression, the verb *to be* needs to be put into the past or future tense as appropriate, e.g.:

Нам **бы́ло** óчень интерéсно.	*We found it very interesting.*
	(lit.: *to us it was very interesting*)
Бýдет хóлодно у Иры́.	*It will be cold at Ira's house.*

1 Some complaints! Translate them into Russian.

   1 *I am hot.*
   2 *He feels worse.*
   3 *Katya feels better.*
   4 *The children were bored.*
   5 *They will find it unpleasant.*

b) with the **infinitive** in expressions of possibility, impossibility, necessity

The infinitive is used in phrases to mean *it is possible, it is impossible, it is necessary* and *it is time to.*

The key words expressing possibility and permission, impossibility and prohibition, necessity are:

мо́жно	*it is possible, one may*
нельзя́	*it is impossible, one may not*
на́до	*it is necessary*
пора́	*it is time to*

NB Возмо́жно means *it is possible* and is an alternative to мо́жно only in the sense of possibility (not in the sense of permission).

These words are all followed by infinitives and are used with the dative of the person being advised of possibility, permission, etc.:

Нельзя́ кури́ть!	*No smoking! (it is not possible to smoke)*
Здесь мо́жно фотографи́ровать?	*Is it possible to take photographs here?*
Мне на́до спать	*I need to sleep (for me it is necessary to sleep)*

In the case of нельзя́ the choice between imperfective or perfective infinitive affects the meaning:

- *Imperfective*: Вам нельзя́ выходи́ть сего́дня! *You can't go out today!* (i.e. because you are ill, not allowed to).

- *Perfective*: Нельзя́ вы́йти. *You can't go out.* (i.e. it is not possible to go out, e.g. because someone has lost the key).

Ну́жно, like на́до, refers to necessity:
Что на́до де́лать?   *What is it necessary to do?*

Пора́ means *it is time to* and occurs in phrases such as:
Нам пора́ идти́.   *It's time for us to go.*

This is often abbreviated to Нам пора́ and sometimes just пора́.

To put expressions of possibility, permission, etc. into past and
future contexts, use the past and future tenses of быть:

Что на́до бу́дет де́лать?　　*What will it be necessary to do?*
Мне на́до бы́ло спать.　　　*I needed to sleep.*

2 Choose the appropriate word from the box to give the required
sense.

> мо́жно　нельзя́　на́до　пора́

1 Нам _____ верну́ться домо́й.
2 Спортсме́ну _____ кури́ть.
3 Где _____ купи́ть моро́женое?
4 Почему́ нам _____ чита́ть э́ту кни́гу?
5 К сожале́нию, _____ позвони́ть отсю́да.

1 *It's time for us to return home.*
2 *A sportsman shouldn't/mustn't smoke.*
3 *Where can one buy ice-cream?*
4 *Why must we read this book?*
5 *Unfortunately, it's not possible to ring from here.*

3 Translate into Russian.

1 *He must rest in hospital.*
2 *It was time for us to go.*
3 *It will be possible to swim.*
4 *No, you can't watch television.*
5 *Yes, you must work.*

c) with verbs in the third person singular

Many impersonal constructions involve the third person singular of the verb and the dative case. Here are some common examples:

каза́ться/показа́ться *to seem*	Мне ка́жется, что он прав. *It seems to me that he is right.*
надоеда́ть/надое́сть *to bore, tire*	Мне надое́ло рабо́тать. *I am/was fed up of working.*
нра́виться/понра́виться *to please*	Вам нра́вится танцева́ть? *Do you like dancing?*
Удава́ться/уда́ться *to be successful, manage*	Нам удало́сь найти́ их дом. *We managed to find their house.*
хо́теться/захо́теться *to feel like*	Тебе́ хо́чется пить? *Do you feel like a drink? (=are you thirsty?)*

d) expressing pity, feeling sorry for

The dative case is used with **жаль** (an impersonal predicate) to mean *sorry*:

Нам жаль ба́бушку.   *We feel sorry for granny.*

Notice that the person you feel sorry for is in the *accusative* case.

Insight

Нра́виться means to please. **NB!** the object of the English sentence (*book*) is the subject of the Russian sentence (the thing that does the pleasing).

Мне нра́вится кни́га.	*I like the book* (lit.: *to me the book is pleasing*)
Вам понра́вились кни́ги?	*Did you like the books?*

4 Make sentences from the words in the box which correspond to the translations.

жаль	мне	надое́ло✓	нам✓	хо́лодно	ску́чно
им	хо́чется	ей	удало́сь	ему́	нра́вится
тебе́	пить	вам	соба́ку	найти́ ключ	пла́вать

e.g. *We're fed up.* → Нам надоéло.

1 *They are bored.*
2 *I am cold.*
3 *She feels sorry for the dog.*
4 *He likes swimming.*
5 *Do you (sing.) feel thirsty?*
6 *Did you (pl.) manage to find the key?*

5 Build sentences explaining who likes what/whom, using the English as a guide.

e.g. Кáтя/нóвая пьéса → Кáте нрáвится нóвая пьéса. *Katya likes the new play.*

1 Он/актрúса	*He likes the actress.*
2 Врач/больнúца	*The doctor likes the hospital.*
3 Профéссор/студéнты	*The professor likes the students.*
4 Вы/экскýрсия	*You liked the excursion.*
5 Я/онá	*I like her.*

> ➤ **For dative case of nouns, see Sections 2.13–2.14; for dative case of adjectives, see Sections 3.12–3.13; for declension of personal pronouns, see Section 7.1.**

10.6 Indirect statement and question

A direct statement is what someone actually says; a report of what someone has said is an indirect statement. Look at the following examples and notice that in English there is a change of the tense of verb between direct and indirect statement:

In direct speech	*'I <u>am going</u> to St Petersburg,' he said.*
In indirect speech	*He said he <u>was going</u> to St Petersburg.*
In direct speech	*'I <u>will go</u> to St Petersburg,' he said.*
In indirect speech	*He said he <u>would go</u> to St Petersburg.*

| In direct speech | 'He <u>has already gone</u> to St Petersburg,' we said. |
| In indirect speech | We said that <u>he had already gone</u> to St Petersburg. |

In Russian the tense in the indirect statement remains the same as it was in the direct statement (although, as in English, there may be some change of the person of the verb):

Direct speech	«Я éду в Санкт-Петербу́рг» сказа́л он.
Indirect speech	Он сказа́л, что он éдет в Санкт-Петербу́рг.
Direct speech	«Я поéду в Санкт-Петербу́рг» сказа́л он.
Indirect speech	Он сказа́л, что он поéдет в Санкт-Петербу́рг.
Direct speech	«Он ужé поéхал в Санкт-Петербу́рг» сказа́ли мы.
Indirect speech	Мы сказа́ли, что он ужé поéхал в Санкт-Петербу́рг.

Note that Russian always needs the word for *that* (что) in an indirect statement, preceded by a comma.

Insight

Certain verbs 'trigger' indirect statements and are all essentially different ways of 'saying': e.g. *to claim*, *declare*, *explain*, *promise*, etc.:

Он объясни́л, что забы́л день рождéния жены́. *He explained that he had forgotten his wife's birthday.*
Он обеща́л, что бóльше не забу́дет. *He promised he would not forget it again.*

1 Match the sentences with their translations.

1 Профéссор сказа́л, что лéкция начнётся в два часа́.
2 Милиционéр объясни́л, что пора́ идти́.
3 Врач обещал, что емý скóро бу́дет лу́чше.
4 Гид не понимал, что тури́сты хотя́т посети́ть.
5 Официа́нт сказа́л, что они́ не заказа́ли суп.

a *The policeman explained that it was time to go.*
b *The guide didn't understand what the tourists wanted to visit.*
c *The professor said that the lecture would begin at 2 o'clock.*
d *The waiter said that they hadn't ordered soup.*
e *The doctor promised that he would soon be better.*

In English we introduce an **indirect question** with the words *if* or *whether*:

Direct question	*'Will you return?' we asked.*
Indirect question	*We asked him whether he would return.*

In Russian, indirect questions must **never** start with the word éсли (*if*), but always with the word ли (*whether*). Just as for indirect statements, Russian keeps the tense of the direct question in the indirect version:

Direct question	«Вы вернётесь?» спроси́ли мы.
Indirect question	Мы спроси́ли, вернётся ли он.

Notice that the word order is usually:

Verb of asking + *comma* + *verb* + ли + *subject*, i.e. Мы спроси́ли + , + вернётся + ли + он.

Я хочу́ знать, прие́дут ли они́ йли нет.	*I want to know whether they are coming or not.*

2 Report on the questions you asked during a conversation, using the English on the right as a guide.

e.g. Он/купи́ть/биле́ты *I asked if he had bought the tickets.* →
Я спроси́л(а), купи́л ли он биле́ты.

1 Бори́с/прие́хать за́втра	*I asked if Boris would arrive tomorrow.*
2 Óльга/заплати́ть за кни́ги	*I asked if Olga had paid for the books.*

3 Клие́нты/пожа́ловаться на това́ры	*I asked if the customers were complaining about the goods.*
4 Бори́с/позвони́ть дире́ктору	*I asked if Boris had rung the director.*
5 О́льга/верну́ться	*I asked if Olga would return.*

3 Rewrite the jumbled sentences in the correct order. Use the English as a guide.

e.g. зна́ю ли я не прие́хал он → Я не зна́ю, прие́хал ли он.
I don't know whether he's arrived.

1 мо́жно мы спроси́ли в 8 часо́в поза́втракать ли.	*We asked if it was possible to have breakfast at 8 o'clock.*
2 спроси́л пошёл конце́рт он друг ли на.	*He asked if his friend had gone to the concert.*
3 когда́ он нам вернётся сказа́л.	*He told us when he would return.*
4 письмо́ ли она́ ты не получи́ла зна́ешь.	*Do you know whether she's received the letter?*
5 я подпи́шет знать ли хочу́ контра́кт дире́ктор.	*I want to know if the director will sign the contract.*

> **For present tense, see Unit 8; for past and future tenses, see Unit 9.**

10.7 Indirect command, wish and purpose (subjunctive)

A **direct command** is what a person actually says when instructing someone to do something: *Go home!* and the imperative is used to express this: Иди́те домо́й! A **direct wish** is what someone actually says they want, and the infinitive is used for this: *I want to go home* – Я хочу́ идти́ домо́й.

In **an indirect command** or **indirect wish**, the subject of the verb in the first part of the sentence is not the same as the subject of the verb in the second half:

They ordered him to (that he should) go home.
I want him to (that he should) go home.

To express this in Russian, use чтобы + past tense (either imperfective or perfective, according to the rules explained in Section 9.1) – this is known as the *subjunctive*.

Insight

Tips for using чтобы:

- It is invariable (i.e. never changes)
- It is used with a <u>past tense verb</u> (not present or future!)
- It is always preceded by a comma.

Indirect command	Они приказáли, чтобы он пошёл домóй.
	They ordered him to (that he should) go home
Indirect wish	Я хочý, чтобы он пошёл домóй.
	I want him (that he should) go home.

Common verbs of commanding, wishing, advising which require the use of чтобы in indirect commands are:

говорúть/сказáть	*to say, tell*
желáть/пожелáть	*to wish*
предлагáть/предложúть	*to suggest*
прикáзывать/приказáть	*to order*
рекомендовáть/отрекомендовáть	*to recommend*
совéтовать/посовéтовать	*to advise*
трéбовать/потрéбовать	*to demand, require*
хотéть/захотéть	*to want*

1 Build sentences to include indirect commands/wishes, etc.

e.g. Он не/хотéть/онá/игрáть в тéннис → Он не хóчет, чтобы онá игрáла в тéннис. *He doesn't want her to play tennis.*

1 Врач/трéбовать/спортсмéн/не курúть.
The doctor demands that the sportsman should not smoke.

2 Гид/рекомендова́ть/тури́сты/обе́дать в рестора́нах.
The guide recommends that the tourists should eat in restaurants.

3 Профе́ссор/тре́бовать/студе́нты/прочита́ть всю кни́гу.
The professor demands that the students read the whole book.

4 Я/хоте́ть/мой сын/стать врачо́м.
I want my son to become a doctor.

5 Де́ти/хоте́ть/роди́тели/купи́ть дороги́е игру́шки.
The children want their parents to buy expensive toys.

2 Form sentences from the following phrases, using the English as a guide.

1 Я хочу́, что́бы он	**a** дал ему́ на чай.
2 Нача́льник приказа́л, что́бы они́	**b** все зри́тели се́ли.
3 Вы хоти́те, что́бы я	**c** рабо́тал усе́рднее.
4 Он сказа́л, что́бы	**d** вы́шел/вы́шла из ко́мнаты?
5 Официа́нт хоте́л, что́бы клие́нт	**e** приходи́ли во́время.

1 *I want him to work harder.*
2 *The boss ordered that they (should) arrive on time.*
3 *Do you want me to leave the room?*
4 *He said that all the audience should be seated.*
5 *The waiter wanted the customer to give him a tip.* (lit.: 'for tea')

Insight

English sometimes uses *should* to express the sense of command/recommendation:

Милиционе́р сказа́л, что́бы они́ отошли́ от две́ри.
The policeman said that they should move away from the door.
Я предлага́ю, что́бы вы всегда́ встава́ли ра́ньше.
I suggest that you (should) always get up earlier.

3 Translate into Russian.

1 *I want you to ring me tomorrow.*
2 *The doctor wants the patient to stay in bed.*

3 *The professor demands that the students work in the library.*
4 *The policeman suggests that you go home.*
5 *I ordered them to sit down.*

A **purpose clause** is part of a sentence which describes an action undertaken to achieve a certain outcome:

a) *I'm ringing you to pass on the news about Tamara.*
b) *I'm ringing Andrei so that he understands what has happened.*

In the first of these examples, the subject *I* is making the call and passing on the news. In the second example *I* am making the call, but *he* (Andrei) is the subject of the verb *to understand*. Чтобы + infinitive are used in both cases:

a) Я звоню тебе, чтобы передать новости о Тамаре.

In English, this kind of purpose clause is expressed as *to, in order to*.

b) Я звоню Андрею, чтобы он понял ситуацию.

In English, this kind of purpose clause is expressed as *in order that, so that*.

Notice that in a) where there is no change of subject, чтобы is used with the infinitive and in b) where there is a change of subject чтобы must be used with the past tense (according to the usual criteria: process or result). The use of чтобы with the past tense is also known as the subjunctive.

NB! Чтобы is usually omitted after verbs of motion:
Он пришёл передать ей хорошие новости.
He came to pass on the good news to her.

4 Why do people want to do things? Build sentences with чтобы. Use the English translations as a guide.

e.g. Он/посещáть музéи/картины/посмотрéть → Он хóчет посещáть музéи, чтобы посмотрéть картины. *He wants to visit the museums (in order) to look at the pictures.*

1 Мы/купить телевизор/смотрéть мáтчи
2 Вы/позвонить другу/пригласить егó на концéрт
3 Ты/написáть письмó/передáть нóвости
4 Они/посетить Москву/видеть интерéсные местá
5 Туристы/посещáть пляжи/отдыхáть

1 *We want to buy a television in order to watch the matches.*
2 *You want to ring (your) friend in order to invite him to the concert.*
3 *You want to write a letter in order to pass on the news.*
4 *They want to visit Moscow in order to see some interesting places.*
5 *The tourists want to visit the beaches in order to relax (rest).*

5 Boris has rung for a variety of reasons. Build sentences using чтобы and the past tense.

e.g. я/объяснить проблéму → Борис позвонил, чтобы я объяснил проблéму. *Boris rang so that I should explain the problem.* (for me to explain the problem).

1 онá/отвéтить на вопрóс   *to answer the question*
2 он/извиниться   *to apologize*
3 мы/обсудить ситуáцию   *to discuss the situation*
4 вы/пригласить егó на обéд   *to invite him to lunch*
5 они/заказáть билéты   *to book tickets*

6 Choose the appropriate word or phrase from the box to complete each sentence:

> чтобы позвонить   позвонить   чтобы _____ позвонил

1 Óльга вы́шла _____ дру́гу.

Olga went out to ring a friend.

2 Óльга иска́ла автома́т _____ дру́гу.

Olga was looking for a phone box in order to ring a friend.

3 Óльга хоте́ла, _____ друг _____ ей.

Olga wanted (her) friend to ring her.

> ➤ **For the use of imperfective and perfective aspects, see**
> **Section 9.1; for the imperative, see Section 10.3.**

10.8 Conjunctions

Conjunctions are words which link phrases to make longer phrases or whole sentences (e.g. *and*, *but*, *because*).

The following are the most frequent conjunctions in Russian:

that – **что** is required much more frequently in Russian than in English. It **must not** be omitted in contexts involving *to say*, *to think*, *to believe*, etc.:

Я ду́маю, что э́то глу́пая иде́я.   *I think (that) it's a stupid idea.*

NB что is always preceded by a comma.

Because, since, because of – **потому́ что** (*because*) is usually preceded by a comma (although you can move the comma to the middle of the phrase if you want to give special emphasis to the clause – *because of the fact that*). A comma always precedes **так как** (*since*) and appears in the middle of the phrase **из-за того́, что** (*because of*):

Он не прие́дет сего́дня, потому́ что (так как/ из-за того́, что) он бо́лен. *He won't come today because he's ill.*

NB Remember that prepositions are for use with nouns, not verbs. This is why an extra phrase is introduced between из-за (*because of*) and что. This is called a *compound conjunction* (i.e. because it is made up of *preposition* + *appropriate case of* то + что (*or* как *in time phrases*) + verb. Here are some more examples:

Preposition + noun: До обе́да мы лежа́ли на пля́же. *Before lunch we lay on the beach.*

Time preposition phrase + verb: До того́, как мы пошли́ в рестора́н, мы лежа́ли на пля́же. *Before we went to the restaurant we lay on the beach.*

And (**и, а**) and *but* (**а, но**).

И (*and*) is used to introduce extra information:

Я игра́ю на кларне́те и на фле́йте.
I play the clarinet and the flute.

It is not preceded by a comma unless it links phrases with different subjects:

Ма́льчик пла́кал, и никто́ не слы́шал его́.
The boy was crying and no one heard him.

А can be translated as *and* or *but*; it gives information which contrasts with other information given, but does not contradict it. It is preceded by a comma.

Я преподаю́ ру́сский язы́к, а он преподаёт биоло́гию.
I teach Russian but/and he teaches biology.

Но means *but* when the ideas described are not compatible; it has a sense of *despite/however*. It is preceded by a comma.

Она́ не лю́бит духи́, но он дал ей духи́.
She doesn't like perfume, but he gave her perfume.
Она́ обеща́ла позвони́ть, но забы́ла. *She promised to ring, but she forgot.*

1 Insert commas as necessary.

1 Она́ обеща́ла написа́ть письмо́ но она́ забы́ла.
She promised to write a letter but she forgot.

2 Он изуча́ет матема́тику и фи́зику.
He studies maths and physics.

3 Серге́й печа́лен и никто́ не обраща́ет внима́ния на него́.
Sergei is sad and no one is taking any notice of him.

4 Тури́сты серди́ты потому́ что в гости́нице хо́лодно.
The tourists are angry because the hotel is cold.

5 Дире́ктор ду́мает что клие́нт дово́лен.
The director thinks that the customer is satisfied.

6 По́сле того́ как они́ ушли́ мы поу́жинали.
After they had gone we had supper.

Both ... and (**и ... и**): Он лю́бит и чай и ко́фе. He likes both tea and coffee.

Or (**и́ли**); *either ... or* (**и́ли ... и́ли**):

Вы хоти́те чай и́ли ко́фе? *Do you want tea or coffee?*

Мы пое́дем и́ли в Гре́цию, и́ли в Ита́лию. *We will go either to Greece or Italy.*

NB! No comma before **и́ли**, but there must be a comma between the two parts of a sentence using **и́ли ... и́ли**

Neither ... nor (**ни ... ни**) is used in negative contexts (always a comma between the two parts of the sentence):

Он не пьёт ни ви́ски, ни вино́. *He drinks neither whisky nor wine.*

2 Make sentences.

1 Я пью	*both ... and*	вино́, во́дку
2 Я не игра́ю	*neither ... nor*	кри́кет, футбо́л

3 Я люблю óперу	*and, but*	он, балéт
4 Я не идý на концéрт	*because*	прогрáмма, неинтерéсная
5 Онá не знáла	*where*	он, рабóтает дирéктором

3 Complete the sentences with the appropriate conjunctions from the box.

> из-за тогó, что и́ли ни … ни но а

1 Мáма врач, _____ пáпа программи́ст.
2 Что лýчше, газéта _____ журнáл?
3 Ситуáция серьёзная, _____ трáнспорта нет.
4 Он пригласи́л меня́ в ресторáн, _____ я не хочý.
5 Дéти не хотя́т ___ смотрéть телеви́зор, ___ игрáть в садý.

4 Translate into Russian.

1 *I'm glad because he wants to buy a ticket.*
2 *I want to go to the concert, but there aren't any tickets.*
3 *Do you want two tickets or three?*

> ➤ **For use of чтóбы (in order to/that), see Section 10.7; for use of éсли (if), see Section 10.2.**

10.9 Ten things to remember

1 Never omit **что** when linking phrases involving *to say, think, believe,* etc.: *I think the plan is too complicated* – Я дýмаю, что план сли́шком слóжный.

2 Remember that что is preceded by a comma when it joins two parts of a phrase/sentence.

3 Verbs of motion have three infinitives: two imperfectives (indefinite and definite) + perfective.

4 Идти/пойти is useful in weather phrases: пошёл дождь (*it started to rain*), шёл снег (*it was snowing*), идёт град (*it is hailing*).

5 Prefixed verbs of motion have just one imperfective and one perfective. Remember to learn the prepositions which follow them.

6 There are two kinds of conditional constructions in Russian: open (present tense + present tense or future + future), or closed (conditional + conditional).

7 The conditional is really easy to make – just make the past tense (from either the imperfective or perfective, according to the usual rules: process or result!) + бы.

8 With никто, никогда, etc., always не + conjugated verb; with некто, некогда use infinitive + dative.

9 Never use если in an indirect question (*whether*), always use ли:
Я не знаю, придёт ли он вовремя. *I don't know whether he'll arrive on time.*

10 Wishing, commanding, purpose – if the subject changes in the course of the phrase, you need чтобы + past tense (subjunctive):
Я желаю, чтобы **вы** кончили сочинение. *I want you to finish the essay.*

11

··

Prepositions

11.1 Using prepositions

A preposition is a word used before a noun (or adjective + noun)
or pronoun to show position (answering the question *where?*),
motion/direction (*answering the question where to/from?*), or to
set the scene with extra detail; it defines the relationship of a noun
or pronoun to some other word: e.g. *tea **with** lemon; **towards** the
dacha; **next to** the museum.*

In Russian, prepositions affect the case endings of the nouns/
adjectives/pronouns which follow them. Some prepositions take
different cases depending on their meaning; for example, c +
instrumental = *with*, *accompanied by*, whilst c + genitive = *(down)
from*, or *since*. Some prepositions have alternative meanings when
used with the same case; for example, про́тив + genitive =
opposite (in terms of physical position), and *against* in terms
of opinion (e.g. *to be against* an idea). Sections 11.2–11.5 treat
prepositions according to categories of meaning (prepositions
describing position, motion/direction, time, setting the scene); 11.6
looks at verbs which must be followed by prepositions.

··
Insight

Try learning a phrase for each meaning of each preposition,
to help you remember the case which is required, e.g.:

Спаси́бо **за** прекра́сную карти́ну. *Thank you **for** the splendid
picture!*

Вот но́вые дома́, **за** кото́рыми краси́вый парк. *Here are the new houses, **behind** which there is a beautiful park.*

11.2 Prepositions: place

В means *in* or *at* when it is followed by the **prepositional** case:

Где он? Он в ба́нке.   *Where is he? He's at the bank.*
Официа́нт рабо́тает в   *The waiter works in the/at the*
   ресторáне.   *restaurant.*

На means *on* or *at* when it is followed by the **prepositional** case:

Где ключи́? На столе́.   *Where are the keys? On the table.*
Она́ на рабо́те.   *She's at work.*

The following words **cannot** be used with **в** if you are describing location; instead you must use **на** (even when you want to *say in, at*):

вокза́л	*station*	се́вер	*north*
восто́к	*east*	спекта́кль	*show*
заво́д	*factory*	стадио́н	*stadium*
за́пад	*west*	ста́нция	*station*
конце́рт	*concert*	у́лица	*street*
ле́кция	*lecture*	Ура́л	*Urals*
пло́щадь	*square*	уро́к	*lesson*
по́чта	*post office*	фа́брика	*factory*
рабо́та	*work*	экза́мен	*exam*
ры́нок	*market*	юг	*south*

Вчера́ мы бы́ли на конце́рте.   *Yesterday we were at a concert.*
Ло́ндон на ю́ге А́нглии.   *London is in the south*
                              of England.

Note that the vowel o is sometimes added to the preposition в when it is followed by a word which starts with a cluster of consonants: во Фра́нции *in France*.

1 Build sentences to explain where things are.

e.g. Ключи/стол → Ключи на столе. *The keys are on the table.*
1 Дом/го́род   *The house is in the town.*
2 Це́рковь/дере́вня   *The church is in the village.*
3 Кни́га/шкаф   *The book is in the cupboard.*
4 Автомоби́ль/у́лица   *The car is in the street.*
5 Компью́тер/о́фис   *The computer is in the office.*
6 Бри́столь/за́пад А́нглии   *Bristol is in the west of England.*
7 По́езд/ста́нция   *The train is at the station.*
8 Тигр/зоопа́рк   *The tiger is in the zoo.*
9 Почтальо́н/по́чта   *The postman is at the post office.*
10 Пиани́ст/конце́рт   *The pianist is at the concert.*

За means *behind* or *beyond* when it is used with the **instrumental** case:

За на́шим до́мом большо́й сад.   *There's a big garden behind our house.*

За по́лем нахо́дится лес.   *Beyond the field there's a forest.*

Пе́ред means *in front of* and it is used only with the **instrumental** case:

Автомоби́ль стои́т пе́ред до́мом.   *The car is standing in front of the house.*

Ме́жду means *between* and it is only used with the **instrumental** case:

Актёр стои́т ме́жду актри́сой и продю́сером.   *The actor is standing between the actress and the producer.*

Над means *above* and it is used only with the **instrumental** case:

Карти́на виси́т над ками́ном.   *The picture is hanging above the fireplace.*

О́коло means *near* or *by* and is used with the **genitive** case:

Омасиде́ла о́коло посте́ли   *She was sitting by the bed.*

Под means *under* when it is used with the **instrumental** case:

Ко́шка сиди́т под столо́м.   *The cat is sitting under the table.*

Ря́дом с means *next to/beside/alongside* and it is used with the **instrumental** case:

Дире́ктор сиде́л ря́дом со мной.   *The director was sitting next to me.*

У means *by* or *at the house of* and is used with the **genitive** case:

Вы сто́йте у две́ри.   *You are standing by the door.*

Вчера́ мы бы́ли у ба́бушки.   *Yesterday we were at granny's.*

2 Olga's not sure where things are ... Build sentences explaining where she should look:

e.g. О́льга/ко́шка/дива́н/дверь
→ О́льга ду́мает, что ко́шка под дива́ном, но она́ у две́ри.
Olga thinks the cat is under the sofa, but it is by the door.

1 О́льга/ру́чка/кни́га/
телефо́н

Olga thinks the pen is under the books, but it is by the telephone.

2 О́льга/биле́ты/зе́ркало/
па́спорт

Olga thinks the tickets are behind the mirror, but they are under the passport.

3 О́льга/автомоби́ль/
дом/ дом

Olga thinks the car is in front of the house, but it is behind it.

4 О́льга/портре́т/ками́н/стол

Olga thinks the portrait is above the fireplace, but it is above the table.

5 О́льга/холоди́льник/шкаф/
дверь

Olga thinks the fridge is between the cupboards, but it is behind the door.

> For prepositional case of nouns, see Sections 2.17–2.18; for prepositional case of adjectives, see Sections 3.16–3.17; for instrumental case of nouns see Sections 2.15–2.16; for instrumental case of adjectives, see Sections 3.14–3.15; for genitive case of nouns, see Sections 2.10–2.12; for genitive case of adjectives, see Sections 3.10–3.11; for declension of personal pronouns, see Section 7.1.

11.3 Prepositions: motion/direction

The preposition **в** means *into* or *to* when it is followed by the **accusative case** (i.e. when direction, rather than position, is important):

Куда́ он идёт? В банк?	*Where's he going? To the bank?*
Официа́нт вхо́дит в рестора́н.	*The waiter is going into the restaurant.*

The preposition **на** means *onto* or *to* when it is followed by the **accusative** case (i.e. when direction, rather than position, is important):

Он положи́л ключи́ на стол.	*He put the keys onto the table.*
Она́ идёт на рабо́ту.	*She is going to work.*

The following words **cannot** be used with **в** if you are describing direction; instead you must use **на** (even when you want to say *into, onto, to*):

вокза́л	*station*	се́вер	*north*
восто́к	*east*	спекта́кль	*show*
заво́д	*factory*	стадио́н	*stadium*
за́пад	*west*	ста́нция	*station*
конце́рт	*concert*	у́лица	*street*
ле́кция	*lecture*	Ура́л	*Urals*
пло́щадь	*square*	уро́к	*lesson*
по́чта	*post office*	фа́брика	*factory*
рабо́та	*work*	экза́мен	*exam*
ры́нок	*market*	юг	*south*

These nouns all combine with the preposition с (+ genitive case) if you want to say *from* (он с Урáла, *he is from the Urals*).

Note that the vowel о is sometimes added to the preposition в when it is followed by a word which starts with a cluster of consonants: во Фрáнцию *to France*.

1 Make sentences to explain who is going where.

> e.g. Врач/больнúца → Врач идёт в больнúцу. *The doctor is going to the hospital.*

1	Секретáрь/рабóта	*The secretary is going to work.*
2	Вúктор/стадиóн	*Viktor is going to the stadium.*
3	Учúтель/шкóла	*The teacher is going to the school.*
4	Студéнт/лéкция	*The student is going to the lecture.*
5	Собáка/сад	*The dog is going into the garden.*

За describes the direction *behind/beyond* when it is used with the **accusative** case:

Вор спешúт за дом. *The thief hurries behind the house.*

Под means *under* and it is used with the **accusative** if **motion** is involved:

Я кладý ведрó под стол. *I am putting the bucket under the table.*

До means *as far as* and it is followed by the **genitive** case:

Идúте до пáрка и вы увúдите цéрковь. *Walk as far as the park and you will see the church.*

Из means *from* in the sense of *from, out of* and it is followed by the **genitive** case:

Врач выхóдит из больнúцы. *The doctor comes out of the hospital.*

Борúс из Москвы́. *Boris is from Moscow.*

К means *towards* or *to the house of* and it is always followed by the **dative** case:

Милиционéр спешúт к хулигáнам.	*The policeman hurries towards the hooligans.*
Сегóдня мы идём к друзья́м.	*Today we are going to some friends (to the house of friends/ to see friends).*

Мúмо means *past* and it is always followed by the **genitive** case:

Студéнты прохóдят мúмо университéта.	*The students are walking past the university.*

От means *from* in the sense of *away from*:

Официáнт отошёл от столá.	*The waiter moved away from the table.*
Онá получúла письмó от дрýга.	*She received a letter from her friend.*

По means *along* (or *round*, as in the example) and is followed by the **dative** case:

Мы идём по глáвной ýлице.	*We are walking along the main street.*
Он лю́бит ходúть по магазúнам.	*He likes to go round the shops.*

It is also found in expressions with *telephone, television, radio, post*:

говорúть по телефóну	*to speak on the telephone*

Чéрез means *across* (or *through*, as in the example) and it is followed by the **accusative** case:

Бáбушка мéдленно перехóдит чéрез ýлицу.	*Granny walks slowly across the street.*
Мóжно заказáть билéты чéрез гúда.	*You can order tickets through the guide.*

2 Put the word in brackets into the appropriate case.

1 Здесь нáдо переходúть чéрез _____ (ýлица).

2 Подходúте к _____ (кáсса), пожáлуйста.

3 От _____ (кто) вы получи́ли письмо́?
4 Джиова́нни из _____ (Ита́лия).
5 Проходи́те ми́мо _____ (ка́сса) в теа́тр.

Insight

Some prepositions need an added o before a word which begins with a cluster of consonants – this makes for easier pronunciation. For example:

Во вто́рник	On Tuesday
Во вре́мя	During
Во Фра́нции	In France
Со среды́	Since Wednesday
Ко мне	Towards me

3 Use appropriate prepositions to complete the Russian sentences, using the English translation as a guide.

1 Она́ не лю́бит ходи́ть ___ магази́нам. **a** *She doesn't like going round the shops.*

2 Ма́льчик перехо́дит _____ у́лицу. **b** *The boy is crossing the street.*

3 Ученики́ поспеши́ли ___ шко́лу. **c** *The pupils hurried behind the school.*

4 Сего́дня мы идём ___ конце́рт. **d** *Today we are going to a concert.*

5 Они́ бы́стро вошли́ ___ гости́ницу. **e** *They went quickly into the hotel.*

For accusative case of nouns, see Sections 2.7–2.9; for accusative case of adjectives, see Sections 3.8–3.9; for genitive case of nouns, see Sections 2.10–2.12; for genitive case of adjectives, see Sections 3.10–3.11; for dative case of nouns see Sections 2.13–2.14; for dative case of adjectives, see Sections 3.12–3.13; for declension of personal pronouns, see Section 7.1; for verbs of motion, see Section 10.1

11.4 Time

Prepositions used with units of time from a second to a day.

Use **в** and the accusative for *seconds, moments, minutes, hours*:

> В э́тот моме́нт он по́нял,   *At that moment he realized that he*
> что забы́л свой па́спорт.   *had forgotten his passport.*

Days of the week are used with **в** and the **accusative** when they are singular:

в понеде́льник	*on Monday*
во вто́рник	*on Tuesday*
в сре́ду	*on Wednesday*
в четве́рг	*on Thursday*
в пя́тницу	*on Friday*
в суббо́ту	*on Saturday*
в воскресе́нье	*on Sunday*

Note also:

в э́тот день	*on that day*
в мой день рожде́ния	*on my birthday*

When **days** are used in the **plural**, **по** and the **dative** are needed:

по понеде́льникам	*on Mondays*
по вто́рникам	*on Tuesdays*
по сре́дам	*on Wednesdays*
по четверга́м	*on Thursdays*
по пя́тницам	*on Fridays*
по суббо́там	*on Saturdays*
по воскресе́ньям	*on Sundays*

> ## Insight
> Here are some useful time expressions based on the word мину́та *minute*:
>
> | | |
> |---|---|
> | Мину́точку! | *Just a moment!/Hang on a minute* |
> | Си́ю мину́ту! | *This minute!* |
> | С мину́ты на мину́ту. | *Any minute now.* |

1 Complete the sentences on the left and match them with those on the right.

1 В мой _____ я игра́ю в гольф.

2 По _____ я рабо́таю в о́фисе.

3 В _____ зазвони́л телефо́н.

4 В _____ мы идём в кинотеа́тр.

5 По _____ я занима́юсь спо́ртом.

6 По _____ я хожу́ в це́рковь.

7 По _____ он пла́вает в бассе́йне.

8 По _____ гид отдыха́ет до́ма.

9 В _____ мы пое́дем в Гре́цию.

10 В _____ вы пое́дете в Санкт-Петербу́рг.

a *On Wednesdays I do sport.*

b *On Friday we are going to the cinema.*

c *On Sundays I go to church.*

d *On Thursdays the guide rests at home.*

e *On my birthday I am playing golf.*

f *On Friday we are going to Greece.*

g *On Tuesdays I work at the office.*

h *On Saturday you are going to St Petersburg.*

i *On Thursdays he swims in the pool.*

j *At that moment the telephone rang.*

2 Look at Olga's diary for the week and then answer the questions that follow.

ПОНЕДЕЛЬНИК	ПЯТНИЦА
Рабо́та	Рабо́та
ВТОРНИК	**СУББОТА**
Го́род	Рабо́та
СРЕДА	**ВОСКРЕСЕНЬЕ**
Кинотеа́тр	К друзья́м
ЧЕТВЕРГ	
Бассе́йн	

1 В какие дни Óльга рабóтает?
2 В какóй день Óльга идёт в гóрод?
3 В какóй день Óльга идёт к друзья́м?

Prepositions used with *weeks*, *months* and *years*:

English does not always use a preposition with time phrases (such as *this week*, *next year*), but Russian always does.

Weeks are used with **на** and the prepositional case:
на э́той неде́ле	*this week*
на прóшлой неде́ле	*last week*
на бу́дущей неде́ле	*next week*
на сле́дующей неде́ле	*the following week*

Months are used with **в** and the prepositional case:
в январе́	*in January*	в ию́ле	*in July*
в феврале́	*in February*	в а́вгусте	*in August*
в ма́рте	*in March*	в сентябре́	*in September*
в апре́ле	*in April*	в октябре́	*in October*
в ма́е	*in May*	в ноябре́	*in November*
в ию́не	*in June*	в декабре́	*in December*

Note also:
в э́том ме́сяце	*this month*
в прóшлом ме́сяце	*last month*
в бу́дущем ме́сяце	*next month*
в сле́дующем ме́сяце	*the following month*

3 Explain in which month people's birthdays are.

e.g. День рожде́ния/ба́бушка/2 → День рожде́ния ба́бушки в феврале́.

1 День рожде́ния/Сергéй/3
2 День рожде́ния/Áня/4
3 День рожде́ния/Татья́на/9
4 День рожде́ния/сестра́/12
5 День рожде́ния/брат/1
6 День рожде́ния/муж/10

7 День рожде́ния/Ка́тя/8
8 День рожде́ния/Вади́м/5
9 День рожде́ния/Зо́я/6
10 День рожде́ния/И́горь/11

Years are used with **в** and the **prepositional** case:

в э́том году́	*this year*
в про́шлом году́	*last year*
в бу́дущем году́	*next year*
в сле́дующем году́	*the following year*

The same construction is also used for **centuries**:

в двадца́том ве́ке	*in the twentieth century*
в два́дцать пе́рвом ве́ке	*in the twenty-first century*

4 Explain when you will see each other.

e.g. Мы уви́димся/янва́рь → Мы уви́димся в январе́. *We will see one another in January.*

1 Мы уви́димся/э́тот год
2 Мы уви́димся/э́та неде́ля
3 Мы уви́димся/март
4 Мы уви́димся/ию́нь
5 Мы уви́димся/бу́дущий год
6 Мы уви́димся/февра́ль
7 Мы уви́димся/э́тот ме́сяц
8 Мы уви́димся/а́вгуст
9 Мы уви́димся/бу́дущая неде́ля
10 Мы уви́димся/21-й век

5 Translate into Russian (useful vocabulary on the right).

1 *In December we like to ski.*	ката́ться на лы́жах
2 *In August we like to lie on the beach.*	лежа́ть на пля́же
3 *In February we like to stay at home.*	сиде́ть до́ма
4 *In July we like to walk in the country.*	гуля́ть в дере́вне

The prepositions for *during*, *before/until*, *over*, *for ago*, *after*, *since* and *in*:

Во вре́мя means *during* and is followed by the genitive case. (Don't confuse it with **во́время**, *on time*, which is written as one word):

Во вре́мя конце́рта Ви́ктор кре́пко спал.	*Viktor was sound asleep during the concert.*

До means *before* and *until* and is followed by the **genitive** case:

Мы там бы́ли до семи́ часо́в.	*We were there before/until 7 o'clock.*

За explains the *time over which* something is done; it is used with the **accusative** case (sometimes we would say *in* here, rather than *over*):

Она́ написа́ла кни́гу за четы́ре неде́ли.	*She wrote the book in four weeks.*

На is used with the **accusative** case to explain the length of time for which something has been arranged:

Мы пое́дем в Москву́ на два дня.	*We are going to Moscow for two days.*

Insight

Sometimes Russian doesn't use a preposition where English does, e.g.: **no preposition needed if 'for' = duration of time spent:**

Он был в Росси́и две неде́ли.	*He was in Russia for two weeks*
Я живу́ в Яросла́вле три го́да.	*I have been living in Yaroslavl for three years.*

Наза́д (or **тому́ наза́д**) means *ago*. It comes at the end of the time phrase, with the amount of time in the **accusative** case:

Они́ перее́хали в но́вый дом
два ме́сяца/неде́лю наза́д.

They moved to their new house two months/a week ago.

По́сле means *after* and it is followed by the **genitive** case:

По́сле обе́да мы пойдём в го́род.

After lunch we will go into town.

С indicates *since* or *from* a certain time; it is followed by the **genitive** case. Note that it is often used in expressions with the present tense to mean *has been*, *have been*:

Я рабо́таю с ра́ннего утра́.

I have been working since early morning.

Че́рез means *in* of time in the sense of 'after an amount of time has elapsed'. It is followed by the **accusative** case.

По́езд отхо́дит че́рез де́сять мину́т.

The train leaves in ten minutes.

6 Choose the appropriate preposition from the box to match the sense of the phrase (hint: you will need some of them more than once).

до по́сле че́рез наза́д с за во вре́мя

1 _____ экску́рсии тури́сты внима́тельно слу́шали.
2 _____ э́то вре́мя, он никого́ не ви́дел.
3 Поса́дка начнётся _____ час.
4 Фильм науался́ 15 мину́т _____ .
5 _____ ле́кции мы пошли́ в кафе́.
6 ____ утра́ ___ ве́чера.
7 Он прочита́л всю кни́гу ____ два дня.

1 *During the excursion the tourists listened attentively.*
2 *Over this time he saw no one.*
3 *Boarding will start in an hour.*
4 *The film began 15 minutes ago.*

5 *After the lecture we set off to the cafe.*
6 *From morning till evening.*
7 *He read the whole book in two days.*

7 Complete the sentences on the left and match them with those on the right.

1 _____ обéда он ничегó не ел.	**a** *He repaired the car in an hour.*
2 Он отремонтúровал машúну ___ час.	**b** *They left two hours ago.*
3 Автóбус приéдет _____ 20 минýт.	**c** *No smoking during the flight.*
4 Онú ушлú два часá _____.	**d** *During lunch he ate nothing.*
5 ____ ýжина мы спáли.	**e** *The bus will arrive in 20 minutes.*
6 Я здесь ___ утрá.	**f** *You wrote the letter in an hour.*
7 Вы написáли письмó ___ час.	**g** *Before supper we slept.*
8 _____ полёта не курúть!	**h** *I have been here since the morning.*

➤ **For telling the time according to twelve- and twenty-four hour clocks, see Section 6.5; for dates, see Section 6.6.**

11.5 Setting the scene

The prepositions in this Section give additional detail about what/who is being described.

Без means *without* and is followed by the **genitive** case:
чай без сáхара *tea without sugar*

За is followed by the **accusative** case when it means *for* in the sense of **on behalf of, in support of, in response to:**

| Спаси́бо за пода́рок. | *Thank you for the present.* |
| Я за э́то предложе́ние. | *I'm for this suggestion.* |

Для means *for* in the sense of **meant for, intended for** and it is used with the **genitive** case:

| Э́тот пода́рок для вас. | *This present is for you.* |

К is used to describe the object of attitudes and feelings, and is used with the **dative** case:

| интере́с к живо́тным | *interest in animals* |
| любо́вь к приро́де | *love of nature* |

Кро́ме means *except(for)/apart from* and it is followed by the **genitive** case:

| Кро́ме Ви́ктора, все пришли́ во́время. | *Except for Viktor everyone arrived on time.* |

На means *for* (in the sense of **intended for**) and is used with the **accusative** case:

| Где биле́ты на конце́рт? | *Where are the tickets for the concert?* |

О means *about* in the sense of *concerning* and it is followed by the **prepositional** case:

| Мы говори́ли о пого́де. | *We talked about the weather.* |

Note that those nouns which have the irregular prepositional ending in -ý (саду́, *in the garden*) form their prepositional regularly with the preposition о: он говори́т о са́де, *he is talking about the garden.*

Óколо means *about/approximately* and is followed by the **genitive** case:

| Мы бу́дем в Но́вгороде о́коло трёх неде́ль. | *We'll be in Novgorod for about three weeks.* |

По is used with the **dative** case and means *according to:*

| по стати́стике | *according to the statistics* |
| по-мо́ему | *in my opinion (according to me)* |

При is followed by the **prepositional** case and has several meanings: *by, near, attached to, in the presence of, during the reign of.* For example:

Он сказа́л э́то при мне.	*He said this in my presence.*
При коммуни́зме.	*Under (i.e. during the time of) communism.*

Про́тив (sometimes **напро́тив**) means *opposite* or *against* (in the sense of *opposed to*) and is followed by the **genitive**:

Шко́ла нахо́дится про́тив теа́тра.	*The school is situated opposite the theatre.*
Я не про́тив э́того.	*I am not opposed to this.*

Insight

Want to go somewhere special? – **на** and the accusative/**в** and the accusative mean *for* in the sense of *to gain admission to* an event or place:

Он купи́л ей цветы́ и биле́ты на са́мый популя́рный спекта́кль.	*He bought flowers for her and tickets for the most popular show.*

С means *with* when it is used with the **instrumental** case, but only in the sense of 'accompanied by', e.g.

Он предпочита́ет отдыха́ть с друзья́ми.	*He prefers to go on holiday with friends.*
Мне, пожа́луйста, чай с лимо́ном.	*I'll have tea with lemon, please.*

Note that when *with* indicates 'by means of' (e.g. *I write with a pen*), then just the instrumental should be used: Я пишу́ ру́чкой.

Insight

The preposition **на** works hard! Here it is in some useful phrases, used with the **prepositional** case to set the scene:

На моро́зе	*in the frost*
На со́лнце	*in the sunshine*

На откры́том во́здухе — *in the open air*
На све́жем во́здухе — *in the fresh air*

....

1 Choose the appropriate preposition from the box to match the sense of the phrase.

> без в для за кро́ме на о по при про́тив

1 Он лю́бит всех компози́торов, _____ Бетхо́вена.
2 Э́то кни́га _____ меня́? Спаси́бо!
3 Он всегда́ пьёт ко́фе _____ молока́.
4 _____ на́шего до́ма краси́вый парк.
5 Вы уже́ купи́ли биле́ты ___ музе́й?
6 _____-мо́ему, э́то непра́вда.
7 Мы до́лго говори́ли ___ пого́де.
8 Он целова́л её ____ всех.
9 Спаси́бо ____ де́ньги.
10 Где биле́ты ___ матч?

1 *He loves all composers except Beethoven.*
2 *Is this book for me? Thank you!*
3 *He always drinks coffee without milk.*
4 *Opposite our house there's a beautiful park.*
5 *Have you already bought the tickets to the museum?*
6 *In my opinion this is not true.*
7 *We talked for a long time about the weather.*
8 *He kissed her in front of (in the presence of) everyone.*
9 *Thank you for the money.*
10 *Where are the tickets for the match?*

2 The following sentences have been jumbled. Put the words in the correct order and match the sentences with their translations.

1 мы за поблагодари́ли пода́рок её

a *They live in a house opposite the hospital.*

2 до́ме они́ в напро́тив живу́т больни́цы

b *Are you for or against this idea?*

3 и́ли за иде́й про́тив э́той вы

c *They went to the disco without me!*

4 все Бори́са дово́льны кро́ме

d *We thanked her for the present.*

5 меня́ ходи́ли концерт они́ на без

e *Apart from Boris everyone is content.*

> **For use of prepositions with verbs of motion, see Section 10.1; for case endings for nouns, see Unit 2; for case endings for adjectives, see Unit 3; for declension of personal pronouns, see Section 7.1.**

11.6 Prepositions which follow verbs

A number of common verbs must be followed by a preposition; the key things to remember are:

- Which verbs?
- What do these verbs mean? (**NB!** The verb for *to play*, for example, is used in different senses, depending on the preposition which follows it.)
- Which preposition must follow?
- Which case must be used after the preposition?

B is used with the **accusative case** after the following verbs:

игра́ть to indicate which *game* or *sport* is being played (e.g. игра́ть в гольф, *to play golf*, игра́ть в ка́рты, *to play cards*).

смотре́ть to indicate something *looked through* or *into* (e.g. смотре́ть в окно́, *to look out of the window*, смотре́ть в зе́ркало, *to look into the mirror*).

3a and the **accusative case** is used with the following verbs:
благодари́ть за (e.g. пода́рок)   *to thank for (e.g. a present)*
нака́зывать за (e.g. оши́бку)   *to punish for (e.g. a mistake)*

| платить за (e.g. покупки) | to pay for (e.g. the shopping) |
| продавать за (e.g. 50 рублей) | to sell for (e.g. 50 roubles) |

К is used with **dative case** with the following verbs:

| готовиться к (e.g. экзаменам) | to prepare for (e.g. exams) |
| относиться к (e.g. другим) | to behave towards (e.g. others) |

На is used with the **accusative case** with the following verbs:

жаловаться на (e.g. службу)	to complain about (e.g. the service)
надеяться на (e.g. лучшее)	to hope for (e.g. the best)
отвечать на (e.g. вопрос)	to answer (e.g. a question)
сердиться на (e.g. меня)	to get cross with (e.g. me)
смотреть на (e.g. карту)	to look at (e.g. the map)

На is used with the **prepositional case** to indicate which *musical instrument* is played:

| играть на клариете | to play the clarinet |
| играть на гитаре | to play the guitar |

От is used with the **genitive case** after the following verbs:

избавляться от проблём	to get rid of problems
отказываться от приглашения	to refuse an invitation
отличаться от кого-нибудь	to differ from someone
страдать от мигрени	to suffer from migraine

С is used with the **genitive case** in the phrase *to begin at*:

| Давайте начнём с начала. | Let's begin at the beginning. |

У is used the **genitive case** after verbs of *taking, buying, stealing, requesting* to indicate the person from whom something is *taken, bought, stolen, requested*:

| Он взял у меня 10 рублей. | He took ten roubles from me. |
| Мы купили у Ани бутылку молока. | We bought a bottle of milk from Anya. |

1 Choose the appropriate preposition from the box to complete the sense, then match each sentence with its translation.

> в за к на с у

1 Он игра́ет ____ футбо́л.

2 Мы купи́ли маши́ну ___ Бори́са.

3 Ка́тя игра́ет ___ фле́йте.
4 Ты поблагодари́л нас ___ приглаше́ние.
5 Мы на́чали ___ пе́рвой страни́цы.
6 Врач о́чень хорошо́ отно́сится ___ свои́м пацие́нтам.
7 Посмотри́те ____ окно́!

8 Посмотри́те ___ фото́графа!

a *Look out of the window!*
b *The doctor behaves very well towards his patients.*
c *He plays football.*
d *Look at the photographer!*
e *Katya plays the flute.*
f *We bought the car from Boris.*
g *We began at the first page.*
h *You thanked us for the invitation.*

2 Look at the drawings and make sentences with the verb игра́ть to describe what they are doing.

1 Бори́с игра́ет _____.
2 Татья́на игра́ет _____.

3 Translate into Russian.

1 *We are cross with you.*
2 *We are hoping for the best.*
3 *He is answering my question.*
4 *It is not necessary to complain about the letter.*
5 *Pay for the books at the cash desk.*
6 *They are selling the chair for 200 roubles.*
7 *We are buying the chair from Anya.*
8 *Do you play the guitar?*
9 *Look at the dog!*
10 *We usually start at the first page.*

> **For prepositions used after verbs of motion, see Section 10.1; for compound conjunctions, see Section 10.8.**

11.7 Ten things to remember

1 Prepositions precede nouns (or adjective + noun) and pronouns. It is important to learn which case each preposition takes, as well as its meaning.

2 The verb to *play* (играть) is followed by **в** + accusative when talking about games/sports, and **на** + prepositional when talking about musical instruments.

3 The most common prepositions used with the dative case are
к and **по**. **К** means *towards* or *to the house* of, but it is also
used about attitudes and feelings (*interest in, love for, etc.*).
По either means *along* or *according to*.

4 Prepositions are very useful indeed in time phrases! Different
prepositions and cases are needed for different amounts of
time: **в** 8 часо́в; **в** сре́ду; **на** про́шлой неде́ле; **в** э́том году́.

5 If you are talking about *where* something/someone is, use the
prepositional case with **в** or **на**; **у/ о́коло** with the genitive
case; and the instrumental case with **за, ме́жду, над, под,
пе́ред, ря́дом с**.

6 Three different words for *from*, all of which take the genitive
case: **из** = *from (out of)*; **от** = *(away) from*; **с** = *(down)
from*.

7 С and the instrumental case means *with*, and supplies extra
detail about something/someone: Да́ма с соба́чкой – *Lady
with the little dog* (the title of one of Chekhov's most famous
short stories); чай с варе́ньем – *tea with jam*.

8 Don't try to use a preposition immediately before a verb; you
need a compound conjunction to do this (see Section 10.8):
до обе́да – *before lunch*; до того́, как мы обе́дали – *before
we had lunch*.

9 У and the genitive case can mean *at someone's house* (У А́ни –
at Anya's).

10 If you want to say *into, onto, to* remember to use the
accusative case after **в** and **на**.

Taking it further

And finally, here are details of books and websites to help you
develop your command of the Russian language:

Books

The first of the four books below deals with language to
approximately GCSE standard; the others take you to a more
advanced level.

Complete Russian, by Daphne West, Hodder & Stoughton,
2001 (ISBN 0 340 80156 5)

A Comprehensive Russian Grammar, by Terence Wade, Blackwell,
1996 (ISBN 0 631 17502 4)

Using Russian Vocabulary, by Terence Wade, CUP 2009
(ISBN 978 0 521 61236 4)

Using Russian, by Derek Offord and Natalia Goglitsyna, CUP2,
2005 (ISBN 978 0 521 54761 1)

Modern Russian Grammar Guide, by John Dunn and Shamil
Khairov, Routledge 2009 (ISBN 978 0 415 39750 6)

Tranzit, by Daphne West and Michael Ransome, Bramcote Press,
1996 (ISBN 1 900405 00 8)

Kompas, by Michael Ransome, Daphne West and Rachel Smith,
Bramcote Press, 2002 (ISBN 1 900405 08 3)

Navigator, (CD-ROM) ed. Michael Ransome, Bramcote Press,
2009 (ISBN 978 1 900405 17 1)

Websites

The following websites will be helpful in finding out more about Russian language, culture and society:

www.ssees.ac.uk/directory.htm

www.crees.bham.ac.uk/links.htm

www.langlink.net

www.gramota.ru

www.rian.ru

www.ucis.pitt.edu/reesweb

www.russophilia.wordpress.com

....

Key to exercises

Unit 1

1.1 **1** 1 e, 2 a, 3 b, 4 d, 5 c   **2** 1 у, 2 т, 3 ж, 4 н, 5 р, 6 а, 7 ф, 8 к, 9 е, 10 б   **3** 1 11.30, 2 1 (ОРТ)   **4** 4

1.2 **1** 1 актри́са 2 балери́на 3 банки́р 4 вода́ 5 до́ктор 6 журнали́ст 7 Ита́лия 8 компью́тер 9 ме́неджер 10 но́вый 11 пиани́ст 12 профе́ссор 13 соба́ка 14 студе́нт 15 тури́ст **2** 1b, 2d, 3a, 4e, 5c

1.3 **1** Ваня наконец спрашивает Машю (*never* ю *after* ш! *write* у *instead!*   «Где собакы?» (*never* ы *after* к! *Write* и *instead!*)   «Почему они молчáт?» (*never* я *after* ч! *Write* а *instead!*) Маша не отвечает.   Ваня берёт свои книгы́ (*never* ы *after* к! *Write* и *instead!*)   и ухóдит к лýчшому (*never unstressed* о *after* ш! *Write* е *instead!*)   дрýгу, Сашé. *Vanya finally asks Masha 'Where are the dogs? Why are they silent?' Masha does not reply. Vanya takes his books and goes off to his best friend's, Sasha.*

Unit 2

2.2   **1** 1 ср, 2 м, 3 ж, 4 ж, 5 ж, 6 ср, 7 ср, 8 ж, 9 м, 10 м
2 1 компью́тер (м) 2 рáдио (ср) 3 собáка (ж) 4 дéрево (ср)
5 автомобúль (м) 6 лáмпа (ж)   **3** In list M the rogue is вúза (ж),
in list ж the rogue is инженéр (м), in list CP the rogue is энéргия (м)

2.4   **1** 1 husband 2 Viktor 3 Olga 4 dog 5 student   **2** 1 собáка
2 теáтр 3 концéрт 4 кнúга 5 сын e.g. *Usually Vladimir holidays in Yalta. 1 The dog is playing in the garden. 2 The theatre is very beautiful. 3 When does the concert start? 4 Where is my book? 5 My son is a very good footballer.*   **3** 1 Лéкция 2 мéсто
3 Студéнт 4 Дéдушка 5 Автомобúль 6 стадиóн

2.5   **1** 1 газéты *Most of all Viktor likes to read newspapers.*
2 мáрки *Stamps are expensive.* 3 компью́теры *I don't know where the computers are.* 4 кинофúльмы *Yes, I often watch films.*
5 телесериáлы *I don't understand why he watches television serials.*   **2** 1 балерúны 2 журналúсты 3 собáки 4 самолёты
5 истóрии 6 свидáния 7 инженéры 8 мéсяцы 9 буты́лки
10 пúсьма   **3** 1 жéнщины 2 мáльчики 3 дéвушки
4 мужчúны 5 кóшки 6 лóшади 7 моря́ 8 декларáции
9 здáния 10 герóи   **4** 1 c, 2 a, 3 b

2.6   **1** 1c, 2a, 3e, 4b, 5d   **2** 1 брáтья 2 именá 3 дéти
4 мáтери 5 адресá 6 глазá 7 дерéвья 8 друзья́ 9 лю́ди
10 городá

3 Кроссво́рд

				⁴у		⁶м		⁸ц		⁹в
				ч		е		в		р
¹в	и	с	к	и		т		е		е
				т		р		т		м
²п	р	о	ф	е	с	⁵с	о	⁷р	а	
о				л		ы		а		н
е				я		н		⁵д	о	м	а
з		³л				о		и		о
д		е				в		о		
а		с				ь				
⁴б	р	а	т	ь	я					

2.7 **1** 1 television 2 water 3 cat 4 Kremlin 5 watch **2** 1 d 4, 2 a 1, 3 e 5, 4 b 2, 5 c 3 **3** 1 дочь 2 ба́бушку 3 мать 4 дя́дю 5 тётю 6 стол 7 по́ле 8 (откры́тку) 9 ло́шадь 10 бра́та

2.8 **1** 1 телефо́ны 2 зда́ния 3 буты́лки 4 поля́ 5 ма́рки **2** 1 Underline boats, circle seagulls 2 underline tickets 3 underline purchases, circle customers 4 underline books and newspapers 5 circle dogs **3** 1 инжене́ров 2 медсестёр 3 футболи́стов 4 балери́н 5 враче́й **4** 1 коро́в 2 музыка́нтов 3 ло́дки 4 магази́ны 5 птиц

2.9 **1** Что вы лю́бите бо́льше, 1 дере́вья/берега́ 2 поезда́/ трактора́ 3 сту́лья/цвета́ 4 дома́/города́ **2** 1 b 4, 2 e 3, 3 a 5, 4 d 1, 5 c 2 **3** 3 города́, дома́, люде́й и номера́ 6 поезда́ и вечера́

2.10 **1** 1 cheese 2 ham 3 Italy 4 tourist 5 Igor, paper **2** 1 Э́то соба́ка Бори́са 2 Э́то автомоби́ль Андре́я 3 Э́то телефо́н А́нны 4 Э́то ра́дио и́горя **3** 1 вина́ 2 сы́ра 3 икры́ 4 ча́я 5 во́дки **4** 1 ветчины́ 2 пи́ва 3 хле́ба 4 говя́дины 5 шокола́да

2.11 **1** 1 ма́льчиков 2 студе́нтов 3 книг 4 ма́рок 5 помидо́ров **2** 1 часо́в 2 рек 3 музе́ев 4 танцо́ров 5 двере́й 6 мо́оérей 7 гости́ниц 8 ня́нь 9 геро́ев

10 строи́телей   **3** 1 апельси́нов 2 конфе́т 3 спи́чек
4 сигаре́т 5 бана́нов   **4** 1 мно́го ста́нций 2 буке́т роз
3 нет ма́рок 4 гру́ппа враче́й 5 па́чка докуме́нтов

2.12 **1** 1 бра́тьев 2 сту́льев 3 дете́й 4 поездо́в 5 городо́в
6 англича́н 7 сынове́й 8 дочере́й 9 гра́ждан 10 ли́стьев
2 1 яи́ц 2 апельси́нов 3 откры́ток 4 блу́зок 5 конве́ртов
6 ру́чек 7 сувени́ров 8 домо́в 9 я́блок 10 пи́сем   **3** 1 де́рево
2 мать 3 гости́ница 4 англича́нин 5 фотогра́фия 6 у́хо
7 бу́лка 8 автомоби́ль 9 вре́мя 10 челове́к

2.13 **1** дру́гу Ви́ктору тёте дя́де племя́ннику   **2** 1 Он дал кни́гу
Светла́не 2 Дочь дала́ духи́ ма́тери 3 Он дал цветы́ медсестре́
4 А́ня дала́ мотоци́кл Андре́ю 5 Она́ дала́ письмо́ дире́ктору
3 1 врачу́ 2 журнали́сту 3 и́горю 4 по́лю 5 у́лице 6 Ита́лии
7 Зо́е 8 ку́хне 9 писа́телю 10 свекро́ви   **4** ма́тери Татья́не
бра́ту Константи́ну дру́гу Анто́ну

2.14 **1** 1 e 3, 2 a 1, 3 d 5, 4 c 4, 5 b 2   **2** 1 трамва́ям
2 дере́вьям 3 карти́нам 4 худо́жникам 5 сыновья́м
6 почтальо́нам 7 преподава́телям 8 зда́ниям 9 лошадя́м
10 официа́нткам **3** 1 Касси́рша даёт сда́чу клие́нтам.
2 Ученики́ даю́т кни́ги учителя́м. 3 Медсестра́ даёт лека́рство
пацие́нтам. 4 Гид даёт биле́ты англича́нам. 5 Он даёт пода́рки
друзья́м.

2.15 **1** *In the evening I am going by train* with *Elena to
Viktor's. Viktor works in Novgorod, as an architect. Viktor's
interested in sport. In summer he plays tennis with Sasha twice
a week, when it's fine.* **2** Ве́чером я е́ду по́ездом с Е́леной к
Ви́ктору. Ви́ктор рабо́тает в Но́вгороде архите́ктором. Ви́ктор
интересу́ется спо́ртом. Ле́том он игра́ет в те́ннис с Са́шей два
ра́за в неде́лю. **3 a)** 1 хле́бом 2 сала́том 3 карто́шкой
b) 4 молоко́м 5 лимо́ном 6 пече́ньем   **4** 1 и́горем
2 профе́ссором 3 Мари́ей 4 дру́гом 5 Ка́тей

2.16 **1** 1 Ири́на интересу́ется симфо́ниями. 2 Валенти́н
интересу́ется фи́льмами. 3 Архите́ктор интересу́ется о́кнами.

4 Гитари́ст интересу́ется гита́рами. 5 Студе́нт интересу́ется писа́телями. **2** 1 апте́ками 2 зда́ниями 3 предме́тами 4 писа́телями 5 откры́тиями 6 дере́вьями 7 друзья́ми 8 экску́рсиями 9 дочерьми́ 10 компью́терами **3** 1 суп с помидо́рами 2 сала́т с огурца́ми (fleeting vowel! see Section 2.5) 3 торт с оре́хами 4 моро́женое с фру́ктами

2.17 **1** 1 Врач рабо́тает в больни́це. 2 Архите́ктор рабо́тает в зда́нии. 3 Моря́к рабо́тает на мо́ре. 4 Официа́нт рабо́тает в рестора́не. 5 Учи́тель рабо́тает в шко́ле. **2** 1 Самолёт в аэропорту́. 2 Ви́за в па́спорте. 3 Шу́ба в шкафу́. 4 Компью́тер на столе́. 5 Мадри́д в Испа́нии. **3** 1 ме́сте 2 бассе́йне 3 автомоби́ле 4 лаборато́рии 5 саду́ 6 музе́е 7 трамва́е 8 по́чте 9 ку́хне 10 по́ле **4** 1 c, 2 a, 3 e, 4 b, 5 d

2.18 **1** 1 Продавцы́ рабо́тают в магази́нах. 2 Студе́нты у́чатся в университе́тах. 3 Фе́рмеры рабо́тают на фе́рмах. 4 Хи́мики рабо́тают в лаборато́риях. 5 Учителя́ рабо́тают в шко́лах. **2** 1 дере́внях 2 города́х 3 це́нтрах 4 стра́нах 5 места́х 6 парфюме́риях 7 портфе́лях 8 поля́х 9 номера́х 10 сту́льях **3** Тури́сты живу́т в гости́ницах и в ке́мпингах. Они́ прово́дят ие́которое вре́мя в музе́ях, в галере́ях, в собо́рах и к концу́ дня, в универма́гах. Они́ то́же прово́дят ие́которое вре́мя в клу́бах, в са́унах и в рестора́нах.

2.19 **1** 1 бра́та 2 телеви́зор 3 сту́лья 4 друзе́й (animate!) 5 ку́рицу **2a)** 1 d 3, 2 a 5, 3 e 4, 4 c 2, 5 b 1 **2b)** 1 Genitive plural 2 a врач b актёр c профе́ссор d компью́тер e учи́тель **3** 1 Серге́й лю́бит де́рево. 2 Мы живём в го́роде. 3 О́льга дала́ Вади́му карти́ну. 4 Я зна́ю студе́нтов. 5 Я люблю́ е́здить по́ездом с друзья́ми. 6 Он смо́трит фильм с бра́том. 7 А́нна рабо́тает медсестро́й в больни́це.

Unit 3

3.3 **1** 1 му́дрый 2 но́вый 3 лёгкий 4 све́жий 5 интере́сный **2** 1 высо́кая стро́йная же́нщина 2 ма́ленький то́лстый мужчи́на **3** 1c, 2a, 3d, 4e, 5b **4** 1 краси́вая шко́ла 2 жёлтое окно́ 3 све́жее молоко́ 4 хоро́ший журнали́ст 5 до́брое у́тро

3.4 **1** 1 плоха́я 2 прямы́е 3 молоды́е 4 родно́й 5 большо́е 6 передова́я 7 други́е 8 сухо́е

3.5 **1** 1 у́треннюю 2 ни́жняя 3 си́няя, ле́тняя 4 сосе́дний 5 за́втрашняя **2** 1e, 2a, 3d, 4c, 5b

3.6 **1** 1 на́ши 2 ва́ши 3 Мо́я 4 твой 5 Наш 6 Моя́ 7 Твой 8 Наш **2** 1c 2d 3b 4a 5e **3** 1 ваш 2 мой 3 ваш 4 моя́, мой **4** 1 моя́ 2 на́ши 3 ваш 4 твой 5 их

3.7 **1** *Last year we set off on holiday in <u>our</u> car. Unfortunately Ivan lost <u>his</u> passport before we reached <u>our</u> destination. My brother, Nikolai, tried to help him find it. Nikolai is a very impatient person and soon lost <u>his</u> patience with Ivan. Whilst they were arguing, I looked in his suitcase and found that his passport was right at the bottom. How I love <u>my</u> brothers!* **2** 1 Её 2 свой 3 мой, свой 4 На́ши, свой 5 Их, своё **3** 1 Их дом в го́роде. 2 Они́ лю́бят свой дом. 3 Мы лю́бим ваш дом. 4 Их мать лю́бит наш дом. 5 Дом Ива́на? Я люблю́ его дом!

3.8 **1** на́шего, краси́вые, но́вый, дороги́е, шика́рный **2** 1 большу́ю соба́ку 2 но́вый дива́н 3 пуши́стого кро́лика 4 деревя́нный стол 5 но́вое окно́ 6 вку́сный торт 7 шика́рную ю́бку 8 интере́сную кни́гу 9 купа́льный костю́м 10 си́нюю бро́шку **3** 1 мою́ сестру́ 2 молодо́го профе́ссора 3 дре́внего писа́теля 4 интере́сную актри́су 5 ску́чного журнали́ста

3.9 **1** 1 иностра́нные 2 краси́вые 3 ле́тние 4 истори́ческие 5 больши́е **2** 1 больши́х соба́к 2 краси́вых лошаде́й 3 зелёные дере́вья 4 дре́вние дома́ 5 стра́нных птиц 6 свои́х бра́тьев 7 молоды́х ко́шек 8 ма́ленькие кварти́ры 9 свои́х друзе́й 10 изве́стных писа́телей **3** 1 ма́леньких соба́к 2 хоро́шие костю́мы 3 ва́ши кни́ги 4 но́вые о́кна 5 интере́сные газе́ты

3.10 **1** 1 красивого 2 этого 3 моего 4 моего 5 старшего
2 1 русской водки 2 жареной курицы 3 гречиевой каши
4 вкусной ветчины 5 свежей колбасы **3** 1 это собака высокой
стройной женщины 2 Это кошка маленького толстого
мужчины

3.11 **1** 1 Налево от иностранных газет 2 Направо от
новых велосипедов 3 Направо от дорогих юбок 4 Налево от
деревянных стульев 5 Налево от огромных зданий
2 1 группа итальянских туристов 2 группа известных врачей
3 группа наших студентов 4 группа пожилых людей 5 группа
древних зданий **3** 1c 2a 3d 4h 5b 6g 7e 8f

3.12 **1** 1 Татьяна идёт к красивой картине. 2 Игорь идёт к
древней вазе. 3 Вадим идёт к большому мосту. 4 Аня идёт к
соседнему дому. 5 Павел идёт к новой лаборатории.
2 1 Женщина даёт конфету большой собаке. 2 Мужчина даёт
рыбу маленькой кошке. **3** 1 моему 2 новому 3 зелёному
4 соседнему 5 нашему **4** 1 русскому студенту 2 больной
старушке 3 прежнему менеджеру 4 нашей матери
5 молодому пианисту

3.13 **1** 1b 2d 3e 4a 5c **2** 1 твоим дочерям 2 нашим
учителям 3 маленьким собакам 4 прежним директорам
5 русским студентам **3** 1 Официант подходит к большим
столам. 2 Архитектор подходит к маленьким окнам. 3 Татьяна
подходит к новым офисам. 4 Катя подходит к своим детям.
5 Иван подходит к старым друзьям.

3.14 **1** 1 Кофе с холодным молоком 2 Чай со свежим
лимоном 3 Чай с белым сахаром 4 Чай с малиновым
вареньем **2** 1 Я еду ранним поездом. 2 Я пишу
дешёвой ручкой. 3 Надо мыть посуду горячей водой.
4 Я открываю дверь моим ключом. 5 Он гладит рубашку
новым утюгом. **3** 1 Врач хочет пойти в театр с красивой
медсестрой. 2 Иван хочет пойти в театр с английским
туристом. 3 Журналист хочет пойти в театр с известным

политиком. 4 Евге́ний хо́чет пойти́ в теа́тр с мое́й сестро́й.
5 Муж хо́чет пойти́ в теа́тр с молодо́й жено́й. 4 1 све́жей
ветчино́й 2 копчёной ры́бой 3 зелёным огурцо́м (fleeting
vowel, see Section 2.5) 4 дороги́м майоне́зом

3.15 1 1 но́выми друзья́ми 2 иностра́нными гостя́ми
3 ва́жными клие́нтами 4 молоды́ми учителя́ми 5 пожилы́ми
тури́стами 6 ста́рыми пенсионе́рами 7 двою́родными
сёстрами 2 1d 2c 3a 4b 3 1 интере́сными кни́гами
2 больны́ми пацие́нтами 3 но́выми студе́нтами 4 хоро́шими
газе́тами 5 на́шими компью́терами

3.16 1 1 ста́ром 2 дре́внем 3 шу́мном 4 краси́вом
5 совреме́нном 2 1e 2a 3d 4c 5b 3 1 зелёном па́рке
2 Кра́сной пло́щади 3 чёрном портфе́ле 4 жёлтой ю́бке
5 си́нем не́бе

3.17 1 1 серьёзных пробле́мах 2 иностра́нных города́х
3 ночны́х клу́бах 4 совреме́нных авто́бусах 5 плохи́х
положе́ниях 2 1b 2g 3e 4d 5a 6c 7h 8f 3 1 Он рабо́тает
на шу́мных заво́дах. 2 Она́ де́лает поку́пки в дороги́х
магази́нах. 3 Мы чита́ем но́вости в вече́рних газе́тах.
4 Вы обе́даете в ма́леньких рестора́нах. 5 Они́ отдыха́ют
в краси́вых па́рках.

Unit 4

4.1 1 *Svetlana walks into the house and notices that all the
doors and windows are* <u>open</u>. *The new curtains are blowing about
in the wind. The kitchen door, however, is* <u>shut</u>. *On the table the
cat lies, howling. It is clearly* <u>glad</u> *to see her. She is* <u>furious</u> *when
she realizes that her son has gone out without feeding the cat. 'He
is so* <u>unreliable</u>!' *she thinks.* 2 1 Э́то ме́сто свобо́дно. 2 Его́
автомоби́ль нов. 3 На́ши де́ти здоро́вы. 4 Все о́кна откры́ты.
5 Ка́ша вкусна́. 3 1d 2a 3e 4b 5c 4 1 ра́ды 2 согла́сный,
откры́тый, закры́тый, за́нятый

4.2 **1** 1g 2j 3i 4a 5h 6b 7c 8f 9e 10d **2** *My (younger) sister, Masha, really likes shopping. Yesterday she bought a (bigger) bag, a newer car, a more expensive radio, a more interesting book and a (smaller) mobile telephone* **3** Моя́ мла́дшая сестра́, Ма́ша, о́чень лю́бит де́лать поку́пки. Вчера́ она́ купи́ла бо́льшую су́мку, бо́лее но́вый автомоби́ль, бо́лее дорого́е ра́дио, бо́лее интере́сную кни́гу и ме́ньший со́товый телефо́н **4** бо́лее приле́жный, ни́зшие, бо́лее интере́сное, бо́лее серьёзный

4.3 **1** You could use the short form comparative in 1, 3, 6, 7, 9, 10 **2** 1 Мой брат умне́е. 2 Э́та кни́га ме́нее ску́чная. 3 Его́ маши́на деше́вле. 4 Мы купи́ли бо́лее но́вый дом. 5 Вы не зна́ете, где бо́лее удо́бный стул? 6 Э́то про́ще. 7 До Москвы́ да́льше. 8 Мы получи́ли бо́лее ва́жное письмо́. 9 Э́то письмо́ коро́че. 10 Э́то ра́дио доро́же. **3** 1 Вади́м 2 Ива́н

4.4 **1** 1b 2d 3a 4e 5c **2** 1 О́льга намно́го добре́е Ири́ны. 2 Андре́й намно́го серьёзнее Константи́на. 3 Он намно́го энерги́чнее меня́. 4 Мой брат намно́го лени́вее мое́й сестры́. 5 Ба́бушка намно́го моло́же де́душки. **3** 1 Э́то бо́лее серьёзная пробле́ма, чем его́/пробле́ма у него́ 2 Го́род Москва́ бо́льше, чем Но́вгород. (Го́род Москва́ бо́льше Но́вгорода). 3 Он ста́рше меня́. 4 Ваш телеви́зор лу́чше моего́. 5 Его́ соба́ка бо́лее энерги́чная, чем её (Его́ соба́ка энерги́чнее, чем её).

4.5 **1** 1 Э́то са́мый краси́вый парк. 2 Ива́н и Андре́й са́мые тала́нтливые футболи́сты. 3 Вот са́мая энерги́чная медсестра́. 4 Я чита́ю са́мую интере́сную кни́гу. 5 Он живёт в са́мой ма́ленькой кварти́ре. **2** 1 Зима́ са́мое холо́дное вре́мя го́да. 2 Са́мый жа́ркий кли́мат. 3 Во́дка са́мый кре́пкий напи́ток. 4 Э́то са́мая краси́вая кварти́ра. **3** 1 Он оди́н из (са́мых) лу́чших гитари́стов. 2 Э́то са́мый краси́вый пляж. 3 Чисте́йший вздор! 4 Где ближа́йшая остано́вка авто́буса? 5 Э́то са́мая серьёзная пробле́ма.

Unit 5

5.1 **1** 1 Нет, сего́дня тепло́. 2 Нет, пиани́ст блестя́ще игра́ет. 3 Нет, студе́нт ме́дленно рабо́тает. 4 Нет, де́ти ти́хо игра́ют. 5 Нет, брат энерги́чно игра́ет. **2** 1 глу́по 2 прия́тно 3 хорошо́ 4 тепло́ 5 логи́чески 6 го́рдо 7 впечатля́юще 8 саркасти́чно 9 эгоисти́чески 10 ще́дро 11 ти́хо 12 шу́мно **3** 1 Испа́нец говори́т по-испа́нски. 2 Ру́сский говори́т по-ру́сски. 3 Англича́нин говори́т по-англи́йски. 4 Япо́нец говори́т по-япо́нски.

5.2 **1** yesterday, early, easily, immediately, smoothly, soon, where, absolutely **2** 1d 2a 3e 4c 5b

5.3 **1** 1 Пиани́ст хорошо́ игра́ет, но гитари́ст игра́ет ещё лу́чше. 2 Мой брат лени́во игра́ет, но твой брат игра́ет ещё лени́вее. 3 Тенниси́ст энерги́чно игра́ет, но футболи́ст игра́ет ещё энерги́чнее. 4 Баскетболи́ст глу́по игра́ет, но хоккеи́ст игра́ет ещё глу́пее. 5 Игро́к в гольф ме́дленно игра́ет, но игро́к в кри́кет игра́ет ещё ме́дленнее. **2** 1 Ка́тя ти́ше говори́т, чем её сестра́. 2 Йгорь гора́здо усе́рднее рабо́тает, чем Валенти́н. 3 Татья́на поёт ещё ху́же, чем Зо́я. 4 Они́ ча́ще пла́вают, чем ра́ньше. 5 Гро́мче, пожа́луйста! **3** 1b 2e 3d 4a 5c

5.4 **1** 1 лу́чше всех **2** лу́чше всего́ **3** лу́чше всех

Unit 6

6.1 **1** 1 сто ми́нус два́дцать бу́дет во́семьдесят 2 два плюс шестна́дцать бу́дет восемна́дцать 3 три́дцать три плюс сто два бу́дет сто три́дцать пять 4 два́дцать де́вять ми́нус пятна́дцать бу́дет четы́рнадцать 5 во́семьдесят пять ми́нус пятьдеся́т четы́ре бу́дет три́дцать оди́н **2** 1b 2c 3e 4a 5d **3** 1 42-93-12 со́рок два девяно́сто три двена́дцать 2 84-53-55 во́семьдесят четы́ре пятьдеся́т три пятьдеся́т пять 3 20-30-40 два́дцать три́дцать со́рок 4 36-62-73 три́дцать шесть шестьдеся́т два сéмьдесят три 5 18-11-26 восемнáдцать одѝннадцать двáдцать шесть

6.2 **1** 1 instrumental 2 dative 3 animate accusative, genitive, prepositional 4 animate accusative, genitive, prepositional 5 dative **2** 1 четырёх 2 шестѝдесяти 3 двацатѝ трёх 4 девянóста двух 5 ста **3** 1 сорокá 2 восемнáдцати 3 семѝдесяти трём 4 трёмстáм 5 шестистáм **4** 1 тремя́ 2 десятью 3 двумястáми 4 двадцатью 5 пятью **5** 1 двенáдцати 2 восьмѝдесяти шестѝ 3 сорокá пятѝ 4 одѝннадцати 5 ста пятѝдесяти **6** *Boris recently went to two book shops and bought three books. Yesterday he was reading his new book on chemistry. He read about 600 different experiments in 32 countries. Ninety-six chemists had got results, but in 44 laboratories there had been accidents.*

6.3 **1** 1 Два журнáла 2 Шесть недéль 3 Сóрок человéк 4 Двáдцать три кóшки 5 Одѝннадцать часóв 6 Сто рублéй 7 Девятнáдцать киломéтров 8 Ты́сяча книг 9 Сто четы́ре мáльчика 10 Сто пять дéвушек **2** 1 Две большѝе собáки 2 Три мáленьких теáтра 3 Сто дéсять нóвых студéнтов 4 Пять стáрых домóв 5 Трѝдцать два энергѝчных мáльчика **3** 1 пятѝ стáрым профессорáм 2 двадцатѝ сердѝтым клиéнтам 3 одѝннадцати шýмным хулигáнам **4** 1 The phrase с пятью нóвыми студéнтами is *all* in the instrumental, because of the preposition с, which takes the instrumental. 2 32 students are an animate object. 3 There is an animate accusative for 2, 3, 4 on their own. 4 The preposition о is followed by the prepositional, so the whole phrase is in the prepositional. 5 Books are inanimate – so the numeral and its adjective and noun behave as they would do if the numeral and its phrase were the subject (numeral + nom. pl. adj. + gen. sing. noun).

6.4 **1** 1 Апрéль – четвёртый мéсяц гóда. 2 Ноя́брь – одѝннадцатый мéсяц гóда. 3 Áвгуст –восьмóй мéсяц гóда. 4 Май – пя́тый мéсяц гóда. 5 Июль – седьмóй мéсяц гóда. **2** 1 Вадѝм купѝл тýфли трѝдцать восьмóго размéра. 2 Татья́на купѝла тýфли тридцáтого размéра. 3 Áнна купѝла туфли три́дцать второ́го разме́ра. 4 Андре́й купи́л ту́фли со́рок тре́тьего разме́ра. 5 Еле́на купи́ла ту́фли три́дцать шесто́го разме́ра. **3** 1 Бага́ж на второ́м этаже́. 2 Фотоаппара́ты на тре́тьем этаже́. 3 Ту́фли на четвёртом этаже́. 4 Кни́ги на пя́том этаже́. 5 Сувени́ры на шесто́м этаже́. **4** 1 Фотогра́фия шко́лы на страни́це пятьдеся́т второ́й. 2 Фотогра́фия теа́тра на страни́це две́сти два́дцать девя́той. 3 Фотогра́фия у́лицы на страни́це во́семьдесят седьмо́й. 4 Фотогра́фия актёра на страни́це шестьдеся́т пе́рвой. 5 Фотогра́фия актри́сы на страни́це деся́той.

6.5 **1** 1 без че́тверти пять 2 де́вять часо́в 3 два́дцать мину́т шесто́го 4 без десяти́ семь 5 полови́на двена́дцатого **2** 1 По́езд в Новосиби́рск отхо́дит в семь пятна́дцать. 2 По́езд в Тверь отхо́дит в четы́рнадцать пятьдеся́т пять. 3 По́езд в Я́лту отхо́дит в два́дцать оди́н три́дцать пять. 4 По́езд в Воро́неж отхо́дит в девятна́дцать три́дцать. 5 По́езд в Ки́ров отхо́дит в семна́дцать де́сять. **3** 1 Он встаёт в семь часо́в. 2 Он за́втракает в че́тверть восьмо́го. 3 Его́ рабо́чий день начина́ется без че́тверти де́вять. 4 Он обе́дает без двадцати́ пяти́ два. 5 Его́ рабо́чий день конча́ется в полови́не шесто́го.

6.6 **1** 1 Сего́дня шесто́е ноября́. 2 Сего́дня два́дцать пя́тое а́вгуста. 3 Сего́дня седьмо́е января́. 4 Сего́дня тре́тье октября́. 5 Сего́дня два́дцать девя́тое февраля́. 6 Сего́дня шестна́дцатое апре́ля. 7 Сего́дня два́дцать пя́тое ию́ня. 8 Сего́дня пе́рвое сентября́. 9 Сего́дня три́дцать пе́рвое декабря́. **2** 1 Деся́того а́вгуста я бу́ду в Вене́ции. 2 Шестна́дцатого а́вгуста я бу́ду в Берли́не. 3 Двадца́того а́вгуста я бу́ду в Москве́. 4 Два́дцать пя́того а́вгуста я бу́ду в Ки́рове. 5 Тридца́того а́вгуста я бу́ду в Но́вгороде. **3** 1 Я пое́ду во Фра́нцию восемна́дцатого а́вгуста. 2 Мы получи́ли письмо́ тре́тьего апре́ля. 3 Он позвони́л мне тридца́того января́. 4 Её день рожде́ния седьмо́го ма́рта. 5 Они́ уе́хали из Герма́нии два́дцать второ́го ноября́. **4** 1 Пу́шкин роди́лся в ты́сяча семьсо́т девяно́сто девя́том году́. 2 Ле́рмонтов роди́лся в ты́сяча восемьсо́т четы́рнадцатом году́. 3 Блок роди́лся в ты́сяча восемьсо́т восьмиде́сятом году́. 4 Ахма́това родила́сь

в ты́сяча восемьсо́т во́семьдесят девя́том году́. 5 Пастерна́к
роди́лся в ты́сяча восемьсо́т девяно́стом году́. 6 Цвета́ева
родила́сь в ты́сяча восемьсо́т девяно́сто второ́м году́.

6.7 **1** 1 Ско́лько сто́ит деревя́нный стол? Ты́сяча две́сти
пятьдеся́т рубле́й. 2 Ско́лько сто́ит япо́нский телеви́зор?
Три ты́сячи рубле́й. 3 Ско́лько сто́ит конве́рт? Три
рубля́ два́дцать копе́ек. 4 Ско́лько сто́ит кра́сная ру́чка?
Пятна́дцать рубле́й пятьдеся́т копе́ек. 5 Ско́лько сто́ит
буты́лка кра́сного вина́? Со́рок рубле́й. **2** 1 четы́ре
килогра́мма хле́ба. 2 полкило́ мя́са. 3 пять килогра́ммов
са́хара. 4 три килогра́мма помидо́ров. 5 шесть килогра́ммов
апельси́нов. **3** 1 Ба́бушке во́семьдесят оди́н год. 2 Ма́тери
пятьдеся́т пять лет. 3 Отцу́ (fleeting vowel!) пятьдеся́т четы́ре
го́да. 4 Сы́ну три́дцать два го́да. 5 До́чери три́дцать лет.
6 Вну́ку двена́дцать лет.

Unit 7

7.1 **1** 1 ты 2 ты 3 ты 4 вы (unless you know your boss very
well!) 5 вы **2** 1 Он 2 Они 3 Вы 4 Мы 5 Они́ **3** 1 Он 2 Оно́
3 Она́ 4 Они́ 5 Они́ **4** 1e 2d 3b 4a 5c **5** 1b 2c 3e 4a 5d
6 1 Сего́дня я звоню́ тебе́. 2 Сего́дня О́льга звони́т нам.
3 Сего́дня он звони́т вам. 4 Сего́дня Са́ша звони́т ей. 5 Сего́дня
ты звони́шь ему́. **7** 1 Я приглаша́ю его́ на вечери́нку.
2 Я приглаша́ю их на вечери́нку. 3 Я приглаша́ю вас на
вечери́нку. **8** 1 У тебя́ боли́т голова́. 2 У неё боли́т голова́.
3 У вас боли́т голова́.

7.2 **1** 1 Ка́тя, вот твоё письмо́. Нет, э́то не моё. 2 Ви́ктор вот
твой сви́тер. Нет, э́то не мой. 3 Са́ша и Аня, вот ва́ши кни́ги.
Нет, э́то не на́ши. 4 Светла́на и Та́ня, вот ва́ши фотогра́фии.
Нет, э́то не на́ши. 5 Андре́й, вот твоя́ руба́шка. Нет, э́то не
моя́. **2** 1 Э́то его́ дом? Да, его́. 2 Э́то их соба́ка? Да, их. 3
Э́то ваш па́спорт? Да, мой (наш). 4 Э́то моё письмо́? Да, твоё
(ва́ше). 5 Э́то на́ша фотогра́фия? Да, ва́ша. **3** 1d 2c 3e 4a 5b

7.3 **1** 1c 2e 3a 4d 5b **2** 1 Какую квартиру вы покупаете? 2 Какой автомобиль вы покупаете? 3 Какое здание вы покупаете? 4 Какой велосипед вы покупаете? 5 Какие книги вы покупаете? **3** 1 Чей это галстук? 2 Чей это чемодан? 3 Чья это юбка? 4 Чьё это платье? 5 Чьи это носки? **4** 1 Какую газету вы читаете? 2 О чём вы думаете (ты думаешь)? 3 С кем вы идёте (ты идёшь) в магазин? 4 Что это? Книга или журнал? 5 Чьи это дети?

7.4 **1** 1 Вы предпочитаете это пальто или то пальто, вон там? 2 Вы предпочитаете эту шапку или ту шапку, вон там? 3 Вы предпочитаете этот шарф или тот шарф, вон там? 4 Вы предпочитаете эту рубашку или ту рубашку, вон там? 5 Вы предпочитаете эти туфли или те туфли, вон там? **2** 1 Кто это? Это наш врач 2 Они живут в этом доме. 3 Вчера мы были в театре с Борисом и Сергеем. Тот работает врачом. 4 Вы уже знаете об этой проблеме? 5 Вот та же книга! 6 Он получил тот же самый галстук. 7 Мы читаем ту же газету. 8 Они работают на этих заводах. 9 Я иду в театр с такими интересными друзьями. 10 Лучшие магазины на этой улице. **3** 1 В каком городе ты живёшь? 2 Кто это? 3 Это такая красивая фотография! 4 Какую шапку ты предпочитаешь?

7.5 **1** 1c 2a 3d 4e 5b **2** 1 в любом магазине 2 в каждом магазине 3 во всех магазинах 4 в некоторых магазинах **3** 1 Можно купить марки в любом магазине. 2 Сам композитор идёт на концерт. 3 Есть такие города по всей Англии. 4 У меня подарки для каждого ребёнка. 5 Он идёт к самому директору. **4** 1 Мы работаем каждый день. 2 Актриса сама идёт в театр. 3 Я подожду у самой библиотеки. 4 Все наши друзья идут на концерт. 5 Какие билеты вы хотите? Любые. **5** 1b 2c 3e 4a 5d

7.6 **1** The tourist came into his room and shut the door behind him*. He saw in front of him* a large room with a bed, a chair and a washbasin, but no towels. He was glad he had brought some with him*. As he was feeling* rather tired, he decided to have a wash and a sleep, although he imagined* that the bed would not be very comfortable.   **2** 1 Что вы купи́ли для себя́? 2 Он ду́мает то́лько о себе́. 3 Я беру́ с собо́й вино́. 4 Мы берём с собо́й соба́ку.   **3** 1 Он хорошо́ ведёт себя́. 2 Я представля́ю себе́, что э́то тру́дно. 3 Закро́й за собо́й дверь! 4 Я пло́хо чу́вствую себя́. 5 Мы купи́ли шампа́нское для себя́.   **4** 1d 2a 3b 4e 5c

7.7   **1** 1 О́льга, кото́рая живёт в Ки́рове, продавщи́ца. 2 На́ши друзья́, кото́рые живу́т в Можа́йске, учителя́. 3 Ви́ктор, кото́рый живёт в Москве́, перево́дчик. 4 Са́ша, кото́рый живёт в Воро́неже, юри́ст. 5 А́ня, кото́рая живёт в Я́лте, медсестра́. 6 Вади́м, кото́рый живёт в О́бнинске, гид.   **2** 1 Велосипе́д, кото́рый О́льга купи́ла, большо́й. 2 Джи́нсы, кото́рые О́льга купи́ла, мо́дные. 3 Цветы́, кото́рые О́льга купи́ла, краси́вые. 4 Ю́бка, кото́рую О́льга купи́ла, коро́ткая.   **3** 1 Друг, к кото́рому мы идём, музыка́нт. 2 Зда́ния, в кото́рых они́ рабо́тают, о́чень больши́е. 3 Врач, с кото́рым она́ говори́ла, о́чень до́брый. 4 Фильм, о кото́ром вы говори́те, не о́чень хоро́ший. 5 Студе́нты, от кото́рых мы получи́ли письмо́, рабо́тают в А́фрике. **4** 1 Соба́ка, кото́рую ты сфотографи́ровал, о́чень ста́рая. 2 Шко́ла, о кото́рой ты говори́шь, о́чень хоро́шая.   **5** 1d 2e 3b 4a 5c   **6** 1 кто 2 кто 3 что 4 что 5 что 6 что

7.8   **1** <u>Someone</u> called to see you this morning. He said <u>something</u> about a meeting tomorrow. For <u>some reason</u> he didn't want to talk to me. He just said that if you can't be on time you should ring anyone in the office   **2** Кто́-то позвони́л тебе́ сего́дня у́тром. Он сказа́л что́-то о совеща́нии за́втра. Он почему́-то не хоте́л говори́ть со мной. Он сказа́л то́лько, что е́сли вы не смо́жете прие́хать (во́время), на́до позвони́ть кому́-нибудь в о́фисе. **3** 1 что́-то 2 когда́-нибудь 3 что́-нибудь 4 где́-нибудь 5 кого́-то 6 како́м-то

Unit 8

8.1   **1** Infinitives: to arrive, to do, to change; Present tense: is, works, is, has, are, loves, does not want.

8.2 **1** 1 Вы слу́шаете ра́дио. 2 Мы игра́ем в те́ннис. 3 Ты
покупа́ешь чай. 4 Она́ понима́ет вопро́с? 5 Я зна́ю дире́ктора.
2 1 покупа́ю 2 отвеча́ет 3 понима́ем 4 игра́ешь 5 гуля́ют
3 1 вы зна́ете 2 ты понима́ешь 3 я ка́шляю 4 она́ рабо́тает
5 они́ отвеча́ют 6 мы спра́шиваем 7 он покупа́ет 8 мы гуля́ем
9 вы слу́шаете 10 ты уме́ешь **4** 1 я молчу́ 2 ты стро́ишь
3 оно́ сто́ит 4 вы ку́рите 5 они́ ва́рят 6 мы гото́вим 7 я лежу́
8 вы кричи́те 9 вы слы́шите 10 ты говори́шь **5** 1 Вы
слы́шите ра́дио. 2 Мы стои́м у окна́. 3 Они́ стро́ят дом. 4 Она́
смо́трит фильм? 5 Ты звони́шь дире́ктору. **6** 1 звоню́
2 слы́шите 3 сто́ит 4 смо́тришь 5 стоя́т

8.3 **1** 1 сиди́т 2 гла́жу 3 во́зит 4 ношу́ 5 лети́те **2** 1 я люблю́
2 я сплю 3 я говорю́ 4 я сижу́ 5 я ла́жу 6 я стою́ 7 я прошу́
8 я смотрю́ 9 я кормлю́ 10 я звоню́ **3** 1b 2e 3a 4c 5d

8.4 **1** 1 мы берём 2 я живу́ 3 вы пьёте 4 они́ кладу́т 5 он
идёт 6 ты поёшь 7 я лью 8 они́ ждут 9 я пью 10 мы живём
2 1 я 2 они́ 3 мы 4 ты 5 они́ 6 вы 7 он (она́, оно́) **3** Ива́н
поёт. Вади́м пьёт **4** 1 Ива́н пьёт во́дку. 2 О́льга живёт в
кварти́ре. 3 Он ждёт в теа́тре. 4 Мы берём биле́ты. 5 Они́ пою́т
сего́дня ве́чером. **5** 1 Я ча́сто пишу́ моему́ дру́гу. 2 Сего́дня мы
е́дем в центр го́рода. 3 Вы не о́чень ча́сто мо́ете посу́ду.
4 Почему́ ты пла́чешь? 5 Они́ и́щут свои́ паспорта́.
6 1 они́ 2 он 3 ты 4 я 5 мы **7** 1 я танцу́ю 2 ты даёшь
3 он рекоменду́ет 4 мы встаём 5 вы сове́туете 6 они́
риску́ют 7 она́ узнаёт 8 я испо́льзую 9 мы тре́буем
10 они́ п утеше́ствуют

8.5 **1** 1 Мой брат – инжене́р. 2 Сего́дня хо́лодно. 3 На столе́ есть
ключ. 4 В дере́вне нет магази́нов. **2** 1 У Вади́ма есть дом.
2 У Бори́са нет автомоби́ля. 3 У Та́ни есть телеви́зор. 4 У Зо́и есть
кварти́ра. 5 У И́горя нет ко́шки. 6 У Серге́я нет компью́тера.
3 1e 2d 3a 4c 5b **4** 1 мо́жет 2 хо́чет 3 хочу́ 4 мо́жешь 5 хотя́т

8.6 **1** 1 я умыва́юсь 2 он причёсывается **2** 1 Я одева́юсь
в во́семь часо́в. 2 Он умыва́ется в семь часо́в. 3 Они́

раздева́ются в де́сять часо́в. 4 Конце́рт конча́ется в де́сять часо́в. 5 Вы ложи́тесь спать в оди́ннадцать часо́в. **3** 1c 2a 3f 4j 5d 6b 7h 8e 9i 10g

---

Unit 9

9.1 **1** 1e 2c 3d 4a 5b **2** 1 говори́ть 2 написа́ть 3 чита́ть 4 игра́ть 5 верну́ться **3** 1 Он предпочита́ет чита́ть газе́ты. 2 Я хочу́ посла́ть э́то письмо́ сего́дня. 3 Актёр начина́ет говори́ть в семь часо́в. 4 Мы продолжа́ем смотре́ть телеви́зор. 5 Они́ лю́бят отдыха́ть на пля́же. 6 Я хочу́ взять кни́гу сейча́с. 7 Мы хоти́м купи́ть э́ту соба́ку. 8 Вы предпочита́ете слу́шать ра́дио? 9 Вы хоти́те верну́ться сего́дня?

9.2 **1** will have, will visit, will ring, will use **2** 1 Он ча́сто бу́дет звони́ть дру́гу. 2 Ба́бушка бу́дет отдыха́ть до́ма. 3 Мы бу́дем игра́ть в гольф ка́ждый день. 4 За́втра я бу́ду занима́ться уро́ками. 5 В университе́те он бу́дет изуча́ть исто́рию. **3** 1b 2e 3c 4a 5d

9.3 **1** will ring, will write, will visit, will sign **2** 1 позвоню́ 2 накормлю́ 3 пообе́даю 4 куплю́ 5 вы́учу **3** 1 Во вто́рник я куплю́ пода́рки. 2 В сре́ду я позвоню́ ма́ме. 3 В четве́рг я напишу́ письмо́ бра́ту. 4 В пя́тницу я вы́учу грамма́тику. 5 В суббо́ту я отремонти́рую маши́ну. 6 В воскресе́нье я закажу́ биле́ты.

9.4 **1** used to live, was, was, loved, was barking, was **2** 1 О́льга за́втракала. 2 Меня́ зову́т Еле́на, я мы́ла посу́ду. 3 Он игра́л в ка́рты. 4 Мы смотре́ли телеви́зор. 5 Вы возвраща́лись в о́фис. 6 Они́ писа́ли пи́сьма. 7 Бори́с и Светла́на гото́вили обе́д. **3** 1 рабо́тал: process, not necessarily complete; it went on for 2 hours 2 игра́ла: action of playing is interrupted 3 бы́ли: description of where you were; быть exists only in imperfective 4 шли: action of walking is interrupted 5 де́лали: habit in the past

9.5 1 had finished, rang, refused, had agreed, rang, hung up, rushed, have brought, asked, said **2 1** Хорошо́! Вади́м уже́ вы́мыл посу́ду. **2** Хорошо́! вы уже́ пригото́вили обе́д. **3** Хорошо́! они́ уже́ сде́лали поку́пки. **4** Хорошо́! На́дя уже́ накорми́ла соба́ку. **5** Хорошо́! И́горь уже́ вы́стирал бельё. **3 1** Игорь и Зо́я ремонти́ровали автомоби́ль, когда́ Бори́с позвони́л. **2** Игорь и Зо́я стира́ли бельё, когда́ стира́льная маши́на слома́лась. **3** Игорь и Зо́я сажа́ли дере́вья в саду́, когда́ ихсын верну́лся. **4** Игорь и Зо́я де́лали поку́пки, когда́ Зо́я потеря́ла де́ньги.

Unit 10

10.1 1 1 е́здил **2** бе́гает **3** пла́вал **4** лета́ем **5** возит **2 1** е́дет **2** бежи́т **3** плывёт **4** лете́ли **5** везла́ **3 1** пое́дет **2** побегу́ **3** поплывёт **4** полете́ли **5** повезла́ **4 1** несёт **2** понёс **3** нёс **5 1** выхожу́ **2** подхожу́ **3** приезжа́ет **4** вхожу́ **5** приезжа́ю **6** выхожу́ **7** прохожу́ **8** вхожу́ **6 1** в **2** к **3** до **4** из **5** на **6** из **7** ми́мо **8** с **9** от **10** че́рез **3 1** Я вхожу́ в теа́тр. **2** Он вно́сит кни́ги в ко́мнату. **3** Мы выбега́ем из па́рка. **4** Они́ перево́дят соба́ку че́рез у́лицу.

10.2 1 1 напи́шет **2** пропылесо́сит **3** вы́стирает **4** вста́нет **5** почи́стит **2 1** прие́дет во́время **2** не забу́дет свои́ де́ньги **3** позвони́т профе́ссору **4** напи́шет письмо́ (своему́) бра́ту **5** прода́ст (свой) мотоци́кл **6** даст мне пода́рок **7** зака́жет биле́ты **8** ку́пит соба́ку **9** сде́лает поку́пки **10** вернётся ра́но **3 1** We are always glad if they send us a card ✓ **2** They will not be pleased if you don't send them a card ✗ **3** You are never satisfied if the food is cold ✓ **4** If you don't ring me tonight I will be furious ✗ **4** 1b 2e 3a 4c 5d **5 1** Е́сли бы у них бы́ли де́ньги, они́ постро́или бы да́чу. **2** Е́сли бы у нас бы́ли де́ньги, мы купи́ли бы пода́рки для друзе́й. **3** Е́сли бы у него́ бы́ли де́ньги, Па́вел сиде́л бы до́ма. **4** Е́сли бы у неё бы́ли де́ньги, Ка́тя купи́ла бы но́вую оде́жду. **5** Е́сли бы у вас бы́ли де́ньги, вы доста́ли бы биле́ты в Большо́й теа́тр. **6 1** Е́сли бы то́лько

мы не забы́ли, А́ня не рассерди́лась бы на нас. 2 Если бы то́лько
она зна́ла об э́том, она́ позвони́ла бы ему. 3 Если бы то́лько мы
пришли́ во́время, мы уви́дели бы их. **7** 1 Бы́ло бы лу́чше, е́сли
бы она́ согласи́лась на э́то. 2 Бы́ло бы лу́чше, е́сли бы у него́ был
лэпто́п. 3 Бы́ло бы лу́чше, е́сли бы я знал/зна́ла его́ а́дрес.

10.3 **1** 1h 2c 3j 4a 5f 6b 7i 8g 9d 10e **2** 1 спи 2 напиши́
3 бери́ 4 купи́ 5 поблагодари́ **3** 1 забу́дьте 2 отдыха́йте
3 слу́шайте 4 рабо́тайте 5 улыба́йтесь **4** 1 Не забу́дьте
биле́ты! 2 Не кури́ть! 3 Переда́йте ключ, пожа́луйста.
4 Дава́й/Дава́йте позвони́м Та́не!

10.4 **1** 1c 2e 3b 4a 5d **2** 1 Ви́ктор никогда́ не поёт пе́сни.
2 Ви́ктор нигде́ не слу́шает поп-му́зыку. 3 Ви́ктор ни с кем не
слу́шает поп-му́зыку. 4 Ви́ктор ничего́ не знает о му́зыке.
3 1 Я не люблю́ смотре́ть фи́льмы. 2 Здесь нет кинотеа́тра.
3 Я ниче́м не занима́юсь в свобо́дное вре́мя. 4 Я нигде́ не
люблю́ отдыха́ть. **4** 1b 2c 3d 4e 5a **5** 1e 2a 3h 4b 5g 6j 7i 8f 9c
10d **6** 1 Ива́ну и Мари́и не́когда смотре́ть телеви́зор. 2 Ива́ну и
Мари́и не́чем писа́ть пи́сьма. 3 Ива́ну и Мари́и не́кого приглаша́ть
на обе́д. 4 Ива́ну и Мари́и не́чего пить. 5 Ива́ну и Мари́и не́кому
звони́ть. **7** 1 Вам не́чего бу́дет де́лать. 2 Не́ за что. 3 Не́чего
есть. 4 Врачу́ не́когда бы́ло отдыха́ть. 5 Нам не́чего бы́ло чита́ть.

10.5 **1** 1 Мне жа́рко. 2 Ему́ ху́же. 3 Ка́те лу́чше. 4 Де́тям
бы́ло ску́чно. 5 Им бу́дет неприя́тно. **2** 1 пора́ 2 нельзя́
3 мо́жно 4 на́до 5 нельзя́ **3** 1 Ему́ на́до отдыха́ть в больни́це.
2 Нам пора́ бы́ло идти́. 3 Мо́жно (возмо́жно) бу́дет пла́вать.
4 Нет, вам (тебе́) нельзя́ смотре́ть телеви́зор. 5 Да, вам (тебе́)
на́до рабо́тать. **4** 1 Им ску́чно. 2 Мне хо́лодно. 3 Ей жаль
соба́ку. 4 Ему́ нра́вится пла́вать. 5 Тебе́ хо́чется пить? 6 Вам
удало́сь найти́ ключ? **5** 1 Ему́ нра́вится актри́са. 2 Врачу́
нра́вится больни́ца. 3 Профе́ссору нра́вятся студе́нты. 4 Вам
понра́вилась экску́рсия. 5 Она́ нра́вится мне.

10.6 **1** 1c 2a 3e 4b 5d **2** 1 Я спроси́л(а), прие́дет ли Бори́с
за́втра. 2 Я спроси́л(а), заплати́ла ли О́льга за кни́ги.
3 Я спроси́л(а), пожа́ловались ли клие́нты на това́рь 4 Я

спроси́л(а), позвони́л ли Бори́с дире́ктору. **5** Я спроси́л(а), вернётся ли О́льга. **3 1** Мы спроси́ли, мо́жно ли поза́втракать в 8 часо́в. **2** Он спроси́л, пошёл ли друг на дискоте́ку. **3** Он нам сказа́л / Он сказа́л нам, когда́ вернётся. **4** Ты не зна́ешь, получи́ла ли она́ письмо́? **5** Я хочу́ знать, подпи́шет ли дире́ктор контра́кт.

10.7 **1 1** Врач тре́бует, что́бы спортсме́н не кури́л. **2** Гид рекоменду́ет, что́бы тури́сты обе́дали в рестора́нах. **3** Профе́ссор тре́бует, что́бы студе́нты прочита́ли всю кни́гу. **4** Я хочу́, что́бы мой сын стал врачо́м. **5** Де́ти хотя́т, что́бы роди́тели купи́ли дороги́е игру́шки. **2** 1c 2e 3d 4b 5a **3 1** Я хочу́, что́бы вы позвони́ли (ты позвони́л/а) мне за́втра. **2** Врач хо́чет, что́бы пацие́нт лежа́л в посте́ли. **3** Профе́ссор тре́бует, что́бы студе́нты рабо́тали в библиоте́ке. **4** Милиционе́р предлага́ет, что́бы вы пошли́ (ты пошёл/ты пошла́) домо́й. **5** Я приказа́л(а), что́бы они́ се́ли. **4 1** Мы хоти́м купи́ть телеви́зор, что́бы смотре́ть ма́тчи. **2** Вы хоти́те позвони́ть дру́гу, что́бы пригласи́ть его́ на конце́рт. **3** Ты хо́чешь написа́ть письмо́, что́бы переда́ть но́вости. **4** Они́ хотя́т посеща́ть Москву́, что́бы ви́деть интере́сные места́. **5** Тури́сты хотя́т посеща́ть пля́жи, что́бы отдыха́ть. **5 1** Бори́с позвони́л, что́бы она́ отве́тила на вопро́с. **2** Бори́с позвони́л, что́бы он извини́лся. **3** Бори́с позвони́л, что́бы мы обсуди́ли ситуа́цию. **4** Бори́с позвони́л, что́бы вы пригласи́ли его́ на обе́д. **5** Бори́с позвони́л, что́бы они́ заказа́ли биле́ты. **6 1** позвони́ть **2** что́бы позвони́ть **3** что́бы друг позвони́л

10.8 **1 1** Она́ обеща́ла написа́ть письмо́, но она́ забы́ла. **2** Он изуча́ет матема́тику и фи́зику. **3** Серге́й печа́лен, и никто́ не обраща́ет внима́ния на него́. **4** Тури́сты серди́ты, потому́ что в гости́нице хо́лодно. **5** Дире́ктор ду́мает, что клие́нт дово́лен. **6** По́сле того́, как они́ ушли́, мы поу́жинали. **2 1** Я пью и вино́ и во́дку. **2** Я не игра́ю ни в кри́кет, ни в футбо́л. **3** Я люблю́ о́перу, а он лю́бит бале́т. **4** Я не иду́ на конце́рт, потому́ что програ́мма неинтере́сная. **5** Она́ не зна́ла, что он рабо́тает дире́ктором. **3 1** а **2** и́ли **3** из-за того́, что **4** но **5** ни … ни **4 1** Я рад (ра́да), потому́ что (так как/из-за того́, что) он хо́чет купи́ть биле́т. 2 Я хочу́ пойти́ на конце́рт, но биле́тов нет. 3 Вы хоти́те два биле́та и́ли три?

_____

Unit 11

11.2 **1** 1 Дом в го́роде. 2 Це́рковь в дере́вне. 3 Кни́га в шкафу́. 4 Автомоби́ль на у́лице. 5 Компью́тер в о́фисе. 6 Бри́столь на за́паде А́нглии. 7 По́езд на ста́нции. 8 Тигр в зоопа́рке. 9 Почтальо́н на по́чте. 10 Пиани́ст на конце́рте. **2** 1 О́льга ду́мает, что ру́чка под кни́гами, но она́ у телефо́на. 2 О́льга ду́мает, что биле́ты за зе́ркалом, но они́ под па́спортом. 3 О́льга ду́мает, что автомоби́ль пе́ред до́мом, но он за до́мом. 4 О́льга ду́мает, что портре́т над ками́ном, но он над столо́м. 5 О́льга ду́мает, что холоди́льник ме́жду шкафа́ми, но он за две́рью.

11.3 **1** 1 Секрета́рь идёт на рабо́ту. 2 Ви́ктор идёт на стадио́н. 3 Учи́тель идёт в шко́лу. 4 Студе́нт идёт на ле́кцию. 5 Соба́ка идёт в сад. **2** 1 у́лицу 2 ка́ссе 3 кого́ 4 Ита́лии 5 ка́ссы **3** 1 по 2 че́рез 3 за 4 на 5 в

11.4 **1** 1 день рожде́ния , e 2 вто́рникам, g 3 э́тот моме́нт, j 4 пя́тницу, b 5 сре́дам, a 6 воскресе́ньям, c 7 четверга́м, i 8 четверга́м, d 9 пя́тницу, f 10 суббо́ту, h **2** 1 в понеде́льник, в пя́тницу и в суббо́ту 2 во вто́рник 3 в воскресе́нье **3** 1 День рожде́ния Серге́я в ма́рте. 2 День рожде́ния А́ни в апре́ле. 3 День рожде́ния Татья́ны в сентябре́. 4 День рожде́ния сестры́ в декабре́. 5 День рожде́ния бра́та в январе́. 6 День рожде́ния му́жа в октябре́. 7 День рожде́ния Ка́ти в а́вгусте. 8 День рожде́ния Вади́ма в ма́е. 9 День рожде́ния Зо́и в ию́не. 10 День рожде́ния И́горя в ноябре́. **4** 1 в э́том году́ 2 на э́той неде́ле 3 в ма́рте 4 в ию́не 5 в бу́дущем году́ 6 в феврале́ 7 в э́том ме́сяце 8 в а́вгусте 9 на бу́дущей неде́ле 10 в два́дцать пе́рвом ве́ке **5** 1 В декабре́ мы лю́бим ката́ться на лы́жах. 2 В а́вгусте мы лю́бим лежа́ть на пля́же. 3 В феврале́ мы лю́бим сиде́ть до́ма. 4 В ию́ле мы лю́бим гуля́ть в дере́вне. **6** 1 во вре́мя 2 за 3 че́рез 4 наза́д 5 по́сле 6 с … до 7 за **7** 1 во время, d 2 за, a 3 через, e 4 наза́д, b 5 до, g 6 c, h 7 за, f 8 во время, c

11.5 **1** 1 кро́ме 2 для 3 без 4 про́тив 5 в 6 по 7 о 8 при 9 за 10 на   **2** 1d Мы поблагодари́ли её за пода́рок. 2a Они́ живу́т в до́ме напро́тив больни́цы. 3b Вы за и́ли про́тив э́той иде́и? 4e Кро́ме Бори́са все дово́льны 5c Они́ ходи́ли на конце́рт без меня́!

11.6 **1** 1 в c, 2 у f, 3 на e, 4 за h, 5 c g, 6 к b, 7 в a, 8 на d **2** 1 Бори́с игра́ет в футбо́л. 2 Татья́на игра́ет на фле́йте. **3** 1 Мы серди́мся на тебя́/вас. 2 Мы наде́емся на лу́чшее. 3 Он отвеча́ет на мой вопро́с. 4 Не на́до жа́ловаться на письмо́. 5 Плати́те за кни́ги в ка́ссу. 6 Они́ продаю́т стул за две́сти рубле́й. 7 Мы покупа́ем стул у А́ни. 8 Вы игра́ете на гита́ре? 9 Посмотри́те на соба́ку! 10 Обы́чно мы начина́ем с пе́рвой страни́цы.

Glossary of grammatical terms

adjective   A word which describes a noun: a *boring* film.

adverb   A word which gives us information about the way in which an action is carried out: he sings *well*; she sings *very badly*.

animate noun   A person or an animal.

article   Words meaning *a, an, the, some*. There are no articles in Russian.

aspects   Most Russian verbs exist in two forms, imperfective and perfective. The imperfective is concerned with process or description and the perfective is concerned with result and successful completion.

case   There are six cases in Russian – nominative, accusative, genitive, dative, instrumental, prepositional. A case indicates what role nouns, adjectives and pronouns are playing in the sentence and the endings of these words change according to their case.

clause   A group of words that contains a verb. A main clause can be followed by a subordinate clause: *Champagne is a drink* (main clause), *which I love* (subordinate clause).

comparative   Adjectives and adverbs in the comparative indicate *more/less*: This is a *more* boring film; he sings *less* well than his sister.

conjugation   The way verb endings change when in a tense.

conjunction   Words which link sentences or phrases (e.g. *and, but, because*).

declension   The way noun, pronoun or adjective endings change when not in the nominative case.

gender A category of noun. In Russian there are three categories: masculine, feminine and neuter.

infinitive The form of the word meaning *to* (e.g. *to do, to read, to write*). In Russian most verbs have two infinitives, the imperfective and the perfective.

negative A word or phrase denying or contradicting something: I *never* watch television; he *can't* sing.

noun Word used to name a person, an animal, a place, an object or an abstract quality: *Viktor, Moscow, postman, happiness.*

object Person or thing that has an action done to it.

preposition Word used before a noun or pronoun to show position, time, method: *in, at, from, with.*

pronoun A word used in place of a noun or phrase: *him, she, this, which, who*

relative clause Part of a sentence introduced by a relative pronoun: These are my friends *who live in Russia.*

subject Person or thing doing an action.

superlative Adjectives and adverbs in the superlative indicate *most: This is the most boring film; he sings best of all.*

tense Tells us when the action of the verb takes/took/will take place:

He reads	present tense
He will read	future tense
He was reading	past tense
He read	past tense
He had read	past tense

verb Words which describe actions, feelings and states.